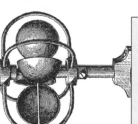

JONATHAN FISK

BROKEN

7

"CHRISTIAN" RULES THAT EVERY CHRISTIAN OUGHT TO BREAK AS OFTEN AS POSSIBLE

CONCORDIA PUBLISHING HOUSE • SAINT LOUIS

For you.

Published by Concordia Publishing House
3558 S. Jefferson Avenue, St. Louis, MO 63118-3968
1-800-325-3040 • www.cph.org

Text © 2012 Jonathan M. Fisk

All rights reserved. Unless specifically noted, no part of this publication may be reproduced, stored in a retrieval system, or transmitted, in any form or by any means, electronic, mechanical, photocopying, recording, or otherwise, without the prior written permission of Concordia Publishing House.

Scripture quotations are from the ESV Bible® (The Holy Bible, English Standard Version®), copyright © 2001 by Crossway Bibles, a publishing ministry of Good News Publishers. Used by permission. All rights reserved.

The quotations from the Lutheran Confessions are from *Concordia: The Lutheran Confessions*, second edition; edited by Paul McCain et al., copyright © 2006 Concordia Publishing House. All rights reserved.

Hymn texts with the abbreviation *LSB* are from *Lutheran Service Book*, copyright © 2006 Concordia Publishing House. All rights reserved.

The quotations from Luther's Works in this publication are from the American Edition: vol. 27 © 1964 by Concordia Publishing House. All rights reserved.

Cover image © Shutterstock.com

Manufactured in the United States of America

Library of Congress Cataloging-in-Publication Data

Fisk, Jonathan M.
    Broken : 7 "Christian" rules that every Christian ought to break as often as possible / Jonathan M. Fisk.
      p. cm.
    Includes bibliographical references and index.
    ISBN 978-0-7586-3101-5 (alk. paper)
1. Christian life. 2. Conduct of life. 3. Postmodernism--Religious aspects
    --Christianity. I. Title.
    BV4501.3.F5765 2012
    248.4--dc23

                              2012027057

8 9 10 11 12 13 14 15   22 21 20 19 18 17 16 15 14

{ Jesus answered him, "If anyone loves Me, he will keep My word." }

John 14:23

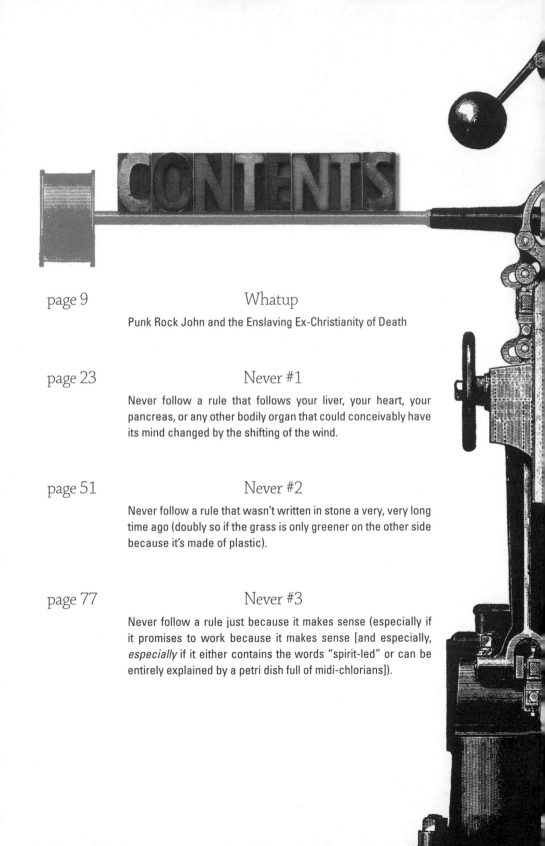

CONTENTS

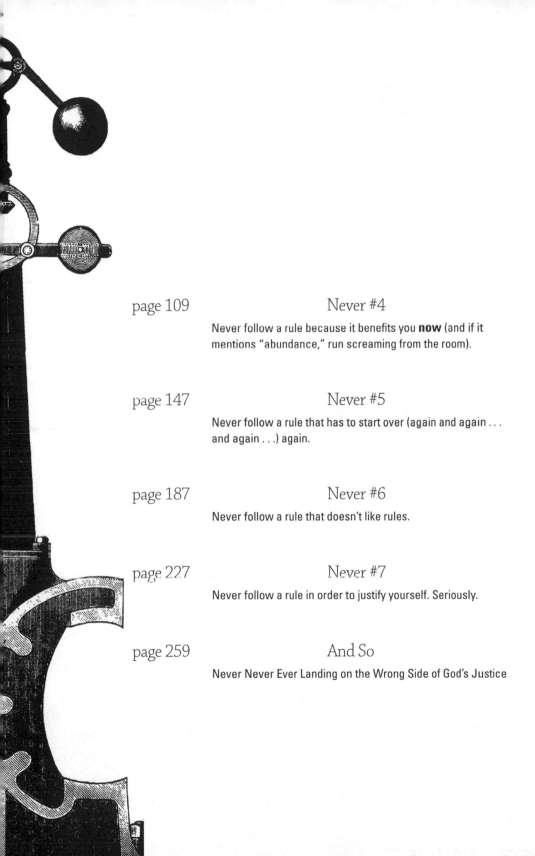

Whatup

Punk Rock John and the Enslaving Ex-Christianity of Death

Christian Punks Are Posers

He was a good kid. He played in a punk rock band and worshiped with punk rock style. He was a good kid. He didn't just go to church, but he was a Christian, on fire and unafraid to step out of the box for Jesus. That was what the Church needed: less fear, less hesitancy, more living by the Spirit, more **real** religion.

He was a good kid. He played in a Christian band. He hung out with Christian friends. He lived the Christian life. He worked hard to get people saved. He struggled after God's will for his life. He set aside time for prayer. He set aside time to play his guitar. He mixed the two together and sang out songs of praise to his heart's content. Soon he'd go to college, and then he'd marry his girlfriend. Maybe he'd be a pastor. Maybe he'd be a worship leader. All he knew was that what he wanted for the rest of his life was to feel this way, to live this life, to know what he knew, and to find a way to help more people do the same.

Then he met a missionary.

It all started innocently enough. He was online, the way he often was, surfing the punk rock forums in search of a few new chord progressions. He clicked a link. It took him to a punk rock site. There was an Ⓐ in the corner and a pretty girl with blue hair on the sidebar . . .

No biggie. He'd been to these sites before. This was the punk rock world. Nothing wrong with it. Well, there were all sorts of things wrong with it. That's why he played **Christian** punk rock.

9

But there really wasn't anything wrong with blue hair or sweet riffs. He was about to click back when something else caught his eye—not the girl or the paraphernalia—but some words. Words he didn't like. Words that made him angry. Words that made him click the link.

"Christian Punks Are Posers"

It was written by the missionary. It was written with passion and zeal. But it was the wrong mission. The missionary said Christian punk rock was a **lie**. True punk rock was anti-authority, anti-prejudice, anti-conformity, anti-establishment. And what could be a more authoritative, prejudiced, conformist establishment than Christianity? What was more, the missionary said, Christians were all idiots living in a total delusion about reality. They didn't just deny science, they based all their decisions on feelings and blindness.

He was a good kid. He wanted his heart to break over how wrong the missionary was. But what scared him more than anything ever had, what terrified him till his pulse quickened, was that his heart wasn't breaking the way it should. He wasn't feeling the way he was supposed to feel. Instead, he was thinking the things he wasn't supposed to think: the missionary made sense. The missionary sounded **right**.

He turned off the computer as fast as he could. He got out his Bible, and he tried to pray. It was always hard to pray because the emotions never came easily. That's why he needed music—for the emotions. He tried to pray, but the feelings didn't come. "God, are You there?" he asked.

It wasn't long before he was back on the same site, reading more. It was like a light had dawned. He started posting in the forum, asking questions, looking for guidance. He learned a lot in the next few months. He watched *Zeitgeist: The Movie* on YouTube and learned that Jesus was just another version of the pagan gods. He read about Martin Luther and how he was a Nazi. He wanted to stop. He wanted to find something to tell him that what he read was wrong. So he went and talked to his youth pastor.

"I think I'm becoming an atheist," he confessed in the eerily warm stuffiness of the office, sweat beading uncomfortably under his arms. The couch had always felt so welcoming and hip, but now it felt too large.

He was sinking in it. He wished he could sink in it—and hide. "I found all these arguments on the Internet. They make a lot of sense. I don't know what to do. I don't want to be an atheist. I used to be on fire. What happened? I don't understand."

"Is there sin you've been hiding?" the youth pastor asked.

"No!" he said right away. He felt guilty saying no, even though he couldn't think of a good reason for it. Maybe he **did** have hidden sin. "I just need answers," he said, shoving the thought away. "I learned that Christmas is just Roman sun worship and that our church body is sexist. I don't know what to think or feel."

"I understand," the youth pastor said. "There are a lot of Satan's messengers out there. They will say all sorts of worldly things to plant doubts in you. You just can't trust them."

"But how can I know that? How do I even know that God is there?"

"Just look at the world. How could it exist without God?"

"I don't know. Evolution?"

"Listen, God loves you. He wants you to have a good life full of purpose and meaning. Trust me. Just pray about it. God will give you the answer you need."

"But I have prayed."

"Pray more. God loves you. He will answer."

But . . . God . . . didn't . . . answer.

He was still a good kid, but now he was an atheist. He got rid of his Christian T-shirts and deleted his Christian punk rock MP3s. It took him a while, but he eventually told his parents. They took it hard. He understood. But they were deceived. They believed in faith, but faith didn't have answers. Science had answers. Now he had answers too. And he had a new community that supported him, accepted him for who he was, without insisting he conform to their standards.

"But weren't you on fire for Jesus?"

"I thought I was. But it was just a show. It was just make-believe."

He was a good kid. But his faith in Christianity was **BROKEN**.

Dirty Crow Tricks

The story of Punk Rock John is fictionalized, but it also is terribly, terribly true. I've heard different versions of it multiple times from too many real people. "What happened to my kid? I don't understand. He used to be so in love with church. He went on mission trips. He went to youth group. He was on fire for Jesus. I don't know where it went wrong."

A sower went out to sow. And as he sowed, some seeds fell along the path, and the birds came and devoured them. Other seeds fell on rocky ground, where they did not have much soil, and immediately they sprang up, since they had no depth of soil, but when the sun rose they were scorched. And since they had no root, they withered away. Other seeds fell among thorns, and the thorns grew up and choked them. Other seeds fell on good soil and produced grain, some a hundredfold, some sixty, some thirty. He who has ears, let him hear. (Matthew 13:3–9)

One of the darkest secrets of Christianity in America is that we are losing our kids. We hide it with light shows and Christian dance video games, but it's true, and it is nothing new. It has been happening for more than fifty years. It is still happening right this very moment.

Worse than that, it's not just happening to kids. It's happening to college students and senior citizens. It's happening to emerging adults and the midlife-crisied. Christians are losing faith. Christians are falling away. Christians once on fire are **burning out**.

Jesus knew about this problem. He once told a story about it. He said the Christian faith was like seeds being planted. Many people would believe in Him, but for too many, their faith would then die. The cares and trials of this world would overwhelm them and choke them. Missionaries for atheism or Buddhism or some secret mystery would find them and convince them that they could get a better deal than Jesus somewhere else. Although they once sprang up with joy and grew like they could never grow enough, their roots would suddenly find themselves trying to creep through a layer of bedrock. They would be thirsty, but no one would give them a glass of water. They would wither. They would die. Their faith in Christianity would be **BROKEN**.

The story about Punk Rock John is not unique, and according to Jesus' parable of the sower, there's more going on than meets the eye. Not only do the cares and trials of this life present a real threat to Christianity, but there is also the role that the devil plays in undermining the Christian life. Long before the roots of faith dry up under persecution or the dangers of American culture choke faith to death like a weed, the devil has first achieved victory with his primary strategy—his most essential tactic. Like a dirty crow he has swept in from above and stolen away the **source of faith**. The devil's primary goal is to make the Christian forget about the Sower's **seed**.

Martin Luther once wrote that the old serpent, the devil, first converted Adam and Eve to unbelief by making them "enthusiasts." By **"enthusiasts,"** he meant that the devil convinced them that the real source of **goodness** was not in **God's Word**. It was in **themselves**. They should be enthusiastic about their own abilities to discern good and evil, to learn of it, and to rule by it. "The old devil . . . led them away from God's outward Word to spiritualizing and self-pride. And yet, he did this through other outward words" (Smalcald Articles III VIII 5).

This means that long before the devil ever breaks the faith of well-meaning Christians with his lies, he first must teach them **"enthusiasm"** as if it were genuine Christianity. Long before a missionary for atheism deceives you with plausible arguments based on merely human thinking, the devil first teaches you to try growing your faith on something other than **God's pure Word**. He teaches you that the Holy Scriptures are not the real place to find the Holy Spirit, that the human words in the Bible are flawed, that the Church is full of errors and confusion. He teaches you a counterfeit Christianity.

Ironically, this hardly keeps him silent, but like a dirty crow, he caws constantly, filling the world with a stream of yapping, twisting, and wily black words. "It is the spirit that you really need," he says to Christians. "It is the renewed life. Abundant living. The next step." With all the noise made by the flapping of his jowls and wings, many well-meaning Christians hardly notice that the seed from which their faith first grew is slowly stolen away, swallowed in a maw of black feathers. Before you know it, belief in a pure Word from God is simply **gone**.

A Famine Not of Bread

Behold, the days are coming, declares the Lord GOD, when I will send a famine on the land—not a famine of bread, nor a thirst for water, but of hearing the words of the LORD. They shall wander from sea to sea, and from north to east; they shall run to and fro, to seek the word of the LORD, but they shall not find it. (Amos 8:11–12)

This is nothing new. It has happened before, and it will happen again. But every time it happens, every time Christianity declines in a society, it happens for the same reason: because genuine believers tried laying a foundation on something other than God's Word. Like the people of Israel in the days of the prophet Amos, they might still be saying, "God surely lives!" and "I know the Way!" But their stomachs still rumble. There is no wheat growing in the fields to harvest. The seed has been stolen away, and suddenly even pastors of the Church struggle to give a satisfying answer for the hope within them.

FAMISHED

Our world has always been **insane**. Previous ages were tough. There is nothing new under the sun, and the heart of man is always and only continually evil from youth. But there is something doubly gnarly about our wild Western civilization of the twenty-first century. A cultural perfect storm shreds the spiritual landscape of the United States. It blows on the winds of a growing ignorance of history and the Bible. It drips with the dew of an insatiable appetite for entertainment and leisure. It billows on the clouds of a mounting desperation for success, even as civilization slips into streamlined decline. Into this chaos the remnant of the Church of Jesus Christ stumbles.

What is the Church's status at this party? Theoretically, the "modern era" of the last century was supposed to show her the door. (That's what all the well-paid scholars thought, at least.) "Soon," they taught, "that pretentious old nun will be gone." But then, she didn't go away. She stuck around. She tried really hard. She bought some new clothes. She learned a few dance moves. But is she attracting a crowd because she's really the life of the party, or is she just drunk? It's hard to tell.

The Church has buildings and storefronts, radio stations and cable channels. But at the same time, she seems a little strung out. She's the girl who tries so hard to be cool and convince everyone she belongs that she ends up making everyone who talks to her feel uncomfortable. Her lipstick is too red, and the low-cut bodice doesn't flatter her body type. Even her friends are kind of embarrassed by the way she dances when she's left alone with the wrong sort of guys. Sure, the Church hasn't died and gone away like the twentieth-century atheists predicted, but neither has she achieved wild success the way so many of her own leaders prophesied. Evangelism didn't explode. Each one didn't reach one. Mission wasn't multiplied. New technology did not complete the Great Commission.

The Church didn't change the world. Worse, the world appears to be growing daily more content to keep going on its merry way, ignoring her best dancing. To make matters worse, the world appears to have changed her, and not for the better. The expensive new hairstyle looks downright forced, and her refusal to face the music is beginning to appear manic. Meanwhile, good Christian people like Punk Rock John find themselves overtired, frustrated, and confused. The clothes have been changed so many times, the next step taken so many times, the future predicted so many times, that they're no longer sure why they came to the party as a Christian at all. Didn't it have something to do with Jesus?

The DJ plays a dirge, but the Church dances. Then he plays the flute, but she weeps. She stumbles through the steps. Her body is anemic. Her breath is growing short. Did she survive the Enlightenment after all? How do we know this is even the **real** Church? Maybe you're not even a **real** Christian. Maybe Christianity isn't real to begin with . . .

The old serpent is up to his same old tactic. He's a talented pony, but he's got only the one trick.

Postmodernism: The dominant philosophical system of twenty-first-century American thought, combining multiple previous systems of thought under the central notion that all methods of thinking are merely "constructions" of a culture, holding in themselves no universal meaning. Where the modern world would say, "Truth is always true," the postmodern world says, "Truth is always (only) your opinion."

For all the perfect storm of our hypercultural age, for all the distractions and amusements and cares of this American life, for all the scorching pressures of conforming to the modern world and the postmodern mind, it is still only the one foil the devil is using to attack the faith. It's the same foil the youth pastor (unwittingly) taught to Punk Rock John as if it were God's own gospel truth. It's the same foil countless well-meaning Christian pastors preach and Christian people try a little harder to believe every single week. It is the **lie** that

"God wants you to find Him somewhere other than in His Word."

"Pray," the devil said to Punk Rock John. *"Pray, and God will answer."* He wasn't told "God has given you answers to your questions. Look, here they are written in His Word." He wasn't told "The idea that Jesus is based on Roman sun worship is a joke of pseudo-scholarship. Here, let me show you what Scripture says . . ." He wasn't told "Luther wasn't perfect, but he wasn't a Nazi either. But Jesus of Nazareth **was** perfect, and there are good historical reasons to believe it. Here, let me show you what Scripture says . . ." He wasn't told "Yeah, sometimes I find it hard to believe that God is there because it doesn't always feel like He is. But here, let me show you what Scripture says . . ." Nope. For Punk Rock John and countless other American Christians there aren't any real answers being given, just a warmed-over, squishy-spiritual sermon of **Rely on Yourself** done up with enough lipstick and a low-cut bodice to keep them coming back because there's no one else to dance with anyway.

This is why Christians are losing faith in our age. They give up on dancing with the Church because the kind of Christianity she is preaching is **BROKEN**. This is why our children are leaving the Church and heading to the after-party somewhere else. A bent version of Christianity isn't capable of giving them a Jesus worth believing anymore. This is how you risk losing your faith. A superficial spirituality filled with words that are **not** the words of the Bible is a counterfeit Christianity.

Behold the Cow of God

[Aaron] received the gold from their hand and
fashioned it with a graving tool and made a golden calf. . . .
And Aaron made a proclamation and said, "Tomorrow
shall be a feast to the LORD." (Exodus 32:4–5)

The old crow never tells you he is stealing your corn. He knows
you know your first love once was the words of and about Jesus. He
knows you know that you need these words, these Scriptures, in order
to remain a Christian. But he also knows you are human, which means
you are forgetful, distracted, and more than a little lazy. He's a one-trick
pony, but it's a darned good trick. With a sleight of hand, he fans into
flame a fire in your heart that he tells you is "for Jesus," but he slips into
your fire fuel for something else—**anything** else. He even doesn't mind
if you call your shiny, new golden cow "Jesus," because he knows that
once you've started fueling your faith with something other than the
real Jesus' words, it's only a matter of time before you wake up to find
your faith beat up, burned out, **BROKEN**, and without a single clue **how
it happened**. He knows, at that moment, you'll be ready to believe
anything in the world he tells you, especially if it gives you a reason to
leave behind your messed-up excuse for a religion. "It's not your faith in
God that's broken," he says then. "It's **Christianity**. Christianity is the
problem. The Bible is the problem. Even Jesus would never have wanted
it to be this way. Even Jesus would be proud of you for walking away
before it gets any worse."

This is a bitter potion the devil brews, a clever web he weaves. But
it is still and always the same **trick**. It is the same **Lie**. I'm sick of it. I'm
not going to sit back and take it anymore.

THE GOLDEN COW'S NEW CLOTHES

There once was an emperor who wanted the finest clothes money could buy. In his luxury, he hired two weavers who promised him the most exquisite clothes of all: a robe that could be seen only by people cool enough to see it. It would expose all liars, posers, and idiots, and show him who the true royalty were. You can imagine the emperor's distress when they first presented him with the outfit, and he could not see it himself. He could lose his kingdom over this! So he pretended it was the most amazing article of clothing he'd ever seen. He looked around and found that all his ministers agreed with him. He nodded and smiled, his fear mounting with every step. Next thing he knew, he was dressed to impress the world and embarking on a grand parade through his capital city. All the people were captivated. It must be a truly extraordinary design! But the silence was deafening. Why did they not cheer? Then a single, solitary voice rang loud and clear throughout the citadel. A child was laughing and calling to his mother, "Why does the emperor have no clothes?!"

The classic tale by Hans Christian Andersen is not supposed to be about Christianity. But it is. It is the tale of a Christianity that has forgotten her first love because her first love was stolen by thieves and liars. It is the tale of countless faithful Christians who feel in their gut something is terribly wrong, but who are frozen into silence by the fact that everyone else (just like them) is pretending not to notice. It is a tale of blindness, arrogance, and paranoia, of teachers who don't teach and believers left with nothing to believe. It is a tale of willful ignorance, of failure to face the cold truth about the situation, and of the refusal to repent. **And**, it is the tale of a child's faith, the simple, wonderful, naïve gift of calling a thing what it **is**.

My goal is to call with that infant's voice. I make no claim to some personal, grandiose insight into the deep and hidden things of God. I am no more than a child astride the hip of his mother. But her lullaby has been filled with words that never change. Her song transcends time and space, culture and style, with words of eternal meaning. She sings of an enemy, an ancient foe, whose guile and great might are armed with cruel hate. There is no equal to him in all the earth. So fierce is his warfare that with all human might there is nothing to be done. Soon were our loss effected! But my mother's song is not only of the danger. She croons also of the valiant One, a man (and more than a man) who fights for us, whom God Himself elected. Who is this? He is the King of kings! Christ Jesus, Mighty Lord. The God who is **the Word**, the Word you can sink your faith into and never have it drown. He holds the field forever.

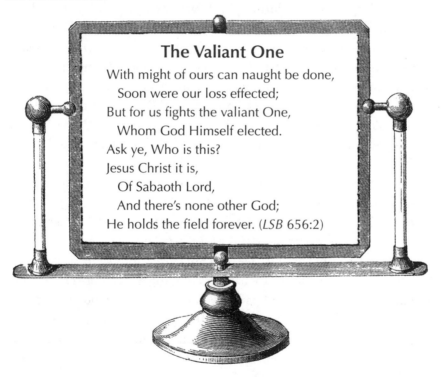

The Valiant One

With might of ours can naught be done,
　　Soon were our loss effected;
But for us fights the valiant One,
　　Whom God Himself elected.
Ask ye, Who is this?
Jesus Christ it is,
　　Of Sabaoth Lord,
　　And there's none other God;
He holds the field forever. (*LSB* 656:2)

There is only one attack the devil uses to destroy the Church of Jesus Christ—remove Jesus. He does this by removing the way Jesus reigns: by removing Jesus' words. There is nothing new to this. He's been a liar from the beginning. But he always tells the same lies. We can learn them. We can discern them. We don't have to believe them.

As the crow sweeps in to steal the seed, we can recognize his caw and learn to fight back by scattering the seed all the more.

How Dumb Do We Have to Be?

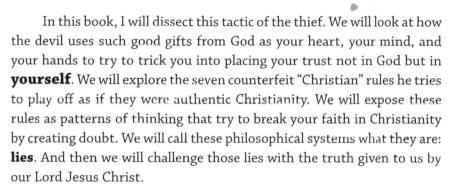

I am astonished that you are so quickly deserting Him who called you in the grace of Christ and are turning to a different gospel—not that there is another one, but there are some who trouble you and want to distort the gospel of Christ. But even if we or an angel from heaven should preach to you a gospel contrary to the one we preached to you, let him be accursed. (Galatians 1:6–8)

In this book, I will dissect this tactic of the thief. We will look at how the devil uses such good gifts from God as your heart, your mind, and your hands to try to trick you into placing your trust not in God but in **yourself**. We will explore the seven counterfeit "Christian" rules he tries to play off as if they were authentic Christianity. We will expose these rules as patterns of thinking that try to break your faith in Christianity by creating doubt. We will call these philosophical systems what they are: **lies**. And then we will challenge those lies with the truth given to us by our Lord Jesus Christ.

The crow comes cawing, promising you freedom, but telling you that **you** must earn it. He promises you supernatural wisdom, but tells you that **you** must figure it out. He promises you comfort, but insists that **you** find it inside yourself. He tells you that you're just on the other side of glory, if only **you** can create it. He offers you the world, but he leaves you hanging on a cross all by yourself, fed up with it all and wondering in anger and frustration where Jesus is. He was supposed to make it all better.

He does this the only way he can: he steals Jesus' words, and he uses **you** to do it. I am not going to let that happen. The house may have grown dirty, but we are going to sweep it clean, and once we do, we're not going to leave it empty so the one-trick pony can slip in and start excreting his filth all over again. Oh, no. We are not going to reduce this Good News to a one-hit wonder. Under the cross of Jesus, we will find emotion kindled on a fire that doesn't burn out. In the resurrection of Jesus, we will find a good reason for faith that answers the toughest questions. In the pure Word of God, we will find true purpose for our lives built on a foundation infinitely more solid than the shifting sands of "me."

For all of you Punk Rock Johns out there who aren't sure how much longer you can hold on: hang on for one more round. This book is written for you.

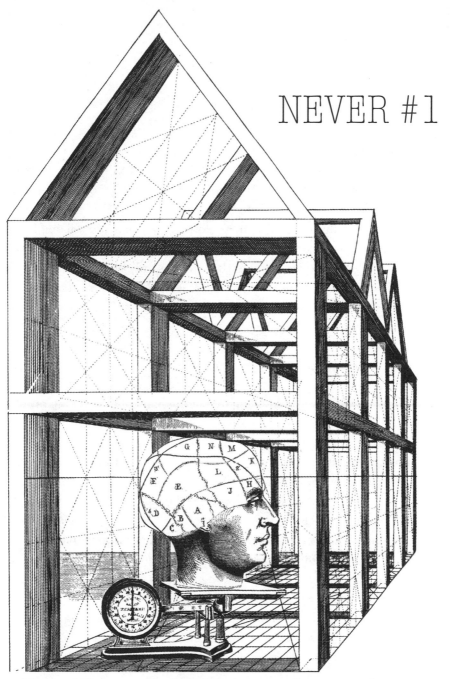

Never follow a rule that follows your liver, your heart, your pancreas, or any other bodily organ that could conceivably have its mind changed by the shifting of the wind.

THE DEVIL'S FIRST RULE

There are only two kinds of spirituality in the world. One is wrong and one is right. One is false and one is true. One is a lie and one is real. One takes the form of the countless spiritualities that have gone out into the world as manifestations of the Antichrist, and the other is God's own holy spirituality. But which is which? How can you learn to tell one from the other?

Let's begin by understanding that there is only one attack the devil uses in his war to destroy the Church of Jesus Christ. It's an attack he uses over and over again, but it is just one attack. The one-and-only attack the devil uses to destroy the Church is to remove Jesus. This is the devil's first rule.

But there is only one way to remove Jesus, and it's not the way that most people think. As far as the devil is concerned, it's perfectly cool to have a picture on the wall of a guy in a white bathrobe with long brown hair and a beard. It's even perfectly cool to call that guy in the picture "Jesus" and tell all the children that this "Jesus" guy loves them. The devil doesn't care whether you keep that picture up or take that picture down, because the devil's first rule is that he must remove Jesus—not just some idea about some imaginary guy named "Jesus," but the actual, real Jesus. There is only one way to do that: remove the actual, real Jesus' **words**.

The devil's first rule is to get us to forget all the things that the real Jesus actually said. The best way to do that is not to take down all the pictures of that long-haired guy walking through fields with some sheep, but to start replacing His words with other words. Our words. Other spiritualities. A counterfeit Christianity. By slowly leaching away the real Jesus' words and replacing them, one by one, with his own, the devil can eventually lead us into worshiping a guy named "Jesus" who is not actually there.

But first, if the devil is ever to slip in his own words as if they were Jesus' words, he must get us to trust him. You might think that would be quite a challenge, but in the end it is actually very easy.

All he has to do is **lie**.

The devil really has only one lie. It is **The Lie**. It's the same Lie he has been telling ever since the beginning (John 8:44; Genesis 3:4–5). As a result, he's very practiced at it. He's learned that there's more than one way to put a little spin on the same deception. He dresses up The Lie in new clothes, and he gives The Lie a new name. And at the drop of the hat, he can do it again. And again. And again. First he points you left. Then he points you right. But both directions are off the path and lead down into a bog, where the waters are muddy and fog blurs the sight. Slogging through those waters gets tough, but then along comes The Lie again (the same lie, but this time with a pretty wig and some fake eyelashes), whispering for you to try yet another direction. Not back to the path— no, never that! Just, "This way." "Over yonder."

With each new step, the fog gets denser, and memories of the path grow dim. Your hands rub raw on the weeds and thorns. Your feet bruise on the stones sunk beneath the mud. Your conscience feels ragged and tired. Then here comes The Lie again (it's the same lie, but now with a top hat, a monocle, and a refined, compelling accent), and this time he says, "You know, you have that cursed path to blame for all of this. If you'd never been on that path in the first place, none of this would have happened to you."

You would think we humans, after all we've been through, might start to recognize that we've fallen for the same dupe so many times before. But the devil is the master of disguising his Lie. He is like a cook preparing immaculate masterpieces worthy of gobbling up to the last delicate crumb. To the unwary, each dish looks like a new creation, something never before seen or tasted. That is the true talent of The Lie. Even so, just as with any other kind of ingredient for a meal, there are only so many things you can do with The Lie. No matter how many spices you add to a tomato base, you can take it only so far, and after all that, it is still going to taste like tomatoes. For all the countless tweaks the devil stirs in to spice up his dish, at the end of the day it's the same old ingredients in the same old recipe.

For the next six chapters, I am going to break down the devil's recipe book. We are going to examine the six primary spices he uses to disguise the flavor of his food, not fragrant leaves and ground-up seeds, but **words**. Words are what the devil uses to mask The Lie until he convinces the world that it is the truth.

There are only two kinds of spirituality in the world. One is right and one is wrong. The goal of the wrong one is to convince you that it is the right one; to get you to eat The Lie, to swallow his dish whole, digest it, and then, despite the stomachache, go back for seconds. The devil's goal is to convincingly replace Jesus' words with his Lie so that you arrive at the place where you trust in his rules—rules that he teaches as if they were God's rules. Every Christian must learn these rules of the devil, these rules that are designed to remove the words of Jesus, not that we would follow the devil's rules, but rather, **so every Christian might break them as often as possible**.

Deconstructing Emo Greek Mythology

Punk Rock John once had a friend. His name was Emo Dan. Emo Dan starred in a five-minute segment on a DVD produced by a superchurch out California-way. It was edgy and cool-ish, marvelously shot and edited. But, despite all its best intentions, it was also **godless**.

Picture this: Our hero Emo Dan stands on a blacktop court somewhere in suburbia. Time-lapse photography paints clouds rolling overhead in an azure sky. The grass waves a deep, organic green. Light shifts from midday to late afternoon, while acoustic guitar and hidden keyboard swells tear at your heart before a word is even uttered.

"I was in a really dark place." Emo Dan's slightly awkward teen voice raises the tension further, begging you for authenticity and understanding. "I grew up in Church, but I didn't know if God was real. I was alone one afternoon, walking out on a playground." The music grows more raw. You feel like crying for him. "Then, just as I was really questioning and doubting, a cloud covered the sun completely and left me all alone in the darkness. And it was, like . . ." he pauses. The timed-lapse stills roll into overcast. The colors fade, and the green grass goes pale and pasty. "It was like God had abandoned me."

"But then!" Emo Dan's voice tears apart the melancholy melody, while bright, immaculate images flash on the screen, and a fresh new riff lifts up the beat. "Right then! Right when I was ready to give up, the sun came out again!" Dan's happiness is tangible. Everything is right with the world again! "I could feel the sun's warmth on my face, and I knew—I just knew! I knew that God was there."

As I sat in my apartment, watching the video for the first time, I almost dove off the bed yelling at the monitor: "*Which God?!* **Which God?!**" But that was it. That was the end of the segment. The rest of the video brought us no more knowledge of the life and times of Emo Dan. After all his pain, after all his doubt, Emo Dan made peace with his spirituality by learning how to worship **the sun**.

It's not a terribly new idea. Sun worship has been around since before we started recording history. In ancient Greece, for example, Apollo was the god of the sun, and he pretty much rocked. Every morning, he took his chariot of fire out for a ride across the sky. At night, he and his solar steeds returned to Mount Olympus to rest. This meant that whenever the perturbed and moody ancient cousin of Emo Dan—let's call him Emo Danomidious—started to question his family's belief in Apollo, all Papa Danomidious had to do was take his son out in the field on a sunny day, point at the sky, and say, "Watch. There goes Apollo. See how he moves. He is watching us. He is protecting us. He is real." And Emo Danomidious could feel the warmth on his face and know, just know, it was true.

Seriously, if you are ever going to be a pagan, Apollo is a pretty sweet god to have. Besides being tough when it comes to a fight, he also holds the superpowers of light, knowledge, medicine, and music.[1] The

---

1.   Would you believe that Apollo's avatars were often either a serpent or a raven? But who's paying attention to coincidences?

other gods have a lot to offer too, but for the average Joe, Apollo is about as sweet a deity as you can hope to have turn his balmy eye your way any lonely afternoon on the blacktop. There's just this one thing that really isn't so hot about worshiping Apollo: Apollo is not actually God. He's not even really *a* god. The sun is a burning ball of gas in outer space, and the stories of Apollo are just that—stories.

But here's the thing. Emo Dan knew this just as well as you do. Yet that didn't stop him from building his faith on the sun anyway. One pivotal afternoon he put all his hope and trust in the chance movements of the clouds and called those movements "God." More than that, his church decided to make a DVD to teach youth groups everywhere that they should do the same.

But this is not quite fair. Emo Dan wasn't really teaching kids everywhere to put their faith **only** in the sun. He wasn't saying that God will always prove Himself to you in the exact same, mildly surprising happenstance event involving the sun and the clouds. No. He was just saying that God will always prove Himself in mildly surprising, happenstance events. So he wasn't really preaching Apollo. He was only preaching **Mysticism**.

Consumer-Market Mystics

The first rule that every authentic Christian ought to fight to the death (in order to break as often as possible) is **Mysticism**. Mysticism is like a seductive woman, sitting at a sidewalk café watching everyone who passes by. She is always dressed in the latest fashions and styles, and while she rarely yells, her voice is always heard above the crowd. *"Whoever would be spiritual, let him talk to me,"* she says. *"Learn from me my spiritual disciplines. I will teach you to experience God. Let me teach you my newfound methods. I will help you learn to discover God through what you feel. Follow me and my advice, and I will show you the trick to finding God **in your heart**."*

> **Mysticism:** The belief that direct knowledge of God can be attained through your subjective experiences of God or something godlike. Mysticism, then, is nothing more than worship of your emotions.

Mysticism has found many ready listeners in American culture because American culture is a melting pot of trying to **feel good**. Humans have always made feeling good a high priority, but in our age we have made it an art form. Both Christians and non-Christians alike spend most of the waking day trying to feel good. When we feel bad (which happens a lot), we begin casting around the market for something new to consume in order to try and feel better. Once we find an answer, we remain as diligent in trying to make the feeling better last as long as possible. This is our way of life. It is our economy, our national pastime, and our greatest export. We believe, teach, and confess that the key to happiness is managing discomfort by increasing good feelings instead, and we are so successful at it that we've also come to assume God approaches religion the very same way. Why wouldn't God want me to be happy? Why wouldn't God want to meet my needs, take away my cares and worries, and lift me up? Why wouldn't a truly good God want me to find Him by learning to **feel** the goodness of His presence? It only makes perfect, heartfelt sense.

For this reason, all over America, every week, a vast number of the most well-meaning of us congregate in special houses that we have built for the sole purpose of trying to feel God together. By combining applied motivational speeches and creative musical arrangement with the latest and best gimmicks of technology, we listen to the promise that we can and will feel good by finding God (and find God by feeling good). We consume these carefully manufactured divine experiences like any other product, expecting them to be over on the hour so that we still have plenty of time to trot back to our lives of buying, selling, and trying to feel even more good in all the ways we possibly can. Fresh off the assembly line, we don't mind applying whatever bits of

29

personal skill development the preacher told us was this week's key to directly enhancing our experience of God. None of us feel manipulated. We would be angry if you told us we were just consumers being sold a fast-food religion. "Mysticism" is just a big word without any meaning to us. But every week we buy it anyway. We go to our churches in search of a better feeling, and when we find it, we believe we have found the real presence of God.

THE ROAD TO NOWHERE

But the righteousness based on faith says, "Do not say in your heart, 'Who will ascend into heaven?'" (that is, to bring Christ down). (Romans 10:6)

There are two main problems with this mystic pursuit of God through feeling. The first (and the biggest for Christians) is that Jesus never actually taught it. The Bible never tells you that the path to finding God lies hidden within positive experiences. It's not that Jesus has a problem with hearts or emotions in general; after all, He created them. But He didn't create them in order to speak to us through them. That was why He created **words**.

The second problem with believing that we can find God in our hearts is that human emotions always have an unintended side effect: **they wear off**. Feelings can come with extraordinary strength. They can be as real and potent as the sun warming your face. They can fill you with confidence, conviction, and daring. They can motivate you, get you to turn your life around, and press you to achieve things you never thought possible. But they inevitably also do what emotions always do— **change**. One week you wake up to discover that the methods once so good at helping you feel God last week—the songs, the advice, the practices, and all the other things that gave you such strong comfort and assurance—suddenly don't quite lift you up the way they used to.

They feel muted. The experience is dulled, if only slightly. At this point, the trained mystic begins seeking, casting about for a new source of feeling better—a catchier song, a more vintage or innovative practice, some new, compelling advice. It really doesn't matter what. If the sun breaking through the clouds holds the potential to help you feel your way past the tolerance you have built up to the rush you believe is the presence of God, Mysticism is more than happy to let you find God in the sun.

This is precisely where Mysticism is the most dangerous (and a little scary). Once you've given her your heart, she is more than content to show you God's presence in just about **anything**. She knows a time is coming when seeking God in your emotions will start to build up a tolerance. She knows you will start to shift from feeling lifted up to feeling tired, from being purposeful to being worn thin, and from experiencing conviction to experiencing a nagging hint of betrayal. After all the work she has done to get you this far, the last thing she wants to do is risk that in your moment of weakness someone else might tell you the mistake you have made is trying to find God in your heart. So she's ready, right there beside you, to whisper her lie, only spiced with different colors. *"This is the moment we've been waiting for,"* she says. *"You weren't ready to* **truly** *experience God before. First, you had to grow and learn. But now you are ready. All of this is just a test you are facing because you have come so far. Now is the time to take finding God in your heart* **to the next level**."

That next level might still include the name Jesus, or it might not. It might come with a few verses quoted from the Bible, or it might not. It doesn't matter so long as you dig into the pie and start practicing the new practices, applying the new methods, and putting your trust in the new promises that you will and can find God in what you feel. *"This time it will be for real. This time the feelings will last. This time you will really, really learn to experience God."*

Mysticism was waiting for Emo Dan on that cloudy day, ready to bring a ray of sunshine into his angst-filled life as a promise that his personal experiences were the key to knowing God and to knowing how God feels about him. But I wonder what would have happened if the weather vane didn't turn. What if it had started to rain instead? Having been promised that life with God is about feeling good, now suddenly convinced by the bad feeling of an overcast sky that God is not real, what will Mysticism offer him next? For a great many people, experimentation with sex, alcohol, and drugs (or some combination of the three) is the natural answer to the quest of feeling better. After all, there aren't many more effective ways to manipulate one's emotions than through substance abuse. But these, too, wear off. Tolerances build up. People get strung out. What then? Sometimes you don't have to wait even that long. Just a few years ago in Philadelphia, two high school girls threw themselves in front of a train because their boyfriends had dumped them. They weren't thinking that day. They were **feeling**. They were doing exactly what they had been taught to do: **follow their hearts**. The dark side of Mysticism wasn't sleeping, even while the rest of us were. With The Lie spiced just right for the moment, Mysticism was waiting to whisper to those heartbroken children, *"This is the next step. This is the path to feeling better. This is how you get to a better place. Just follow me. Just jump."*

{ Mysticism's lie: You can find God in your heart. }

But the dark side of Mysticism isn't always such an early tragedy. For many, Mysticism dances with them through decades of church attendance, purposeful living, and chasing after a successful life. For many, it isn't until they're sitting alone in a nursing home, forcing down fifteen pills a day, and hoping for a visit from anyone, that the despair and doubts about God buried beneath endless rays of sunshine come flooding back as the perfect storm of a broken life. Sometimes it's later, sometimes it's sooner, but it is inevitable that the lows tip the balance back from the highs. How many times can feelings fix the real questions of faith? What about after the divorce, after the layoff, after the bankruptcy, after the **sin**? What will give Emo Dan hope next?

Though he will rarely admit it to himself, the Mystic Christian wakes up every day feeling a little bit weaker, needing to try something a little bit newer, in order to recover the emotions he was convinced he had finally captured in a bottle the day before. If Emo Dan walks this path long enough, if he eats The Lie long enough, then it is only a matter of time until one of those days he wakes up royally angry (and not quite sure why), filled with a growing awareness that his attempts to feel God just aren't working. Too tired to go seeking yet another emotional proof, unwilling to force-feed himself yet another quest for experience at yet another new church, fed up with believing that this next trick will work when all the others have been such limited failures, Emo Dan will conclude that his problem is God. This is exactly what Mysticism is waiting for. This is her plan. She knows Emo Dan won't take out his anger on her (after all, Emo Dan doesn't even know she is the one he's been worshiping, because all along Emo Dan thinks he has been worshiping the God of the Bible).

On that day, Emo Dan will wake up and blame his failures of trying to feel God on Christianity, because Christianity is what he thinks he has been practicing. He has tried with all his heart and all his mind and all his soul to feel God, and as a direct result he now feels with utmost, experiential certainty that Christianity is the most untrustworthy religion in the world. What will he try next? Maybe a nice, safe religion that promises a better walk with God through healthy living, with some regular stretching and breathing exercises. Maybe he'll go join Punk Rock John at the local Atheistic Apologetics Festival. Then again, maybe his ears will be perked by the latest religion making a splash among young men in Western civilization, the one that guarantees that a real, ultimate God experience comes fastest by strapping explosives to your chest and walking into a café.

This is the great danger of Mysticism. She is terribly powerful. Once you've believed the lie she tells—that you can find God in your heart—she is capable of convincing you to try **anything**.

The Bible Is a Book

But doesn't the Bible teach us that God lives in our hearts? What about a passage like 2 Corinthians 1:21–22, which says, "It is God who establishes us with you in Christ, and has anointed us, and who has also 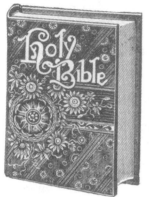 put His seal on us and *given us His Spirit in our hearts* as a guarantee." Doesn't that teach us that it is God's plan for us to feel Him present in our lives?

Well . . . no.

The devil's goal is to make you think that his words are God's words. One of the sneakiest ways to do this is actually to quote God's words, but not quite **all** of them. By taking a sentence from the Bible apart from its context, it's easy enough to squish the words into meaning almost anything. Reading 2 Corinthians 1:21–22 all by itself means you, the reader, must import into it your own definitions for soft, fluid words such as "anointed," "seal," and "Spirit," as well as "in our hearts." Does "in our hearts" mean "in our feelings"? Or does it mean something else entirely, such as "by faith alone"? The only way to know is to read the verse together with its **context**.

Words work this way all the time. It's the nature of language. When you take any sentence out of its context, that makes it difficult to understand what it means. For example, if I were to tell you to "season it with salt," am I saying you should put a pinch of salt into whatever you're cooking? Maybe. Or maybe I mean that you should bring the conversation down to earth a bit more. Or maybe I'm suggesting you should not take the conversation seriously at all. How do you know which? The answer is **context**.

The context of 2 Corinthians 1 doesn't fit well into a bullet-point lecture. It doesn't read like a user manual for finding God. Instead, it reads like a letter, indeed, a very difficult letter to a very in-crisis congregation. In verses 3–11, the apostle Paul confesses his own struggle with anything but good feelings. "We were so utterly burdened beyond our strength that we despaired of life itself," he says. He follows this up in verses 12–14 by explaining that what he is going to say next is the same thing he says in every letter he ever has written, and he asks them in verses 15–18 not to judge this theology he preaches based on his failure to visit them like he had promised to do. After their previous conflict (see 1 Corinthians!) he had truly wanted to come and see them, so that together they could forgive one another face-to-face and thus have a mutual "experience of grace" (2 Corinthians 1:15).

Unfortunately, his plans to visit fell through, but he implores them not to use this as an excuse to think that his words about Christ are **also** untrue. "For the Son of God, Jesus Christ, whom we proclaimed among you . . . was not Yes and No, but in Him it is always Yes. . . . That is why it is through Him that we utter our Amen to God for His glory" (2 Corinthians 1:19–20). It is this same God preached by Paul who has established both him and the Corinthians in Christ and has therefore "anointed us, and who has also put His seal on us and given us His Spirit in our hearts as a guarantee."

So, if we let the context teach us what words such as "anointing" and "in our hearts" mean, then they must relate to Jesus Christ being **proclaimed** by Paul and to the fact that through these words the Corinthians were brought to say **"Amen!"** In the next chapter, Paul continues, "I came to Troas to **preach** the gospel of Christ . . . and through us [God] spreads the fragrance of the **knowledge** of Him [Christ] everywhere" (2 Corinthians 2:12–14). We are "not, like so many, peddlers of God's word," he says, "but as men of sincerity, as commissioned by God, in the sight of God we **speak** in Christ" (2 Corinthians 2:17).

So what is the anointing? What is this seal? And how does the Spirit work? The constant in all these verses is not the feelings or experiences Christians might have, but the words about Jesus that the apostles were sent to preach. It is true that in many and various ways God did speak to people of old through the prophets (Hebrews 1:1). But even then He never once expected the prophets to find Him in the changes of the weather or the shifting of their hearts. More so, in these last days, He has spoken to us through His Son (Hebrews 1:2). He sent His Son into human flesh, and while He was here, He did more than let Apollo shine lazily through the clouds onto Jesus' face one balmy afternoon. Instead, on the banks of the Jordan River in the land of Israel, He ripped the sky in half with a fantastic display of ultracosmic authority, in order to proclaim, "That guy. Right there. That one named Jesus. He is My beloved Son" (cf. Matthew 3:17). And then later, He did it again on a mountain, where He said to the men following Jesus, "Hey, guys. Do you want to know what I think about you? **Listen to Him**" (cf. Matthew 17:5).

This is the reality of how God's way of creating faith strikes at the root of the mystic problem. The Lie first told in the garden of Eden is the same Lie the devil has told ever since. Although God Himself is more than content to make use of real words, the devil keeps coming along with his nifty little trick of asking, "Did God actually say?" (Genesis 3:1). He bends and twists the words until he's spun you around like a blindfolded kid trying to swing a stick at a piñata. He's talked you off the path and into a journey across a bog, convinced that you will be able to find what God really thinks anywhere and everywhere in the universe **except** for the plain and simple, straightforward and sufficient words of Holy Scripture.

I Have Some Wild Geese to Sell You

God made the sunshine. He likes it a lot. But He doesn't want you to use it to listen to Him. That is why He gave you **Jesus**. The plain words of Holy Scripture are the antidote to the poisoned dish of Mysticism. Reading those words carefully and learning their context is to inwardly digest the faith that God is not only real but also gives us real, pure, true answers. God is far more generous to us than to force us to endlessly seek Him in the flurries of the wind and the palpitations of our hearts. He wants us to do far more than merely imagine what His will for us might be. He wants us to be certain. You don't need to wait for a break in the weather to hear and know what God thinks about you.

> ## Crossing Our Hearts
> We ourselves heard this very voice borne from heaven, for we were with Him on the holy mountain. And we have the prophetic word more fully confirmed, to which you will do well to pay attention as to a lamp shining in a dark place, until the day dawns and the morning star rises in your hearts. (2 Peter 1:18–19)

Where should Christians look for the Spirit's guidance? We look to the preached words the apostles left written down for us to stand on, like a foundation laid in rock. What is the anointing that God has given us? In the Bible, to anoint something always refers to the actual **physical** act of pouring something over someone. In the Early Church, the pouring that was always done for new believers involved the waters of Baptism. But here the modern mystic in us senses something sketchy. The sunshine is one thing, but simple water included with God's Word and given at Jesus' own command is another. It's not that the Bible doesn't have plenty of words connecting the Holy Spirit and faith in Jesus with God's activity of Baptism. (It does: Acts 2:38–39; Romans 6:3–4; Galatians 3:26–27; Colossians 2:11–12; and 1 Peter 3:21 are some of the most obvious.) It's that trusting in Baptism doesn't quite **feel** right.

But right there is the very point. Regardless of how it feels, what does the Bible actually say? Mysticism's lie is meant to convince you that what the Bible says matters far less than defending all the emotions you have learned to trust in. *"God's voice is not found only in Scripture,"* Mysticism says. *"The Bible is a matter of your own personal interpretation anyway."*

Just like that, maybe without even realizing it, Christianity is unhinged from the one place the apostles taught was the **actual** working place of the Holy Spirit. Without Scripture interpreting Scripture, words such as "anointed" and "seal" and "Spirit" are made squishy and transformed into hooks used to drag your conscience off into all manner of spiritual jeopardy. With the Spirit no longer found in the words on the page, but instead "over here" or "over there," Mysticism keeps you dangling on an endless journey here and there and everywhere with your hope of eventually finding God boiling down to what's going on **inside of you**.

{ Mysticism is the worship of your emotions.}

*So go look! Find an experience. Join a club. Get excited. Pick a method. Choose a discipline, or three. Even read the Bible if you like. Just make sure you underline all the passages about what **you** are supposed to do to get your walk right. Ignore anything you feel God didn't mean for **you** to believe. And whatever **you** do, don't make the horrible mistake of thinking that anything it says is so universally unchanging and true as to be something like "doctrine." **That** would be close-minded. **That** would limit God, put Him in a box. The Bible is just a book written by men after all. It's a living document. It's not like God really said it all exactly that way on purpose. It's the spirit **behind** the words you're really after, and that spirit will speak to **you** through how you feel, through your experiences in prayer, and through the chance happenings of life.*

At the end of the slogging through that bog, what exactly have you found?

Just you.

you **and your own personal**

"spirituality."

you **and your own personal Bible.**

you **and your own personal Jesus.**

you **and totally you, completely, absolutely,** entirely you

all alone.

BREAKING ALONE

Strangely enough, it is this being alone that plagues the doubts of countless Christians. Our fast-food religion isn't cutting it, and **we know it**. Living in mystic pursuit of an emotion-giving god, we are constantly haunted by the strange **feeling** that after all our efforts, we don't feel closer to God. Not really. Not once the adrenaline wears off. Instead, we feel more alone. It's this loneliness that keeps us susceptible to the latest, greatest marketing techniques and the next bigger, better spiritual deal. If we truly had found God, we could retire to a mountaintop somewhere and bask in His presence. But we're not satisfied with our God experiences. This makes every new worship form, every new program, every new wind that comes down the pike an easy sell. (And believe me, some people are making a real killing in this market.) Christians are starving for something that **this time**

will really, really, *really* work. But like a foolish man adrift on a raft in the ocean, drinking saltwater does anything but quench his thirst. The haunting, back-of-the-heart feeling that went away in a moment of transcendent experience just keeps coming back.

This time, just like last time and just like the next time, it's all the same Lie. It's Mysticism's lie that what **you** manage to feel inside of **you** can make **your** problems go away. It's Mysticism's lie that trying to find God in **your** heart, **your** emotions, and **your** experience (even in a superchurch filled with 20,000 singing people) still boils down to **you** experiencing **your** encounter with **your** god entirely inside of **you** . . . which means . . . entirely . . . all . . . by . . . **your** . . . **self**.

This is Mysticism. This is the rule every authentic Christian ought to fight to the death to break as often as possible. When you are the source, when you are the foundation, when you are the **heart** of your spirituality, you have fallen prey to Mysticism's old lie dressed up as the triumph of the individual (and with it the death of the community) in Western civilization. Worse yet, even if you have also found the true God in American mystical Christianity (because His Word is just that cool, working even through the lies we pile on top of it), the emotions that we confuse with God's presence on a regular basis still always come with a **timer**. One day, no matter how new the trend is, no matter how clever the next gimmick, you're going to go to the trough looking for another meal of mystical food and find out that Christianity just isn't cutting it anymore.

This is what made me angry about that godless video sold by a church looking to make a killing by marketing Mysticism dressed up as Christian subculture. Here, with Emo Dan, was a real chance to preach the real Gospel from the real Bible about the real man Jesus, who came down to earth with divinely perfect, real words that **we still have**. Words that are inspired and inerrant. Spirit-filled words. Words from a man who, as the incarnation of almighty God, wasn't deterred in His perfect faith by a failed Apollo on one more-than-overcast Friday on a not-so-playground Roman hill called Golgotha. For the sole purpose of sparing you from knowing what God really thinks about you, He ignored what He had to feel in order to save you from it. He endured the cross, scorning its shame and pain. He put His will and emotions aside, submitting to the will of His Father. He did not feel joy, but rather believed that joy would come on the other side of His tomb, when He would ascend to heaven and send His Holy Spirit to preach to you that no matter how you feel, the victory is His, and He has committed himself to giving that victory to you as a free gift.

That is what I wanted the video to preach to me. I was starving for it to remind me that Jesus' dying was not just some emo flirtation with darkness, but the ultimate cosmically sacrificial death. It was the pinnacle of all human loneliness and yet the place where man was not alone, but "God with us" (Matthew 1:23). It was the place where Mysticism met her match in a man who could not be tempted to do anything other than trust God despite all that He was seeing and experiencing, including the utter and eternal wrath of God against the sins of the whole world!

Christian spirituality lives from the teaching that Jesus is the place where man is one with God and God is one with us. He took in Himself all our reliance on Mysticism as our hope for finding God, and He let that divided, fractured, idol in our hearts be nailed to the cross in Him. And having given up the Spirit, His real, mortal human heart was pierced through until blood and water flowed from His dead body onto our parched and thirsty ground.

And then . . .
    He didn't . . .
        stay . . .
            dead.

You know the story.

Do you **know** the story?

What was it that Emo Dan had forgotten? Jesus, the man, brought back to life the beating heart of God. "In Christ God was reconciling the world to Himself, not counting their trespasses against them, and entrusting to us the message of reconciliation" (2 Corinthians 5:19). God's act of saving the world did not happen in me, but outside of me. That's the **message**. That's the **Word**. This Word has pure **meaning**. The meaning is more than a mere **story**. This story is humanity's **history**. Our history is not the experience of every individual Christian all **alone**, but an utterly and entirely **shared** faith—not a feeling but a believed **reality**. One set of facts. One result from those facts. One faith. One Lord. One Baptism (cf. Ephesians 4:5).

One God and Father of all has sent one Spirit, who calls to our hearts with one hope that belongs to the preached call—one hope that believes these words: "Hey, you. Yeah, you. I'm Jesus. I died for you. That's right. I'm calling you by name. I'm washing you so that you shall have a part with Me. Just trust Me on this one. You are Mine now."

WHEN GOD AND SPIRIT SMASH, YOU GET JESUS

Dr. Martin Luther (who I happen to think was pretty sweet) once got really frustrated with the pope. That's a long story. But seven years before his death, after a lifetime of terrible struggle against entirely insurmountable odds, Dr. Luther composed and published a short work called the Smalcald Articles. This was a short series of sections (or "articles") briefly describing what Luther believed the Reformation stood for and could not survive without. Granted, it's not the most entirely cool title you've ever heard. You've got to give the guy a break. It was written for a meeting of important nobles and scholars at a place called Smalcald. From there, it gathered dust for a couple of years as matters of Euro-politics took over. But in 1538, battling illness and concerned he would soon die, Luther had it published as his own last will and testament of faith. If you want to know what **the** reformer of the Reformation believed that all Protestants needed to believe, "The Super Fantastic Rock Out Final Declaration of Dr. Luther (of Blessed Memory)," otherwise published as the Smalcald Articles, is the place to go. "In a word," he says, "mysticism" (although he calls it "enthusiasm")

---

dwells in Adam and his children from the beginning to the end of the world. Its venom has been implanted and infused into them [us] by the old serpent. It is the origin, power, and strength of all heresy, especially of that of the papacy and Muhammad. (Smalcald Articles III VIII 9)

God Speaks

It is the Spirit who gives life; the flesh is no help at all. The words that I have spoken to you are spirit and life. (John 6:63)

Therefore, we must constantly maintain this point: God does not want to deal with us in any other way than through the spoken Word and the Sacraments. Whatever is praised as from the Spirit—without the Word and Sacraments—is the devil himself. God wanted to appear even to Moses through the burning bush and spoken Word. No prophet, neither Elijah nor Elisha, received the Spirit without the Ten Commandments or the spoken Word. (Smalcald Articles III VIII 10–11)

Whoa. Dude.

From long experience battling not only the pope on one side but also more radical reformers on the other, Luther came to see that at the end of the day there was a common argument being made by both sides: the Word of God is simply not enough for your spirituality. They argue that something more needs to be added. Scripture alone is **incomplete**. We need **another** testimony from God. Whether that meant a papal bull (which was a really special letter with the pope's seal on it) or visions delivered to "heavenly prophets" ready to lead the peasants of Germany in an uprising against all tyranny, or even the oracles of an Arabian warrior-king, it was the same Lie told over and over again. *"God didn't really say you can find Him completely and totally and sufficiently in His Word alone. You need something more."*

But this is not Christianity. This is our natural religion, which has inherited rebellion against God as our original sin. You don't have to teach your children to think they're right. They do that fine for themselves. You need to teach them they're wrong. You need to teach them that they can be corrected. You need to teach them you will forgive them. You need to teach them Jesus is not about mystic experience. Jesus is about outside-of-you forgiveness.

St. Paul said it best:

All Scripture is breathed out by God and profitable for teaching, for reproof, for correction, and for training in righteousness.

(2 Timothy 3:16)

The words "breathed out by God" are only one word in Greek, an unusual term that many scholars think Paul coined. *Theopneumos* (pronounced thay-oh-noo-mos) is the smashing together of two more common Greek roots: *Theos* means "God," and *pneuma,* while it can mean "breath" or "wind," is usually translated as "spirit." So, literally, St. Paul says, "All Scripture is God's-Spirited." The words of the Bible are the place the Holy Spirit works. The Holy Spirit works using these real words "for teaching, for reproof, for correction, and for training in righteousness."

Each of these words is a powerhouse of meaning. The word "teaching," or *didaskalia,* can also be translated as **doctrine**, which means objective truth that never changes and can be faithfully passed on from one person to another. "Reproof" is about much more than **rebuking** one's behavior. It is about replacing false ideas with true ones. In the same way, "correction" is not only changing the way one acts, but changing the way one thinks, growing from being ignorant to **informed** about God's will. All of these three meet together as training in **righteousness**.

Just as with the words "reproof" and "correction," it is all too easy to hear the word "righteousness" in English and think that it is about being a good person. But this word "righteousness" is based on the Greek root *dikaios,* which is the foundation of a far more exciting word: **justification**. In the New Testament, justification isn't about living a good life but about being declared righteous in God's sight (even though you aren't of your own account) because of Jesus' work on the cross for you. Being declared something is always all about words, which is where St. Paul started us off in the first place.

So when we put it all together, we find that St. Paul and Dr. Luther agree: Holy Scripture is God's own Spirited words, given for the purpose of establishing **doctrine** (eternal truth) that **rebukes** our natural sinful thoughts and **corrects** our ignorance of what God thinks about us by training us to believe we are **justified** for Christ's sake. This Christianity is entirely outside of us, promised to us, a gift you are free to believe by faith.

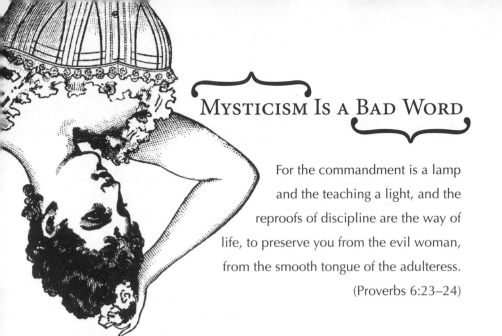

Mysticism Is a Bad Word

For the commandment is a lamp
and the teaching a light, and the
reproofs of discipline are the way of
life, to preserve you from the evil woman,
from the smooth tongue of the adulteress.

(Proverbs 6:23–24)

We live in a sad age, but our age is not so different from every age since the serpent first tempted our forebears to believe God's Word wasn't the only thing worth believing. The lips of Mysticism have always dripped with milk and honey. But Mysticism has also always been a bitter two-edged sword. From her seat at the café she promises life. "*Come in and drink with me*," she says, but she knows nothing (Proverbs 9:13–14), and she holds only death and corruption. She teaches you not to listen to the reproving doctrines of Scripture, but to despise discipline and to hate correction. She closes your ears to any teacher but your own heart and leads you to the brink of utter ruin. Her spirituality is intoxicating, as alluring and seductive as the most beautiful woman mankind has ever seen. But she is no lady. She is a prostitute, and she will make you pay for what she gives, not with gold or jewels, but your very life (Proverbs 9:13–18).

It should shock us all the more that many pulpits in America not only fail to warn us about this adulterous spirituality, but instead **promote it**. The number of mystical "Christian" rules for finding God come in all styles and sizes, but it is always the same lie: "*Your emotions are where you will find God.*" You don't have the answers? Pray and wait for a feeling. You need to figure something out? Go listen to the wind. Not sure if Jesus lives? It doesn't matter if He lives. He lives inside **your heart**.

This is why the first rule that every Christian ought to follow is "Never follow a rule that follows your liver, your heart, your pancreas, or any other bodily organ that could conceivably have its mind changed by the shifting of the wind." Never put your trust in "Christian" disciplines, methods, and traditions that make promises about your relationship with the almighty God founded on what you **feel**. Never put your trust in Mysticism.

The Better to Hear You With

In Him you also, when you heard the word of truth, the gospel of your salvation, and believed in Him, were sealed with the promised Holy Spirit. (Ephesians 1:13)

Emotions are a wonderful gift of the created world. God made them for us. They are part of being human, and Christianity exalts in the redemption that has been purchased for us. But there is a chasm of difference between believing feelings are a gift from God and believing feelings **are** God. Feelings can be good, but feelings are never **the Gospel**. Rules and traditions, methods and disciplines that teach that your emotions are the source of God's revealing of Himself to you confuse Jesus Christ with **you**. As exciting as those kinds of promises might sound, ignore them.

Get real wisdom. Follow the Word of God instead.

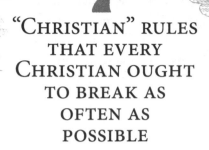

7

"CHRISTIAN" RULES THAT EVERY CHRISTIAN OUGHT TO BREAK AS OFTEN AS POSSIBLE

Never #1

Never follow a rule that follows your liver,
your heart, your pancreas, or any other
bodily organ that could conceivably
have its mind changed by
the shifting of the wind.

The First Rule to be **BROKEN**

Mysticism.

You can find God in your heart: the worship of your emotions.

NEVER #2

Never follow a rule that wasn't written
in stone a very, very long time ago
(doubly so if the grass is only greener on
the other side because it's made of plastic).

ME VERSUS THE HAND-SEWN, NOT-PLASTIC, CARROT

My family has a problem with toys.

Before our first daughter was born, my wife and I visited some friends with a toddler. They were good people. Conscientious. Focused. Goals and dreams. But dear goodness, their living room was a fallout zone from a particle bomb filled with colored plastic made in China. My eyes had to be popping out of my face as I tried to smile through the evening while ignoring the mountains of petroleum-derived, slightly chewable (perhaps toxic) spillage that was growing out of their carpet. We were so traumatized that when we went home that night, our marriage was forever changed. A day earlier it had been "till death do us part." Now, it was "till death do us part, **and without plastic toys**." Reeling with premonitions of latex-laden living, we set out on a marital crusade to hedge in the actual number of toys our children would one day inevitably compile in our home:

"No stockades built of wasted fossil fuels for us!" quoth I.

"Agreed!" parlayed my dear and winsome bride. "Every descendant of our line may retain custody to a maximum equity of seven toys."

"Forsooth!" I returned. "Any toy received above and beyond said holy number shall require barter of one to one, eye for eye."

"Yeah, yeah, and verily indeed," she vowed. "We shall thusly with stated master plan catechize our children unto the true value of material blessings."

"It is most certainly true," I appended.
"To boot! By association with our just fiat we shall also impart to our progeny delayed gratification."

Call us naïve or laugh at our convicted enthusiasm for changing the world one household at a time, but when it comes down to it, there was only one honest-to-goodness, unforeseen flaw in our grand, entirely pragmatic plan: grandparents.

That's not entirely fair; aunts and uncles exist too. But I can count on one hand the number of toys I have personally purchased for my four children combined. Two stuffed bears, one set of blocks and two Lego box sets. My wife has also sewn one stuffed rag doll apiece for our three girls, bringing the grand total to something like eight toys **combined**. But that doesn't matter. My family has a problem with toys. In a four-bedroom house, one half of one entire room is fully devoted to the children's "stuff." Every day, around 7:00 a.m., they wake for a cuddle and then hurry off for "morning session" (their word) in a miniature kitchen replete with all manner of fruits and vegetables, eggs and ham, pots and pans, cups and plates. You name it, there's a version, or they'll make you one out of some combination of cardboard, Lego bricks, and Tupperware pilfered from the kitchen. Tea time? "Why, yes. Earl Grey, hot."

Now, I can't entirely give ourselves up to mockery. There have been minor victories along the way. Plastic makes up only about 7 percent of the current toy contents. (Would you believe that every single one of the endless stream of pretend perishable foods was hand-sewn by Grandma? The carrot comes in four pieces linked by Velcro so it can be cut and served.) Best of all, we technically have stuck to our "seven toys per offspring" covenant. The "morning session" room is held in common. Each child personally owns only a few dolls, easily fulfilling to a pharisaical *T* our despotic requirements.

Even so, not a day goes by that I don't step gingerly over the spillage that trickles into our living space. No matter how I try to justify it, my family has a problem with toys, and this in spite of a near-epic vigilant effort on the part of my wife and me to explain to extended friends and family our household worldview. It doesn't matter. Toys keep pouring in through the cracks in the walls. To paraphrase one philosopher, "The more you tighten your grip, the more Oriental Trading Company gimmicks will slip through your fingers."

Interior Design Legalists

Innocent as our little sociological dilemma may seem, it is also a tidy introduction to the second rule every Christian ought to break as often as possible. While dame Mysticism casually sits on her porch and calls out for you to transcend the pain and suffering of this world with deep emotional experience, the second rule is more like a strongman who patrols the streets, ever ready, hand on his sword and his shield in tow. Like Mysticism, he wears many disguises and changes into as many opinions as there are humans willing to be deceived by him. His name is Moralism, and he cares far less for what he feels and far more for what he believes he can do if only he tries hard enough. *"Follow me,"* he speaks with a firm word, *"and I will show you the real path to God. Heed my advice, and I promise you will build a better world by what you do. Work hard and never say die, and I will teach you to find God **with your hands**."*

{ **Moralism:** The belief that access to God can be achieved through your personal efforts or attempts to improve yourself. Moralism, then, is nothing more than the worship of your works. }

The great weapon of Moralism is that he does not tempt you with evil. Instead, he tempts you with good. With your own fondest dreams, with all your best aspirations for a more perfect world, Moralism promises that you hold in the works of your hands the power to make it all come true. No future possibility is too great. There is nothing you cannot achieve. *"Just **do this**,"* he says, *"and you will live."* The sad reality is that whatever "this" happens to be, no matter how hard you might work at it and how pure your intentions might be, Moralism's "do" is never done. It works like this:

One day you find you hold an opinion. It's pretty normal to do. You believe something is right, or you feel something is wrong. But it's more than that. Because it is right or wrong, you also conclude that to better your life you must also develop a way to live based on your point of view. That is, you make up some **rules**.

Soon enough, your opinions about good order have coalesced into your very own set of personalized, mostly perfect rules. You use these rules to direct your actions for the purpose of building your own personal, mostly perfect responses to any and all situations—responses that ought to lead to a personal, mostly perfect day-to-day life in which things go right (just like you planned) almost all the time.

This is not a total problem. Order and organization are good things. They are gifts of God. Moralism is not simply a matter of planning and acting in a world of rights and wrongs. Moralism is the belief that by living according to our rights and wrongs, we'll somehow create a world in which the only thing left is rights. In the midst of such a spirituality, Moralism also has a more dastardly plan. Waiting patiently for the right moment, he acts as the military commander and cheerleader, urging you on in your pursuits, telling you that you can do it with just a bit more elbow grease. But all the while as he urges you to succeed, he also watches for a moment he knows full well is coming—the moment when you try to live your life by your good rules but stumble into a not quite tragic but still unfortunate mistake.

One day you find that the thing standing between you and a more perfect world is your own set of rules. There in front of you sits the little bar you once set up in the certainty that by jumping over it you would find on the other side a better place than the one you left. You can still see the greener grass, just like you always have, but now the bar looks less like an aid and more like a roadblock. No worries! You take a wild stab at it, running with a full sprint and leaping with youthful vigor. Only . . . **crash**! Your foot is caught and you come smashing down on your face. Disgusted, dusting yourself off, you glance around. Did anyone notice?

Getting over that bar should have been easier, but there isn't time for worrying about that now. You're late for work and have a splitting headache from smashing your face on the ground. There's less time in the day. You're a bit more tired than you were a year ago (or five). There are other things, other rules, other acts you need to do. You just can't quite give the effort to meeting the bar that you once did, that you know you can, that you believe you ought to. More so, not getting over the bar is out of the question. That would be failure. That would mean you are no longer on the side of right but of wrong.

So what do you do? You do what we all do. You make certain the coast is clear, and then you take the fatal plunge. You reach out, lift the latch, make a quick switch, and **lower the bar**. Just this once. Just enough to get you back on track. Just enough so next time you'll be sure to make it over in one leap.

When my wife and I made our seven-toys-per-child covenant, we set in place a bar to jump over. By setting up the bar, we believed that hopping over it we would find slightly greener pastures on the other side (or at least be able to see the carpet in the living room). It seemed pretty simple on the surface. What could be harder than sticking to a number? But then came the day when we opened a box from relatives (who shall remain nameless) and found inside not "plastic toys," but a wooden board with animal shapes cut out as a puzzle for toddlers. With the child already drooling on it, were we really going to throw away a homemade rag doll in order to keep this nontoxic, primarily educational product? Suddenly the bar looked a little higher than we remembered setting it. So what did we do? **We lowered the bar.** Just a little. Just this once. Just for us. But here's the catch: we didn't change the rule because of any grand philosophic epiphany. Our motives were far baser. With the modified bar, we could convince ourselves we weren't really breaking our rules after all.

Coulda, Woulda, Shoulda

Moralism lies in wait for you to lower the bar. In fact, Moralism can't really exist without it. Once he has taught you that your hands are the answer to all your problems, he must also teach you to cheat. Just a little. Just for you. If he didn't, then he would only be **morality**, a belief in good and evil.

Morality is a good thing, a knowledge of the truths created by God to make the world work efficiently and in harmony. But Moralism does not want you to worship God and believe in God's morality. He wants you to worship you. Step 1 is teaching you to trust in morality as the path to finding God's blessings. Step 2 is teaching you to place that morality on your own personal **sliding scale**. Whether it is the Ten Commandments written in stone or your New Year's resolution to eat right, lose weight, or read more books, the moral doesn't matter. The rules you follow can be your own opinions or an eternal truth. What matters is your belief that by following those rules you will alter the course of your life or the universe or both. What matters is that when you find you can't follow those rules perfectly, you find a way to make it look like you did.

In this way, Moralism does not tempt you to believe in good things and do those good things for other people. He tempts you to do good things for **yourself**. The goal is to be good so that you can look at yourself and say, *"Hey, check it out. I'm doin' pretty good."* So when you fail just a little, you change the definition of "good" just a little to convince yourself that you are succeeding in making the world a better place.

The more you bend the "good" to fit yourself in it, the more you believe you actually **have** been a good person. You convince yourself you really **have** done the right thing most of the time. You buy your own illusion that you really are making the world a better place. But the more this happens, the more you also begin thinking everyone else isn't quite living up to their end of the bargain. When you look around, you start to get frustrated that no one else can measure up to the new, mostly good measure of all things: **you.** Having come to the conviction that you are (at least) mostly pleasing God by the actions of your hands, what you can't see is how far you adjusted the meter, how much you nudged the results, how greatly you changed the final score to appear in your favor.

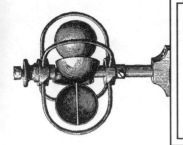

FAULTY MEASURES

When they measure themselves by one another and compare themselves with one another, they are without understanding.

(2 Corinthians 10:12b)

Then, something else happens. One day you wake up, and somewhere deep inside of you something refuses to buy the lie. Moralism's greatest weakness is that while he can fool our heads, he can never entirely fool our hearts. Without Mysticism's help, human hearts can live only so long under Moralism before they begin screaming out that something is wrong. Eventually, the screaming gets loud enough our heads start to take notice.

This nagging awareness of failure does little to slow our addiction to the sliding scale. If anything, it pushes us deeper into the maze of Moralism. *"Shift the blame,"* he says, so we do. *"It's the fault of everyone else,"* he whispers, so we vent our judgments in pursuit of justifying our own actions. *"You've only done your best,"* he smiles. *"You meant well. Everyone deserves a little slack, a pat on the back, so why don't you go ahead and give one to yourself?"* However, regardless of how much you explain to Jenny that everything is Johnny's fault, and even though Jenny agrees with you, your subconscious keeps insisting on brutal honesty. No matter what you say or do, you **feel** deep down in your bones the truth that you are not as innocent as you **think**.

Deceptive as the human heart can be, the truth of right and wrong is still written on it. You can sear the conscience, but the juices are still there on the inside. That is why everyone is always making rules and why we are always trying so hard to keep them and trying even harder to convince everyone else we **have** kept them. If we can convince others, then we can also convince ourselves. The emotions about missing the mark gradually bubble up, like a pot slowly brought to a boil. Teased with bad dreams and shocked by fits of sudden awareness, anger is the most common method for keeping the reality at bay. Fear also helps to build up the walls and block out the obvious. Through it all, Moralism plays you like a pawn, moving you deeper and deeper into the cage of one horrible, endlessly persistent emotion that, no matter how much you do, you can never quite make go away: **guilt**.

The Placebo Defect

Guilt is the firstborn son of Moralism. You set your rules, and then you break them. You put off your judgment by judging others. You slide the scale to make it go away. But following Moralism's rule is like trying to erase answers on the SAT. As hard as you rub the pink rubber eraser, the black number 2 lead still lays ingrained in the page. Deep down you worry the testing machine will judge you in total precision, not sliding the scale a smidgeon to the left or to the right. Someone is keeping score of your life, and not only do you know it, but you also can't help but feel your score is going to be significantly lower than you want it to be.

This is why Moralism is so well loved. He is a strongman, or at least he is a strong pretender. His encouragements are effective, convincing you that your hands are the answer to your problems. So clever are his arguments, so charismatic his personality, many people don't even begin to see the holes in his plan until they lie in a hospital bed with doctors telling them they are at death's door. Then they begin to realize what a flood of conviction they buried behind a dam built of lowered bars and slid scales. Caught in the end-of-life whirlwind, the only answer to the incessant guilt forcing through the dam is to fight back with a catalog of conjured-up memories. Like a man with a set of balances, the dying moralist stacks his lists of the good things he's done on one side, trying to balance against his painful awareness of the good things he hasn't done, not to mention the bad things he has. Doing his best to ignore that he also has his left thumb pressing down on the "good" side of the scale, he whispers to himself and all who visit him, "I kept my rules . . . I did my best . . . I gave my all . . . I did it my way . . ."

"Of course you did," the nurse replies as she gives him his pills. But neither the pills nor the empty words help the moralist psyche one bit. All attempts to justify his life based on technicalities, excuses, and lowered bars haunt him like so many excuses. No matter how many times the moralist asserts his successes, not one of them brings lasting comfort. Every attempt to build a more perfect excuse remains incapable of salving his conscience. The heart can't lie its way out of the tragic truth that he has **broken** all his own rules, not to mention that God's rules have been **broken** too.

Moralism's promise, *"Do this and you will live,"* is never done. The need for law and order is written on every human heart, yet the work of our hands cannot make redemption possible. The result is we take something created for our good—structure, order, goals, rules, beauty—and then we go terribly, horribly, scathingly religious with it. Worshiping our inkling that true good exists and spiritualizing our efforts to make the world full of it, our inbred addiction to considering ourselves the answer to all our problems fails to create a world of innocence and goodness. We bend whatever is needed and redefine our barometer of success at whim. The result is the chaos of millions of people each running around with their own personal measuring sticks, chopping an inch off every time it suits them, but complaining when everyone else's stick doesn't match up to theirs. It all adds up to a world where each of us does as much evil as we can while simultaneously insisting that everyone else learn to call it "good." Real justification, real innocence, real goodness, just gets farther and farther away.

Classic theologians had a term for this dilemma. It was called the OPINIO LEGIS, which is Latin for "the opinion of the law." It's a shorthand way of remembering that fallen humans have a built-in hunch that if we do enough of the right kind of stuff, we'll manage to make ourselves holy and just. Misguided by this natural assumption, even "spirituality" becomes our excuse to use everything we touch, say, or do for individual personal advantage. The lie becomes our greatest hope. Listening to the lie of Moralism, religion becomes a spirituality of what you do.

{ **Moralism's lie:** You can find God in your hands. }

But no matter what we do, the newest car still rusts. Erased pencil still leaves a mark. You can super glue the bite back into the apple, but even you won't want to eat it then. The world is broken, and the reason for that brokenness is the man in the mirror. Even when man tries to change his ways and heal the world in the process, it's only one more of those selfish acts, one more attempt to justify himself, one more cut that drives the rut deeper.

THE CHURCH OF NEVER DONE

The Christian Church is no stranger to this bad habit. Throughout our history, countless styles of Christianity have fallen victim to Moralism's warfare. It's rather amazing when you think about it. Here the world is, offering endless hordes of law-based, do-it-yourself religions, each making up rules for every end of the spectrum. While Hindu gurus teach ascetic living (a life of hyper-spiritualized, intentional hardship), feng shui teaches aesthetic living (a life of hyper-spiritualized, intentional comfort). The specific moral doesn't matter so much as the continual attempt to reach up by any means possible, to pull the goodness of heaven down to earth with our own bare hands. So how is it that the one world religion whose single most important tenet is the exclusive centrality of the **grace** of God ends up also buying and teaching the same lie? The answer is because we are still tempted by the OPINIO LEGIS.

OPINIO LEGIS

For we know that the law is spiritual, but I am
of the flesh, sold under sin. (Romans 7:14)

Even Christians saved by grace alone still dwell with the temptation to believe Moralism's lie that what was begun by the Spirit can be finished by the flesh (Galatians 3:3). Add to this the reality that, revealed in inerrant Scripture, Christianity also has the most pure and perfect set of rules for humans ever written. In the Ten Commandments (and in their summary in Matthew 22:37–40), God delivers to mankind the ultimate order, the true definition of love, and the epic presentation of what human life really could look like in a perfect world. Having such goodness presented in the Law of God is hard to resist. Why would God have given us this perfect picture if He didn't think we could live up to it? But that is exactly the point. Those Ten Commandments are so pure, so perfect, that anyone who sets about trying to keep them, even for one day, soon comes up quite a bit more than a little shy.

Sadly, this means that for many churches and traditions, Moralism's sliding scale must be set straight to work. Having come to a point where we realize that the Ten Commandments are a little narrow to ever be completed with perfect obedience, we abridge them. Or maybe we add an addendum. *"Do what is in you. . . . What matters is that you try. . . ."* We write up a few exceptions with the hardness of our hearts. *"It's only a white lie. . . . It's not adultery if I love her."* We insert those things we feel God surely would have wanted. *"Surely, God wants me to be happy. . . . Surely, God wouldn't expect me to suffer **that**."*

At first glance, our reinterpreted rules look like the kind of bar we can get excited about jumping over. But what appears to be an easier set of rules only ends up being **more rules** for us to break. The next time we look, the bar we thought was lowered is higher than it seemed in the first place. *Well, then*, we think, *I'll just add a few more precautions, polish a few more edges, bring that bar down to our level again.*

The ultimate result of all this is twofold. First, the bar is eventually so low that any actual good you might achieve for your fellow man by jumping over it is practically nil; the bar is only an inch or so off the ground. At the same time, you're also so tired from all the work you've put into lowering the bar you can now do little more than lie there, half your face in the mud, staring up and wondering how you ever got so incapable.

Then the pastor comes in! What will he do? Clearly, he is there to lend a helping hand. He says he is on the other side of the bar, and life really is better over there. With a few words of "do-it-yourself" encouragement, what the pastor has done is place his foot firmly on the back of your neck. "Here. This will help you." In authentic faith, you hope, you listen, you try. But you can't budge. (There it is again: **guilt**.) He begins to jump up and down, all excited and shouting that if only you'll stand up and try again, you can join him. Surely, if he's been able to do it, you can do it too. To his credit, he has no clue that with every helpful bit of advice, he gets closer and closer to breaking your neck. But meanwhile you are secretly starting to think, *"If there really is a God, then I think I'd be better off if I had nothing to do with Him."*

May I Borrow Your Soul for a Minute?

They make much of you, but for no good purpose. They want to shut you out, that you may make much of them. (Galatians 4:17)

If you currently attend a church where the emphasis is on you and all you can do to make your life and your world a better place, don't be fooled. Moralism is never done. The pastor up front is not really on the other side of the bar, no matter how good he's become at faking it. In all likelihood, he's ten times as conflicted as you are. He has slid his scale so often, tweaked the rules so far, that while it may look like he's jumping up and down, the spiritual reality is that his face is fully submerged in the mud and he's starting to have trouble breathing. In fact, that is why he's always so excited when you come around. The reason he is so desperate to convince you to make another run at the bar is because his bar is getting you to try to get over your bar just one more time. For him to believe he is making the world a better place, he needs to get you to do it, to try, to look like you're making an effort. Then he will be able to tell himself that he is closer to getting over his own bar, and for another moment believe that having his face in the mud won't be the end of him.

"If you don't do this, you won't get that." This is the torment of Moralism. This is normal for false religion, but when it sets itself up in the heart of Christianity, it is not normal at all. It adds an addendum to the Gospel that "Jesus has done it" with the Law that "but you've still really got to do it after all." Once that has happened, Christianity can only do one thing: never be done. Far from the good news of a promise about what God has finished, Christianity is perverted into just one more style of religious stepladder for trying to ascend to heaven by the works of your hands. This not only steals the joy and hope right out of the Christian life, but it also has the all-too-common side effect of leaving your faith in Christianity broken.

Jumping over the Moon

The Ten Commandments are the Bible's explanation of what it means to be "good." To be "good" is to truly fear God, to love Him, and to trust in Him at all times and in every moment. The nifty bonus effect of this perfect faith is when you perfectly love God, you also end up perfectly loving your neighbor as yourself. That means you will always do to them only what you would have them do to you. It sounds pretty awesome, and the world would be a much better place if we would just live like that. But that is where the problem comes in.

The unfortunate reality is God's description of perfect goodness doesn't come with the power to carry it out. It's easy enough to say, "Love your neighbor." Sounds sweet. But actually doing it—perfectly, entirely— is another thing altogether. The result is that the more you learn about the Bible's definition of "good," the more you start to realize that, insofar as bars-for-jumping-over go, even Superman would trip on this sucker if he tried to leap over it with a single bound. This can be pretty depressing on the day you finally realize you are standing alone in a field staring up at a bar of "goodness" that would cause even the cow who jumped over the moon to fall short.

Who then can be saved? **No one!** That is the point (Matthew 19:25–26). No one who tries to save himself can do it. It would be easier to move a beach with a pair of tweezers or balance an orange on the end of a toothpick. Using your hands to build up bigger barns and stave off sickness can help keep the despair at bay for a while, but then, suddenly one night, your life is taken from you. Then, all the things you have prepared, whose will they be (Luke 12:18–20)? At that very moment, all the goodness you thought to build up for yourself on earth becomes only one more weight laid on a back full of guilt and trouble. All the while you thought you were building a future by the works of your hands, but in the end you were taking an ax to the root of what you needed to hear.

But there is an alternative. In fact, according to St. Paul, this alternative is the real reason God gave us the Ten Commandments in the first place. God never intended that we use them as our ladder for climbing up to Him with our own bare hands. He gave the Law to "increase the trespass, [that] where sin increased, grace abounded all the more" (Romans 5:20). The Ten Commandments show us just how far we have to go to be the perfect people we all wish that we were. While despair is a common outcome of the Ten Commandments' work to show us our sinfulness, they also create **an awareness of our sin**. Taught by God Himself just how far away you are from not merely fixing the world but also from fixing yourself, you are also able to learn from Him that He doesn't need you to fix the world or yourself anyway. That was why He sent **Jesus**.

Made the Cut!

Let us also lay aside every weight, and sin which clings so closely, and let us run with endurance the race that is set before us, looking to Jesus, the founder and perfecter of our faith, who for the joy that was set before Him endured the cross, despising the shame, and is seated at the right hand of the throne of God. (Hebrews 12:1b–2)

Jesus is the answer to perfection. Where we could never hope to jump over the bar of perfection, God climbed down over the bar to reach you. In Jesus, God puts you on His own shoulders and carries you across the raging flood and storms of sin, death, and the devil's temptation to rely on yourself. Jesus isn't a law for making yourself perfect. He isn't something you have to do. Jesus is someone whom God sent to be perfect **in your place**.

Of course, Moralism can't stand this idea. Moralism would rather have you bend every rule, twist every trick, and shift every principle to convince yourself that you don't need deliverance. *"You are doing just fine. . . . Keep trying. . . . Work harder."* With these diversions, Moralism focuses you on your hands in order to get your eyes off of Jesus. When you take your eyes off of Jesus, you are left alone with the bar that is deathly high, no matter how hard you work to lower it again.

Even though we never manage to get to "good," all humans still have a lingering desire to be "good." We have an inkling that "good" exists, and the inkling is just strong enough to curb us into striving for goodness most of the time. This might keep us from totally destroying one another, but it also becomes yet one more way for us to set up a worship of ourselves. Knowing there is a "**should have been**," we start to believe we are the makers of the "**what will be**." Curved inward on this incessant hope in our own efforts, endlessly trapped in the trials of a broken world, stuck with breaking bodies, breaking relationships, and breaking minds, the best opinion of the "good" Law we can come up with is to use it in the worst possible manner: **for our own benefit**.

The Ten Commandments will always remain the most perfect demonstration of what a world of true love and justice would look like. But Christianity confesses that by means of these works, neither this world nor any individual in it will ever reach the justice we seek. God has created these works. He calls them ultimate goodness, but He has also said they cannot help you stop the world from being broken.

This One Kind of Matters Lots

For by grace you have been saved through faith.
And this is not your own doing; it is the gift of God,
not a result of works, so that no one may boast.
For we are His workmanship, created in Christ Jesus
for good works, which God prepared beforehand,
that we should walk in them. (Ephesians 2:8–10)

In This Corner, the Winner, by Gumming

In one very real sense, the Law of God is the most important teaching one can ever discover in all of life. It grants wisdom, the ability to know right from wrong, and the gift of discerning reality from falsehood. But it also has a limit. It cannot advance you on your way to goodness. So consider this: if God's own perfect, revealed-from-heaven-and-written-in-stone divine Law cannot help you find God with the works of your hands, how much less can your own ideas or dreamed-up schemes for undoing the breaking of our planet, no matter how many times they are pursued, ever help you to achieve that end? Sadly, the Moralism dominating the lives of so many Christians in America isn't rooted in God's morals. Many evangelical Christians can't even name the Ten Commandments, much less do they use them as their guide for Christian living and the new obedience. When we feel guilty (which is often!) it is not over failing to love our neighbor as ourselves. We feel guilty because we don't live up to the squishy hyper-spiritualishness and success we hear preached from our pulpits. We don't "really live what we believe" or we don't "celebrate every Sunday as if it truly were resurrection day." Our preachers harp on us to seek the real faith of "seeing the world through new eyes" or "living without fear" or "daring to hope even when hope seems gone" or "living a transformed life."[2]

But what does any of that mean? Rather than use the real bar of the Ten Commandments, Moralism has set up the sliding scale of meager improvements and silly half laws, dreamed up by guilty pastors who think their job is to try and make Christianity seem real. We slap Jesus' name somewhere on the end of our latest idea, and off we go on a merry romp. But this is precisely where Moralism's knife-in-the-back, assassin-style warfare is equally as deadly as any poison that dame Mysticism might have slipped into your tea. Where the perfect Law of God would stab any thoughts of self-lifting spirituality straight through the heart, self-chosen "good works" lull us into a death of a thousand cuts.

When man peers at himself in the mirror of God's perfect Ten Commandments in an attempt to assess the ways in which he should change, it isn't very long before he realizes that if these are the real scales of God's justice, then he is most certainly in a great deal of trouble if there ever comes a real Judgment Day. The perfect Law pierces his heart in two, and he is left with the growing conviction that while the works of his hands might achieve some authentic good here and there, it will never be enough to save either himself or the world. It is a brutal and glorious honesty the Ten Commandments deliver in all their truth and purity. They are entire. They define "good." Looking to them as our mirror, we get a very clear premonition that we are not so good. We are run through with a truth sword and die quickly, even honorably, under their shadow.

MIRROR, MIRROR IN THE LAW

For I do not do the good I want, but the evil I do not want is what I keep on doing. (Romans 7:19)

---

2   These direct quotes come from the "pastor's message" of a church newsletter I received on the day
     I was writing this portion of the chapter.

For that gory reason, when set next to the Ten Commandments, the weakened strains of Moralism's self-appointed rules look far more appealing. They don't seem so deadly to the conscience. They are less pure and perfect, so they seem more achievable. All the ways we define and redefine what God wants from us, all the plans we make up to fix the world, all the personal improvements we make, all the big next steps and self-helps look like a fight we can win. So, we climb in the ring with Moralism because we think he is a toothless old man compared to the gnarly beast of the Ten Commandments caged over in the corner. But by Round 23, lying flat on our face, out of breath and tired of trying, we find the old man has got himself perched on our back, and he is entirely succeeding in his strategy of gumming us to death.

LONG HAVE DIED THE KINGS

If you don't know who Michael Jackson is, then you are an amazing person. Growing up in the early '90s, I missed most of Michael's earlier achievements. The first (and only) album of his I ever bought was *Dangerous*, which included one of his biggest hit singles of all time, "Black or White," a jiving diatribe against racism. But the album also had a lesser hit single crooned by the ultrafamous media mogul who once insisted that Billie Jean was not his lover. In "Heal the World," the multimillionaire stepped beyond preaching against prejudices to teach us that "if you care enough for the living" you can make the world "a better place for you and me and the entire human race." The music video for "Heal the World" was filled to the brim with images of suffering, impoverished children from every corner of the globe. If only we all could make a real effort, then together we could end world hunger and help the poor in every place everywhere.

The song was an immediate hit. After all, who is so callous as not to appreciate the suffering of others in this world nor want to do something about it? But decades later, there is one itching question you rarely hear anyone talk about. **Why didn't the world change?**

In 2009, Jackson died due to drug-related circumstances. This both shocked the world and semitragically reignited his career, which was in all but tatters. The man who had seen nothing short of the wildest success in both childhood and adult fame had fallen to a point where those enormous victories were horrendously overshadowed by his even greater public failures. From child sexual abuse allegations to failed marriages, from child custody disputes to foreclosure on his Neverland Ranch home, Michael Jackson did not heal the world. The poor man couldn't even heal himself. **Why?**

Why didn't the man who had millions of young people around the planet singing at the top of their lungs about the man looking back from the mirror, the man he asked to change, why didn't that man manage to follow through in his own attempts to escape his past and flaws? Why couldn't the man whose memorial service was attended by so many celebrities that it had to be held at Staples Center in Los Angeles use all of his influence and charisma to make the laudable dream of ending world hunger happen? Why didn't the richest people in the world all singing "Heal the World" together in memorial of their fallen comrade go home that sad day and finally make it happen?

Because "by works of the law no human being will be justified" (Romans 3:20). Because all you build and all you do and all you say still falls victim to the decay eating at our world (Matthew 6:19). Because no matter what Moralism tells you, he is the same old Lie. No matter how hard you try, you cannot build a better world. No matter how good your intentions, you don't have the power to kill the real root of the problem. No matter how talented you are, you cannot remove the curse, which is why no matter what you are able to do you still cannot find God with your hands.

MORALISM IS A BAD WORD

In spite of failure after failure, chasing trend after trend, teaching opinion after opinion about work after work, your hands shoulda, woulda, coulda, but **didn't**. Moralism marches on. Unlike the feigning dame Mysticism in her scarlet dress, Moralism is a man of war. He is justice, righteousness, power. He stands before you and beckons you to a world where the lines are drawn clean, where the laws always work, where what is on the outside defines what is on the inside. He says, *"Do it just like that, and then it will be good. Then it will be just. Then it will be justified."* Yet, man of war that he is, he is also a coward.

A world in which every issue is black and white, where justice is dispensed without mercy, where an eye for an eye and a tooth for a tooth are judged without partiality is a scary world. Who could live in it? Can you imagine what devastation would be wreaked on our bodies if every time we harbored a grudge or looked lustfully at another human or tweaked the truth just a little bit or sloughed off on the work only a tad or simply wanted a better stake for "me and mine," we received only a paper cut as punishment? We would all bleed to death before finishing middle school. With such an ultimately true standard of good and evil, Moralism could never win the war for godhood, and he knows it. So he rewrites the rules.

GRAVE PAINTINGS

Woe to you, scribes and Pharisees, hypocrites! For you are like whitewashed tombs, which outwardly appear beautiful, but within are full of dead people's bones and all uncleanness. (Matthew 23:27)

Nowhere is this sad fact more evident than in the Christianity we Christians prefer to buy. It's common street knowledge the Church is full of hypocrites and self-righteous jerks. It's one of the main reasons people give for never going; they feel judged, not by the preaching of the Ten Commandments, but by the countless, arbitrary rules of a million sliding scales.

The problem is not that American churches are full of sinners. Jesus Christ was crucified to cover all of that. The problem is that our churches have decided they're better off not believing they are full of sinners. Instead, we've marched to war under the banner of Moralism. Whether it is by pushing a sermon series on the dangers of credit card debt or taking action in a movement to end world hunger, churches have become athletic clubs for training the muscles of self-righteousness. Whether selling toned spiritual abs or installing the latest treadmills for sanctification, Moralism means the big business of cleaning the outside until it is spic-and-span in the hopes that a shiny exterior will help us forget that inside we are full of curses and bitterness (Romans 3:14).

These are the reasons Moralism is the second rule every Christian ought to break as often as possible. We cannot let this cowardly man of war steal our faith in the grace of Christ. Our fight back begins by never following a rule that wasn't written in stone a very, very long time ago. It ends in remembering that even when the apostles of the New Testament exhort you to love your neighbor, to pursue gentleness, and to refrain from debauchery, that's awesome, but that's not a way to find God, to please God, or to satisfy God, because God is not found, pleased, or satisfied with the works of your hands.

He is **satisfied** already.
He is pleased **already**.
He has found you
already
in
Jesus.

God is never found in what you **do**. God is found in what Jesus has done for you with His birth, His life, His suffering and death, with His glorious resurrection and ascension, and with the current preaching of who He is and what He has done. That is what those verbally inspired holy apostles really want you to get out of their inerrant letters and Gospels. They knew as well as anyone that virtue and goodness are wonderful gifts. Good deeds are good things God has prepared for us beforehand so that we may do them (Ephesians 2:10). But there is a chasm of difference between believing good works are good and believing you can make yourself good enough for God by doing them.

So, as a Christian, never let anyone tell you Christianity is about what you're supposed to do, even if the rule was written in stone. Tell that warrior-coward to sit on a tack. Rely on the free gift of Jesus instead of relying on your hands.

"You are in Christ Jesus, who became to us wisdom from God, righteousness and sanctification and redemption, so that, as it is written, 'Let the one who boasts, boast in the Lord'" (1 Corinthians 1:30–31). You don't have to heal the world. That work is already done, and the amount of plastic in your living room has nothing to do with any of it. (Thank goodness!)

73

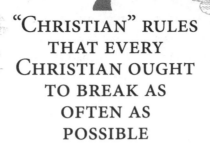

7

"CHRISTIAN" RULES THAT EVERY CHRISTIAN OUGHT TO BREAK AS OFTEN AS POSSIBLE

Never #2

Never follow a rule that wasn't
written in stone a very, very long time ago
(doubly so if the grass is only greener
on the other side because it's made of plastic).

The Second Rule to be **BROKEN**

Moralism.

You can find God in your hands: the worship of your works.

NEVER #3

Never follow a rule just because it makes sense
(especially if it promises to work because it makes sense
[and especially, *especially* if it either contains
the words "spirit-led" or can be entirely explained
by a petri dish full of midi-chlorians]).

THE DAY MYSTICISM DIED OR
WHO LET JAR JAR DRIVE THE X-WING?

I wasn't quite sure why *Star Wars* was ruined. I just knew that it was. After a night spent camping on cement with only Coca-Cola, junk food, and casual geek revelry over sci-fi memories, I and a legion of costumed, painted, paraphernalia-sporting nerds were now rolling out of the theater following the premiere showing of *Star Wars Episode I: The Phantom Menace*. I blinked at the 10:00 a.m. sunshine, a young man whose universe had suddenly become unhinged.

Sixteen years earlier, in 1983, I had been a wide-eyed five-year-old shuffled into a dark theater on my mother's apron strings, fully unprepared for the glory of the third *Star Wars* film, bizarrely numbered *Episode VI* yet enduringly titled *Return of the Jedi*. From Jabba the Hut's palace and Boba Fett's plunge into the sarlacc pit to the Rebel Alliance Fleet massing off Sullust and the deaths of many Bothans who died to help destroy the Death Star, the powerful mythology of a hypergalactic war between good and evil made my journey toward fanboy immediately complete.

I was not alone. *Star Wars* was that once-in-a-generation defining cult movie, an icon that universalized the coming of age for boys across an emerging pop-culture civilization. Movies come and go, but *Star Wars* went on and on. A decade and a half later, when the news came out that the long-hoped-for prequel trilogy of Episodes I–III was in the works, bringing with it the special effects of countless new technological advances and with the budget to cast such names as Liam Neeson and Samuel L. Jackson, an indescribable glee broke out across geekdom. Nothing can summarize it better than the fanfare of millions of giddy, full-grown men and women sleeping on pavement for as long as a week in order to get seats for the premiere showing. My friends who had camped out for two days to hold down our spot were **fiftieth** in line!

Streaming into the theater, an impromptu chorus of the Empire's theme song broke out, heartily sung by all, and not a one of us was surprised when a choreographed, live-action duel broke out between impeccably costumed nerds as precurtain entertainment. What else would you expect from true fans viewing the truest movie in the history of all movie and storydom? This was the climactic moment of civilization, the brink of a new era, the fulfillment of the hopes and dreams of men and boys everywhere. This was sci-fi ecstasy. We roared in applause. The lights dimmed.

And then the movie started.

Two hours later we were a room full of nerds in post-traumatic shock.

"It was good," I said to my friend, trying to mask the sinking feeling as if several of my vital organs had spontaneously shut down.

"It's the setup for the next one," he said. "Just wait. The second one will be sweet."

"Yeah," I said. That was what everyone else was saying too. How could we not? This was our **entire** childhood, our identity as America's next generation of heroes. It was too big to fail.

But the next movie was worse. By the time the third movie rolled around years later, its minor improvement over the previous two was too little too late. For 85 percent of men and boys born between 1968 and 1990, *Star Wars* was over. Ended. Done. The new movies were so ruinous, so completely wrong, an aftershock rippled backward through time, tarnishing even the golden lining of the original movies. Cherished boxed sets were thrown out. Unopened action figures were sold. It may be trite, but it is true nonetheless. Favorite childhood joy embodied in a young man who wielded light in order to vanquish the forces of darkness was now being intentionally forgotten, blocked out of the psyche, because the memory of it was just too painful to bear.

Of course, there are those who disagree with us. Believe it or not, significant ink has been spilled on the topic from blogs to critical essays. From calling out the overuse of incredibly annoying, entirely digitized characters (such as the clown Jar Jar Binks) to in-depth scholarly criticisms based on film theory, it can be boggling to see how grown people could care so much about something that is, in the end, just a fantasy. But I bring it up here because there is also something more going on than the retargeting of an old franchise for a new generation of consumers or the mere development of director George Lucas from a '70s rebel to a kingpin of the establishment. Those who believe the essence of *Star Wars* was betrayed by the new films, amazingly, also bring to light a portal through which we can learn a thing or two about the third rule every Christian ought to break as often as possible. More than a matter of mere differences of generational styles or schools of film, at the heart of the *Star Wars* shift is the clash of two philosophical forces in the heat of a centuries-long war, vying for the very soul of Western civilization. One is our old friend from chapter 2, dame Mysticism. The other is a skeptic of a man named **Midi-chlorians**.

Well, no. The third rule every Christian ought to break isn't really named Midi-chlorians. He is named **Rationalism**. Midi-chlorians are just a bunch of silly science fiction nonsense from the *Star Wars* universe. But as such, they represent an idea, a profound example of the way that Rationalism works, and of how Rationalism's ages-long battle with Mysticism has left Western civilization tottering in their wake. Yet unless you, like me, score a 10 out of 10 on the dork meter, then the word *Rationalism* is only slightly more meaningful to you than the word *Midi-chlorians*, which itself is about as meaningless as bull's eying womp rats in your T-16 back home. So lend me your ear, and see if I can put the puzzle pieces together for you.

Key to Western Civilization: A Three-Part Essay

Part I—The Enlightenment: It Only Makes Perfect Sense

The tale of Rationalism starts with a history lesson. Eighteenth-century Europe found itself on the cusp of a cultural movement that had been building for several hundred years. The schools where the Renaissance had rediscovered ancient Greek and Latin philosophy were giving way to groundbreaking original thinkers. Like men reaching the peak of a mountain they have been climbing all day who suddenly cry out at the view of the world they can now see on the far side, scholars of the 1700s burst forth with a cascade of new discoveries. John Locke, Isaac Newton, François-Marie Arouet (Voltaire), and Immanuel Kant are just a few of the well-recognized names that heralded an era of mind-boggling realization. At the heart of it all, the pioneering thinkers of the world were learning that by following certain rules of thought, it was possible to discover logical answers to nearly every question in the world, with immediate and astounding implications for how to improve the quality of life and society as a whole. So vast was this shift that the ages that came before it were those of darkness by comparison. Now, mankind had begun its **Enlightenment**.

The Enlightenment: A cultural movement in eighteenth-century Europe and America that sought to improve society through the advancement of knowledge.

"I think, therefore I am," wrote René Descartes, a philosopher who with that one statement summed up this new world order of thought. From math to political theory, the power to think reasonably and consistently was spreading with a spirit of great optimism about the powers of the human mind. With the right series of steps, one could search out and know almost anything. Philosophers increasingly believed this new method of study to discover "knowledge" (or *scientia* in Latin and *science* in French) could lead mankind to the learning of **all** truth. Even ancient and holy religion could be subjected to rules of reason and deduction in order to discover its value. Centuries would still pass before atheism would arise to assert that the reason you cannot find or test God is because God does not exist; first, men of reason had to search for Him to see if He was there. The Enlightenment was giving them the tools to do just that. After all, what kind of reasonable God would create a creation that could not understand Him? What kind of rational God would fail to make it possible for you, His creature, to find Him with **your mind**?

This is the third rule every Christian ought to break as often as possible: "You can find God with your mind." **Rationalism.** Where Moralism patrols the streets night and day seeking to mask his cowardice with incessant warfare against decay, and while Mysticism sits on her porch with a bottle of wine and sings, *"Come and rest with me,"* Rationalism is the far more "civilized" face of the devil's original Lie. He is a philosopher-monk whose habit is the scholar's gown. He toils away in the holy rituals of laboratories and libraries, an icon of sacrifice and precision. His great strength is the quiet assurance that he knows the way to knowing better after all. Always. About everything. Especially religion and spirituality. *"Give me facts,"* he tut-tuts, looking down past his long, bespectacled nose. *"Let me touch. Let me see. Let me test. Let me prove. That is the only way of knowing anything we can know."*

Rationalism: The belief that contact with God can be found through the clarity of your observations or the consistency of your logic. Rationalism, then, is nothing more than the worship of your thoughts.

Armed with the annals of history and the microcosms of test tubes, he says, *"I am only a humble realist. Nothing more. A simple logistician. Merely practical. I only ask that everything and everyone be **reasonable**. (And, oh, yes, I will set the standards for what passes as reasonable, thank you very much!) From this I therefore deduce what is only logical: **if** God exists, man will be able to find Him, and the most certain way of finding Him is through the disciplines of the mind."*

Rationalism existed long before the Enlightenment, but the modern era was one that ushered him into a booming business the likes of which he had not seen since the glory days of Athens and Rome. Given how good things were going, he was able to put a few additions on the old homestead, in which he had holed up throughout the medieval ages, renovating his monastery into something more of a cathedral-palace. From this state-of-the-art, eighteenth-century temple, the strictly sensible King of Reason embarked on a mission to reign on high over all future eras of mankind. Little could his graphs and experiments foretell what an irrational blunder his thinking would eventually become.

Part II—Mysticism Strikes Back

All throughout the Enlightenment, Mysticism was certainly on the defensive. With steam and electricity powering the Industrial Revolution, Rationalism's armies pressed forward with little retaliation, sweeping over nation after nation, building a modern world of cogs and gears. *"With another century or two,"* the newfangled "radio" proclaimed, *"our scientific method will lead us to a new era. I promise you a world without hunger, a world without sickness, fatigue, or war. A paradise! An Eden built with the power of human reason. This is the future of the human mind, and nothing can stop its coming."*

Anyone alive and listening had to work very hard to argue against this rising **Modernism**. The coming centuries brought the telegraph, the transcontinental railroad, the assembly line, and revolutions in the practice of medicine. Radioactivity and penicillin were right around the corner. The twentieth century was hailed as the dawn of the moment when the world would change for the good and never look back.

Modernism: The belief that the new economic, social, and political conditions ushered in by the Industrial Revolution made more "traditional" forms of art, literature, architecture, and faith increasingly outdated.

83

But then, the unthinkable happened.

On June 28, 1914, the heir to the throne of the Austro-Hungarian Empire, Archduke Franz Ferdinand, was assassinated in Sarajevo. He was a minor royal in a weak empire, but his death was nonetheless a catalyst setting off a chain of events that ended only after nine million combatants had been killed in a kind of war never before thought possible. Worse, the sheer potency of the modern destructive force that left nearly the entire continent of Europe wrecked was made possible only by the technological advances of science, which had been mankind's great hope. On top of this, the entire ordeal was showcased for the world to see through the modern marvels of photographs and news media. Scholar and dockworker alike were suddenly given enormous pause to wonder about all these claims of a utopian age to be ushered in by the powers of human reason.

Of course, it would be totally illogical to blame science or reason for the terrible display of human depravity revealed in the Great War. But Mysticism has never cared about being logical. This was her moment of chance, and she took it. Her archenemy had pulled out his brand new "Gatling gun of reasonable discovery" and blown off his left foot. Now was the time to strike back.

Not everyone who lived during the Enlightenment had thought adherence to Rationalism was such a great idea. Throughout the movement, pockets of scholars pushed back against the sterilized and calculating cold reliance on reason that increasingly came at the expense of human emotion. Names like William Blake, Ralph Waldo Emerson, Edgar Allen Poe, Wolfgang Amadeus Mozart, Ludwig van Beethoven, and Francisco Goya were the cusp of a powerful counter philosophical and artistic movement called **Romanticism**. Embodied most strongly in visual arts, music, and literature, Romanticism shunned stale, hard factuality in favor of a deeper authenticity rooted in the human experience of **feeling**. Where Rationalism preached his crusade for man to figure the world out through the Enlightenment of the mind, from her barrio stronghold Mysticism rallied an army of underground guerrillas around the heartfelt dream of worrying less about "how life worked" and simply enjoying more of "living life to the full."

Romanticism:

A cultural movement that reacted against the Enlightenment by validating personal experience as a significant source of authority.

Seeds for total revolution were already planted. With the terrors of the Great War as the rally cry to her troops, Mysticism rode the abuses of science and reason straight into the very schools Rationalism had labored so hard to build. With principled dignity, she called the question of Rationalism's extreme optimism and his doctrine of the human mind as the source of future perfection. By the time the Allied Forces were rolling over Berlin in the 1940s and historians were forced to put a "II" behind "World War," the consensus that "logical thinking" and "scientific discovery" were the tools for ending human suffering had met a war-torn, bitter end.

By the 1960s, under a blitzkrieg of "cool man" beatniks and Dadaists, Rationalism appeared increasingly old, tired, and disheveled. Even to the scholar in this new world of **Postmodernism**, knowledge was becoming increasingly suspect. Voluminous tomes poured forth from universities in France and Germany arguing that words did not have any meaning at all. The problem, they said, is the assumption that what "is" can be reasonably known. The true reality, they said, is that nothing can actually be tested and shared in any objective, nonrelative way. Even your daily conversation about how much you love pizza is a facade. What is pizza? Chicago style? New York? All things real are limited to the realm of your personal experience. None of it is true. None of it can be known. *"What is true for me is true for me, but might not necessarily be true for you."* After all, isn't beauty only in the eye of the beholder?

P O S T M O D E R N I S M : Rising in reaction to Modernism, the belief that reality is only apparent, a variety of evolved social constructions, always subject to change.

EXCURSUS

WHATEVER WORKS:
THE OLD MONK TURNS DIRTY

All of this couldn't have been more contrary to Rationalism's well-laid plans. So vast, so far, had his power grown during the Enlightenment that he truly came to believe that his reasonableness would eventually create a world in which Mysticism no longer existed at all. Freed from the deceptive charms of emotion, uplifted by the pure thinking of reason, this paradise was almost within reach as the evening shadows settled over the nineteenth century. So he had summoned to himself his prodigy, an assassin well trained as the ultimate tool for the spreading of logic and perfect thought across the globe. **Education** had been the finest of Rationalism's pupils, his ultimate soldier, a student of all things, diligently applying himself to every facet of art and science. He had mastered every tool at his disposal and was the strongest believer in the logic of all things.

Education: The history, philosophy, sociology, and practicality of deliberately transmitting knowledge, skills, customs, and values from one generation to another.

"Now is our chance," he had whispered. *"Go down from our temple mount to that harlot's brothel in the ghetto, and only come back once you have cut out her 'you can find God in your heart' and impaled it on a spit!"*

The murder of Mysticism was the task for which Education had been born. Without question, he willingly embarked on his mission to slaughter her. But what should have been struck down that day proved herself far more powerful than anyone had ever imagined as she took Rationalism's young apprentice and made him her own.

When he found her, she was neither lounging in the arms of the deceived lower-class brutes nor drunk on the wines of make-believe nor wearing the profane red dress of disrepute. He had been taught to be wary of a whore, but the woman he met was a lady of great refinement and wisdom, dressed dazzlingly in the crimson gown of artistic passion and sipping on the cordial of noble intentions. Perhaps, he thought to himself, I have come to the wrong home.

"*Does Mysticism live here?*" he asked, his heart strangely warmed by the civilized charm of the woman sitting before him on her porch dais.

"*There is no one here by that name,*" she replied to him, piously batting her eyes and setting down her reading, a copy of Homer's *Iliad*. "*There is only I, Romanticism.*"

It was a blatant lie, to deny one name while accepting the other. But with that lie, she won Education's heart. A few more words about honor, virtue, valiant heroism, and the beautiful feeling of true experience, and Education was won entirely to Mysticism's side. Taking her arm, he led her straightway to the temple fortress and presented her before his liege. Rationalism could only sit on his throne in utter dismay, as his would-be assassin stood before the entire court and advocated his King's sworn enemy for her gifts of grace and freethinking. Try as he might, he had little choice but to accede to the lady Romanticism's request to dwell in his palace and to walk daily at Education's side. Worse, he, too, began to find himself increasingly susceptible to her subtle charms. Before he knew it, she was sitting at his side on her own throne, giving out orders in his name, and championing their alliance. Though he still despised her mightily, neither could he drive her away. His jealousy grew more and more until he found (crazy as it might sound) he no longer felt mere covetousness, but true lust.

Rarely (if ever) publicly admitted, a child was soon seen running among the halls of the monastery and in the courtyards of the temple. Trained daily in all skills at Education's feet, he grew in favor and stature. He was more winsome than his father (having received all the charisma of his mother), yet he was more clever than his mother (having received all the practicality of his sire). As the boy came of age, he began to speak openly, saying his father's ideas about reigning from on high in the cold search for pure knowledge was a trivial and heartless pursuit. But just as cavalierly he boasted that his mother worshiped the ancient spirits in tomfoolery and superstition. Neither parent openly objected to these claims, for each saw in him an alliance that had brought to bear one of the deadliest deceivers ever to walk the earth. They named him **Pragmatism**, and he is something more than **a** rule every Christian ought to break, because he is spawned from the mixing of two: "You will find God with your heart **and** your mind, **or** whichever you prefer and whenever you prefer it. Because, after all, **whatever works**."

Pragmatism: The belief that knowledge found by evaluating the consequences of actions can create more efficient or "intelligent" future actions.

Part III—
The Need to Peer behind the Curtain:
May the Midi-Chlorians Be with You

And . . . in all the art, literature, philosophy, chemistry, industry, and history that could be called on to illustrate the practical meaning of this tale for our lives in the twenty-first century, there is no more complete a story than the rise and fall of *Star Wars*. Seriously. Really.

It starts with *Star Wars Episode IV: A New Hope*, the first *Star Wars* movie, being a turning point in history, the first Hollywood film to truly capitalize on the cultural warfare unleashed by Mysticism's "postmodern" push back against Rationalism's "modern" world. When Han Solo looked Luke Skywalker in the eye and said, "May the Force be with you," it was more than just a catchy line. It was the tipping point in Western civilization.

The movie had a million things going for it. New technologies like blue screen special effects were combined with an unforgettable score penned by master soundtrack composer John Williams. To this was added the powerful on-screen presence of world-class actors such as Alec Guinness, Harrison Ford, and the voice of James Earl Jones. But none of these assets were why *Star Wars* stormed the pop world and captured the hearts of an emerging generation. Modern films had long been using good actors, great music, and improving technology. Science fiction was hardly a new thing. But *Star Wars* broke the mold by adding to all these things the experiential promise that the American movie-going soul was beginning to crave incessantly: **emotion** as the key to all truth.

Films before *Star Wars*, though at times aware of Romanticism's war to wrest the American heart from the tightened grip of Rationalism's mind, had nonetheless been unsuccessful at embracing the fight. Films from the 1970s, such as *The Godfather, Rocky,* and *One Flew Over the Cuckoo's Nest*, were triumphs of the art form, but they were stories told in an old world, a world filled with straight lines, stable rules, solid facts, and strict hard work. Even when their protagonists longed to break out of it, they never could. Reality was still **real**.

Star Wars couldn't have taken a more opposite approach. With a good blaster at his side, George Lucas didn't mind relying on luck to shoot his way into a new era of filmmaking. Lucas threw *Star Wars* backward into the Wild West, carrying the melodrama of eighteenth-century opera on his shoulders. At the same time, he jumped at light speed into "a galaxy far, far away," fusing his story to the bizarre and unimagined. But at the heart of all this pulp fiction was the embrace of the one thing all the movies that came before it had only flirted with—complete, mind-adulterating Mysticism.

From its first moments, the enemy is a sterilized, evil empire, powered by storm troopers intentionally modeled after World War II's Nazis and armed with all the modern weapons the Industrial Revolution could ever dream of. They are an overwhelming power pressing down on a minority Rebel Alliance, an alliance embodied by a frail damsel-princess garbed in white and hailing from a planet without weapons. Pulled by her allure, a young hero must lead a band of gunslinging misfits to fight back, and their "new hope" is that he learns to wield the most unmodern of all possible weapons: **religion**.

When Luke Skywalker finally overcomes the modern threat of a space station capable of destroying entire planets, it is only after an aged warrior monk tutors him from beyond the grave to manipulate the magical energy field that holds all things together. He fires two hyper-scientific "proton" torpedoes from his X-wing fighter, but then he literally **prays** them into a ventilation shaft to trigger a chain reaction that catapulted the Rebel Alliance to success and *Star Wars* to the top of the box office.

But this is just science fiction. It's just fantasy, right? Not so fast. Just twenty-nine years after a farm boy from the mythological world of Tatooine destroyed the Death Star, not with his scientific targeting computer but by trusting in his **feelings**, Mysticism was ready to take her show out of the dream world and into the mainstream. In 2006, a book called *The Secret* was recommended by Oprah Winfrey's book club and marketed on her weekday show. This in itself was nothing out of the ordinary. What is extraordinary is the self-help advice contained in this book, gobbled up by twenty-one million real people, taught that the universe is made up of an energy field each individual human can control by exercising a practiced willpower. This is to say twenty-one million American consumers forked over $14.92 each in order to be taught—get this—**the exact same religion** a little green man named Yoda once taught Luke Skywalker in a swamp on Dagobah in backwoods of the *Star Wars* universe. Who would have thought that modern people would believe such a science fiction fantasy? But here was Mysticism, bold and strong, proudly reminding the emerging pragmatic world, *Good. Your feelings make you powerful. So join me, and let us rule the galaxy together.*

But there was a catch. Rationalism had once been the teacher, and even though Mysticism was making a play to become the master, he was still sitting behind her on his lonely throne of test tube glass like a coldhearted crow, and he had one last trick to pull: **midi-chlorians**.

Midi-what?

Well . . . exactly. Mentioned for the first time in the "new" *Star Wars* movies (those same latter films that broke the hearts of original fanboys everywhere), midi-chlorians were something no self-respecting *Star Wars* fan had ever heard of or dreamed of. They are microscopic organisms that live inside Jedi Knights, acting as conduits by which the Force can be used.

But wait a minute. **Huh**? Exactly. The Force was supposed to be an inexplicable, mystical energy field that held all things together and was channeled through sheer strength of will, aided by religious devotion. That is how tiny green Yoda magically lifted a huge X-wing fighter out of a swamp. It's why the aged warrior-monk Ben Kenobi waxed eloquent in catechizing his young apprentice about "letting go" and "trusting feelings."

But, nope. Sorry to disappoint you. As it turns out, that was mostly mumbo jumbo. It was a convenient, if ignorant, lie. Luke Skywalker did **not** guide those two proton torpedoes into the Death Star's exhaust shaft with super tenacious prayer juju. Instead, he merely inherited from his father a very unique (and quite advanced) bacterial infection.

So what this means is that a long, long time ago, one weekend in 1993, Rationalism crushed Mysticism's Rebel Alliance to overthrow pop culture. He did this by convincing the creator of the most anticipated sequel to the most powerfully popular, mystic movie franchise in the history of the world to carve out its heart by explaining away this greatest mystery with a most cold and calculatingly boring kind of laboratory-level logic. It was a barely noticeable, subplot factoid. Most people who saw the movies don't even remember it. Yet with it Rationalism proved, even in the postmodern era, he was the one holding Mysticism's leash. Anything, even the Force, can be explained by science. Midi-chlorians were the proof that in the postmodern age, even Mysticism needs to be **rational.**

This is why when author Rhonda Byrne sold her secret knowledge of "how to manipulate the universe in three easy steps," like *Star Wars* before her, she, too, needed to explain her religious "Law of Attraction" with an appeal to science. The postmodern mystic won't buy just any old voodoo. But a bottle of snake-oil empowered by the marvels of cutting-edge quantum physics? Well, that's a different story! Her quack theories didn't stop book sales. They **increased** them.

Whether it's midi-whatsits or the bizarre tendencies of subatomic particles, Rationalism isn't done tempting Pragmatism's final loyalty. It is a war for the Western soul, raging in both heart and mind. Which shall we make into the greater idol? Our feelings? Or our thoughts? Chances are that for most of us it is a shifting combination of the two. Like good pragmatists, we harness whatever most suits our needs in the present moment and use it for our advantage. Yet, as mystical as our culture has become and as deeply as we rely on our feelings to teach us what is true and what is false, when push comes to shove, we find Pragmatism does have a final allegiance, and it is not to the feelings of his heart but to the limitless trust he will place in the powers of his ability to understand. Worse, far from Rationalism's high-browed, intellectual commitments of the past, the logic of his heir cares far less about the hidden rules that run the universe. His reasoning is far more base, the simple black-and-white science of a banker's ledger.

{ **Rationalism's lie:** You can find God with your mind. }

This is the real point *Star Wars* has to teach us, because whether or not you were disappointed by the new films, whether you think they totally rock or whether you've never seen them, in the end it **doesn't even matter**. Neither what you think nor what you feel about *Star Wars* lore or theory matters. What you think about any film theory or plot theory or music theory or art theory doesn't matter **because** in the postmodern world of Pragmatism, the only thing that matters is whether or not something works, and that means whether or not something sells. It doesn't matter what you think about the new *Star Wars* sequels because they did exactly what they were designed to do: make more money than the original movies ever dreamed possible. This is how all things in a pragmatic culture must be judged. It doesn't matter if millions of geek voices suddenly cry out in terror at their loss of childhood memories, so long as they are just as suddenly silenced by the tens of millions of new fans raised up to take their place. With mass produced lightsabers and spaceships, lunch boxes and Lego kits, the real point is that the coins of **consumerism** are their own form of pure and ruthless **logic**.

This is what makes Pragmatism the postmodern incarnation of the third rule every Christian ought to break as often as possible. Born of the mixing of both Mysticism and Rationalism, in the end he is Rationalism 2.0. He has the advantage of harnessing the allure of his mother whenever it suits him. He is a master of playing with promises made to human emotion, toying with you through your passions and desires so every commercial he produces is targeted perfectly, not at your mind, but at your heart. Yet the targeting system is no mere letting go and trusting in his feelings. It is a hard science, with tests and trials, in which the data speaks for itself and the chief law is the bottom line, which must always make perfect sense.

Under pure and driving reason, not only is every commercial and show, but every thought, word, and deed of every human life in our age, subjected, tried, tested, compared, weighed, and judged for **usefulness**. The only survivors are those who adapt to the ever-changing climate. Trend-asaurus Rex might dominate the food chain today, but he will be extinct tomorrow. Individuals mill here and there, questing, searching, seeking with their minds for a perfect logic that will ensure their hearts and hands will find their way, if not to God, then to something like the world God really ought to have made for them in the first place.

Over this entire roost rules the Pragmatic spirit, the apex of centuries of warfare between heart and mind, searching for the perfect lie with which to tease the human soul away from faith in the one true God. Proving himself most fit, Pragmatism is Rationalism made even stronger, able to live in a truce with Mysticism and use her to continue selling his promises about an entirely human-created, reasonable future.

"You can find God anyway you want," he preaches. *"You can use your heart, or you can use your hands. Only remember the key to making both heart and hands work is the power of your mind."*

"Is this the path to Truth, then?" the common man asks.

"Friend," he replies, *"I'll be honest with you. I'm no theologian. I cannot speak of doctrines. Who am I to put God in a box? But one thing I can tell you: follow me, and you will see* **results***."*

"What of the Scriptures?" the man might ask.

"Those are all well and good!" Pragmatism smiles. *"There is so much we can learn from them. We only must apply our minds, remembering to test the principles we find to see if our use of them is truly Spirit-led."*

"How do we do that?"

"That is easy. Look at what you are doing based on your interpretation of Scripture, and then ask yourself, does it work?"

Sola Infide

Results are always easy to sell. The problem is that whether or not something works, biblically speaking, has never been a very trustworthy measuring stick when it comes to God's Spirit. After all, lying works (if you're good at it) even though it is wrong. Meanwhile, the Trinity doesn't work at all (at least on paper) even though it is God's own revelation of Himself. Having everything make sense may be very appealing, but a God who is completely comprehensible can't be very much of a God. This hardly means being a Christian requires you to check your brain at the door (far from it). But it does mean that you need to check your brain at the limits of your brain. There are some things your brain just isn't capable of perceiving or even knowing. But that does not mean those things don't exist or they are not real or they are not true. It only means you are not God. God is God, and the real God has some things He very much wants to say.

At Cross Purposes

The word of the cross is folly to those who are perishing. . . . For it is written, "I will destroy the wisdom of the wise, and the discernment of the discerning I will thwart." (1 Corinthians 1:18–19)

Strangely, for all the infinite ability to find knowledge that our age attributes to the human mind and heart, we at the same time seem incapable of imagining any kind of almighty God who might also be almighty enough to do something as simple as talk to us with words we can understand. Remember those scholars who worked out the conclusion that human language is so weak that not even two humans speaking the same tongue have the ability to really, actually, truly understand what the other is saying? By playing with the subtleties of language (called **semantics**), these teachers showed how strictly logical and scientifically perfect communication is all but impossible between two humans. But after these scholars, still more scholars took this communicated information (ironically believing they had understood it fully) and did God the favor of projecting our little problem onto Him too. It boiled down to something like this: *"Because it is theoretically possible for me to misinterpret the words of the Bible, this therefore means that the words of the Bible can't actually be received without misinterpretation."*

That may sound abstract, but you've probably been there. It happens in the moment when you're talking to another person about what the Bible says. You say, "The Word was God" or "You shall not commit adultery" or "This is My body," and then the other person smiles, relaxes back in her chair, and says with a calmly level voice, "Yes, but that is only your **interpretation**."

This is insanity. The life, death, and resurrection of Jesus, if they teach us anything, teach us that the almighty God not only **can** speak in human language, but He **does**. When He does, He uses real, true, actual **words**. God believes these words have meaning. He is convinced these meanings are His own power of salvation to all who believe it (Romans 1:16). This faith can be truly received and confessed again to others, not merely as an interpretation, but as the exact same, original oracle of truth (Romans 1:14).

The Day God Broke the Sky

Behold, the heavens were opened . . .

and behold, a voice from heaven said,

"This is My beloved Son, with whom

I am well pleased." (Matthew 3:16–17)

The problem is that the postmodern man isn't listening. He will listen to the wind or study a Pew Forum Poll, and he will try in both to discern what God must be thinking. But he is determined to call "superstitious" and "unbelievable" those things God has actually, audibly said. Postmodernism is so modern that it will trust the mind far more than it will trust even one's own eyes and ears!

Of course, we should hardly think this is some special, once-in-all-history achievement. "Postmodernism" and "modernism" are new words to describe the same old problem. The belief that God's human words don't have real, ultimate meaning is an ancient idea, dating all the way back to where all of our problems got going in the first place. All the rot, the terror, the chaos, and the suffering go back to the very beginning, to the day when the first human first decided the almighty God was not quite capable of always speaking the absolute truth. It was not Adam's pride that caused the fall. Pride was only the result of his first sin:

unbelief.

"You shall not eat [of it]," God had said, "[or] you shall surely die" (Genesis 2:17). The serpent deceived Adam's wife, so she ignored these words. But Adam was not deceived (1 Timothy 2:14). Adam **chose** to not believe God's words. This was not a temptation for higher emotional experience than he could find in God's words (mysticism) or a more perfect obedience than he could find in God's words (legalism.) The thing Adam wanted above all was **knowledge** (Genesis 2:17), and in order to attain it, he was even willing to learn "the knowledge of evil." Irony of ironies, the "knowledge of evil" he learned is the notion that the path to personal godhood can be achieved by learning knowledge. But this notion is a false idea. It is a lie. It is a knowledge that, no matter how much it learns, can never quite be the knowledge of the truth (2 Timothy 3:7).

{ **Rationalism** is the worship of your thoughts. }

This **is** the fall: the theoretical but false knowledge that by worshiping knowledge we shall become ultimately knowledgeable. It was this worship of knowledge that wrought an everlasting curse on Adam's world. It was this worship of knowledge that rained down plagues on Adam's children. It was this worship of knowledge that increased our pain, taught us fearful terror, and brought us under the rule of death. It was this worship of knowledge that taught Adam to think the fruit of the tree of the knowledge of good and evil would make him wiser than God. It was this worship of knowledge that is still taught by the first Lie: "You can find God with your **mind**."

Believing this did more than burden us children of Adam with thorns, thistles, and sweat. It spawned itself as its own horrid consequence. Knowing evil is its own curse. There is no "good" knowledge of evil. You cannot look at it, observe it, test it, and then put it down. The moment Adam ate, he knew the "evil" of his own rebellion against God. This rebellion was founded on a lie, but it was a lie he now **believed** to be trustworthy knowledge. Once learned, the knowledge of evil can only further mislead and deceive because it is, by definition, **false** knowledge. It produces, by definition, only more falsehood.

This is Rationalism, not true reason, but an aged monk of the Enlightenment living vicariously through the pragmatic salesmanship of the postmodern age. He constantly boasts that the cure to the plague of human arrogance is to believe that the plague is its own cure. He teaches that all the problems caused in the past by the arrogance of men who thought their thoughts to be the best shall be overcome in the present by refusing to believe that there are any limitations to how far one can progress in his thinking today. If only the right application is discovered, the right system, the right method, then minds will be freed from mental slavery. But this is our problem. We believe we can shake off the chains and free our minds from mental slavery **by thinking our way out of it**. We are shackled to this foundational, erroneous thought. Like a drug addict getting high in order to stem off the side effects of withdrawal, we cannot see that our attempts to get better are only making the problem worse.

There is a vast market for selling anything that enhances this worship of knowledge, both within and outside churches. It is filled with trend after trend (and scam after scam), each promising this time, this answer, this method, this approach, or this knowledge will be the real silver bullet you've been looking for all along. But all along we are simply taking more of the poison that got us sick as if it were the antidote. We assume if we build up a big enough pool of failure, eventually all our failures will breed success. Like total fools, we believe if we tell enough lies, eventually they will become the honest truth.

This is **un**faith, and this is the problem of the human condition. It is the problem of evil itself. The sad reality is, all science aside, Rationalism will believe **anything** so long as God did not say it. Postmodern people are willing to believe human life was seeded on earth by aliens billions of years ago. They are willing to believe we'll eventually find a pill to keep our bodies in perfect shape without one whit of exercise. They will wax poetic about being a seagull soaring higher and higher into the next life. They will tell stories about how one day man will merge with computer and overcome the grave altogether. They will hypothesize the discovery of the "multiverse," which we will one day open with a wormhole so we might walk directly into a place where the thing we call "God" is just another creature like us, sitting at his desk and working for someone he calls "the man." Postmodern rationalists will even believe the "secret" that the universe is made up of an energy field holding all things together, which you can manipulate by focusing the thoughts of your mind, just like a Jedi.

Rationalism, in the end, is anything but reasonable at all. All of these things are believed, taught, and confessed in the human quest for a reasonable explanation for our problems. It is the everlasting search for a way out of ourselves, into a divinity we can grasp with the mind. On this quest, we are no longer merely discoverers but creators. We are the shapers, the makers of our own identities, the authors of the future that ought to be, the definers of the image of God. Our first premise is that even if God exists, it is obvious He cannot actually speak for Himself, and so we announce that therefore all claims of His speaking (like the claims of Jesus) are self-evident frauds. Because all claims that God has spoken are self-evident frauds, it also becomes most certain that God probably does not exist, or if He did, He is now at the very least dead. And since God does not exist or is at the very least dead, it is also therefore logical to assert we have killed Him.[3]

But, see. Now, we're not talking about reason, logic, or science at all. Now we're just making stuff up and calling it "true."

---

3.   "God is dead. God remains dead. And we have killed him." Friedrich Nietzsche, *The Gay Science*, ed. Walter Kaufmann (New York: Vintage, 1974), 181–82.

The Good Bad News

Placing our hope in the human mind is utter folly. Like our emotions and works, it is part of an originally good creation, but it has been blackened, charred, and diseased by evil. Our lust for knowledge beyond what we are given to know has bred in us a pure discontent with the knowledge of good that God has freely given. So we mar our every attempt to find God with our minds through the irony of that first attempt: *"Trying to find God with my mind, I broke the world. But never fear! I know of a way to fix it!"*

Every effort to do the same, every achievement thus hoped in, and all wisdom and science so abused are nothing but spiritual hypocrisy. So long as we insist that we can know all things while remaining destitute of fear, love, and confidence in the true God, we shall only be brute animals that can do nothing but kill one another and die. We will remain destitute of faith so long as we refuse to believe the one thing faith can believe: God's own, actual, every word.

God's answer to Rationalism's worship of knowledge is the same as His answer to Mysticism's mutiny of our emotions and Moralism's tyranny over our works. Often, the human response to learning about the things we have made into idols is to overreact in the opposite direction, making new idols out of rejecting morality

altogether, avoiding emotion as if it is in itself evil, or scoffing at intelligent thought as somehow "less than spiritual." The history of the churches is peppered with such knee-jerk backlashes, and they have never ended well. But Jesus makes no such overreaction. He neither embraces our sinful idolatry nor rejects the creation we have idolized. The faith He delivers to us comes with (of all things!) the **knowledge** that our abuse of our hearts, minds, and hands has not led Him to destroy them (and us with them). Instead, He has shown mercy. Instead, He has **redeemed** them.

This redemption Christ preaches comes in two parts. That is to say, His words work in two ways. These two active powers of Christ, which He pours down over us, are not two options or two paths, but one path that leads to the other. They are like two sides of the same coin, the total coin of His Word.

When this coin turns tails, we find God speaking about our problem, diagnosing the way sinful humanity abuses His gifts of emotion, thought, and deed. He calls our worship of our hearts and our minds and our hands exactly what it is: false religion. St. Paul calls this "the law of sin" (Romans 7:23), and it is bad news about us. It is the knowledge that we are evil. But this good revelation of the knowledge that we are evil is highly useful in explaining why life on this planet is always such a war. Like a mirror held up to a man whose ear infection has become a cancer covering his entire face, this knowledge helps us see and believe that if we are ever to get out of our problem, the answer needs to come from somewhere outside of us.

Then the coin turns heads, and we see a very different picture. We see an image of what St. Paul calls "the law of my mind," which classic Christianity often called "the rule of faith." But properly speaking, this is neither a law nor a rule.

It is a promise. This promise is "the Gospel," the actions accomplished by Christ on the cross for you. It is knowledge, but it is not "bare" knowledge. It is the power of God for salvation to all people who believe it (Romans 1:16). Jesus of Nazareth, true God, begotten from eternity, yet also true man, born of a virgin, is your Lord. He is mankind's proper King. As King, He has taken it on Himself to redeem you, a traitorous person. He knows your addiction to the knowledge of evil, but that doesn't matter to Him. He purchased you anyway, by great warfare and at immense expense. He won you from your own defection and bought you back from the just sentence for your treason: eternal capital punishment. He did all this not with the black-and-white pragmatism of mammon, but with His holy, precious, divine, human blood, shed in innocent suffering and death.

He did it all for one purpose: **to make you His own**, restoring you to life under His reign and as it was always meant to be. A new world is coming, a world where good never ends, where evil will never begin, where nothing profane exists. Jesus is taking you there. This is His choice. This is His work. This is the Gospel.

This reality is **already true** in Jesus' own personal resurrection over death. His resurrection is a firstfruit of His eternity breaking into the **now**. His resurrection is the proof He has the power to promise the same reality as your personal future too.

The knowledge of the resurrection is not a leap of faith, but a fact of history supported by all the evidence the most reasonable of people could ever ask for. But this amazing act of God for you cannot be known to you through your own reason or strength because of your inbred idolatry of the mind (not to mention the heart and the hands). It is all literally too good to be true. In your knowledge of evil, you could never bring yourself to accept it. A free pardon for your treason seems unreasonable. It would require a love that could halt even the emotions of righteous anger and wrath. It would be a kind of mercy unjustifiable in any court of law. Rationalism will sooner believe in panspermia than concede to this knowledge that "the knowledge of evil" has been overcome with good in such a way.

But Jesus preached and achieved these words as more than mere words. He infused this rule of faith, this promise of His resurrection, with the very person of the Holy Spirit. Just as His own incarnate flesh was not merely human, so now His own human words are still breathed wherever they are spoken with a total, spiritual divinity. Like a dove descending on the wing, the Holy Spirit of God flies on the waves of sound. He lights up the rays that reflect the very ink of this sentence of promise into your eyes in order to call you by means of this Good News, even in the same way Jesus once called Lazarus out of his tomb.

All Scripture is breathed out by God and profitable for teaching, for reproof, for correction, and for training in righteousness. (2 Timothy 3:16)

The bare facts about who Jesus is and what He has accomplished for us achieve what Rationalism's Enlightenment never could—atonement, a restoration to holiness, a return to faith that believes God's words actually mean what they say. This is the literal meaning of Jesus' word "Church," which in the original Greek does not describe a building, much less a club made up of super spiritual, semi like-minded people, but the assembly of those "called out." Not you alone, but **we**, **churched**, "called out." Gathered. Harvested. Illuminated. We who are purified by the **speaking** from God the Father through the words of Jesus the Christ as the real, ultimate power of their very Holy Spirit.

In this preaching, teaching, confessing, proclaiming, **churching**, the divine wind of Pentecost keeps calling us out, regenerating our faith by means of the rule of faith. The words fly wherever the Spirit wishes. We speak them. We hear their sound, though we do not control them. But we know they daily impart to us a rich re-revealing of the forgiveness of sins. They deliver you, me, and other brothers and sisters into a family. This goes on and will go on until the day when we will finally be churched together once and for all. In a blink, our addiction to unfaith will be cured. In the twinkling of an eye, the law of sin, the tears of sadness, the problem of evil, and the fallen flesh that ever dwells in the shadow of death will all vanish. With a sound and a shout, we will be raised by the coming of Christ, the faith we already are given blessed with the sight of seeing what we have relearned to believe: God is true.

Yub Nub

Staring at the heads side of the coin is exhilarating. It is even enough to make one forget about the tails. The Gospel of Jesus Christ is **so** good it can make the Law seem "bad" by comparison (especially since the Law is constantly reminding us we are bad, and being reminded you are bad never really feels good). But this is Rationalism's last gasp. If he is ever to retain his precious "worship of knowledge," he must purge Christianity of the knowledge that "the knowledge of evil" is evil. Using the Gospel that God has forgiven all, his last deceit is to try and remove the Law from God's Word, stopping the Word from exposing our sin. Thus freed from the revelation that exposes us, our knowledge of evil can go right back to being dishonest with itself, all in the name of "Jesus" and His "Gospel." Like a drug addict who claims to be cured of his addiction while he shoots up in front of you, this final kind of Rationalism boasts of a doctor who can heal him, while at the same time letting him remain sick.

Such Gospel reductionism is a shipwreck that inevitably drowns in its own delusions, which is why both sides of the coin of Law and Gospel given in God's Word are constantly needed as the "calling out" of the Church. Luther called the preaching of the Law "a sweat bath of anguish and sorrow under the teaching of the Law." He went on, "[But] without the sweat of the Law, men become fat and comfortable and lose all desire for the Gospel. . . . This preaching is for the thirsty. To them we bring the message [of Christ]."[4]

4.   C. F. W. Walther, *Law and Gospel: How to Read and Apply the Bible.* Reader's edition. (St. Louis: Concordia, 2010), 29.

A perfect mirror with which to look at our hearts, hands, and minds, the Law's pure knowledge of what is good pricks consciences that were born seared by the knowledge of evil, piercing us so the juices of repentance flow down. Faith then stands at a crossroads. Do I seal the breach? Do I put a patch over my conscience? Do I return to my pursuits and my ideals? Do I close my mind to the revelation of God? Or shall I let the blood flow? Shall I learn to believe my mind cannot heal itself? Shall I abandon this shipwreck of thinking that thinking can make me whatever I propose myself to be?

It is with this thirst that Jesus again promises the water of life. It is with these pangs of hunger that Jesus promises the bread from heaven. It is with the knowledge of my depravity that Jesus first gives me the faith to believe I need to be forgiven.

As you sit reading this, Western civilization continues to blunder onward in its addiction to knowledge. It is a cold, raw quest in which the voracious desire to know more at any cost has become the answer to its own question. It is a new mythology built for the postmodern mind: the myth of everlasting **progress**. Fulfilling the destiny of the Genesis curse, we fill our minds with facts we think will eventually be combined into enough theories we can use to transcend our limitations and become like gods. This quest does not serve the human mind. It rules as a brutal tyrant. When the healthy desire for knowledge becomes a lust for it, there is no end to what we will sacrifice, no limit to who we will hurt, no fantasy we will not insist on believing. In willful ignorance, as a law unto ourselves, our desire to know more leads only to knowing more evil at any cost.

The Ultimate Stabilizer

Heaven and earth will pass away,
but My words will not pass away.

(Matthew 24:35)

So, what are Midi-chlorians? They are a bad joke at geek parties. But under the watchful eye of Rationalism, postmodern Pragmatism is the modern world on a hyperdrive of greed set to ludicrous speed, and all this at your personal, spiritual expense. Whether dressed in business casual and preaching principles for a better life now or decked out as the original civilized scholar and holding court in a lecture hall, Rationalism is the belief that the ritual of test and trial will lead to an Enlightenment of all mankind. It is because of this misguided trust in the idea that "**You can find God with your mind**" that Rationalism remains the third rule every Christian ought to break as often as possible.

God does not want you to discover Him through science or history, reason or experiment, logic or philosophy, any more than He wants you to find His Spirit through trial and error, practice and leadership, tactics and methods. God wants you to **know** He already has **found you** in Jesus. And **Jesus speaks**. Real words. Words He has left behind as His testimony. Words that are written.

The final test of all knowledge is black-and-white after all, but it is not a banker's ledger. It is Scripture alone.

7

"Christian" rules that every Christian ought to break as often as possible

Never #3

Never follow a rule just because it makes sense (especially if it promises to work because it makes sense [and especially, *especially* if it either contains the words "spirit-led" or can be entirely explained by a petri dish full of midi-chlorians]).

The Third Rule to be **BROKEN** →

Rationalism.

You can find God with your mind: the worship of your thoughts.

Never follow a rule because it benefits
you **now** (and if it mentions "abundance,"
run screaming from the room).

Ozymandias and Me

I was high, and I was at church.

Born and raised an LCMS Lutheran, baptized on the tenth day, the son of a lifelong LCMS professional church worker and his lifelong LCMS Iowa farm-girl bride, confirmed in the eighth grade, I was clearly able to articulate the grace of Jesus Christ in my "statement of faith." Yet I'm not quite certain what happened. I know that it happened, and I know when it happened. High school was accompanied by an excessive use of pornography leading to adultery. Youth group didn't stop it and possibly aided it. I continued to attend church as a sort of imprisonment forced upon me by my parents. I know I still argued with my atheist best friend about how important it was to believe in "God"; I thought believing in God was necessary to get to heaven. But I was already gone. My Christianity was BROKEN.

When I went off to college, I did not go off to church. Instead, I went off to parties. Parties are where the girls are. Parties also have beer, and beer helps you talk to girls. Some girls not only drink beer, but they do more illicit substances too. So do old friends and new friends alike. Crazy thing about drugs—they might **be** bad, but they don't **feel** bad. Not at first. The problem is once you start using drugs, it's not too long before suddenly, without them, nothing else feels quite as good.

By my junior year, I had replaced weekend binge drinking with being a daily, habitual stoner. I didn't have the money to "smoke two joints in the morning," but I certainly never got out of bed without first "waking and baking." What was wrong with it? I was pulling a 3.9 in English Lit and holding down a part-time job as wait staff. I was on my way through the American dream. So what if the way I'd found to make it all taste sweeter was looked down upon by my culture (not to mention illegal)? Sure, I was still looking for love in all the wrong places, and I was increasingly battling with powerful bursts of depression. Sure, there were some bizarre fits of paranoia after smoking, a few run-ins with ridiculously dangerous people, and a newfound superpower that enabled me to lose my car keys on a daily basis. But Bob Marley kept telling me "everything is going to be all right," and even though Bradley of Sublime was dead of a heroin overdose at an all-too-tragic age, he still was doing a fine job of convincing me through my stereo that a little pot and "lovin' is what I got" was the only way to stay sane in a crazy and hate-filled world.

My conscience worked arduously to justify my habit of self-medication and for good reason: in the back of my mind was an ever-growing awareness that I wasn't just smoking pot in order to relax (like I kept telling myself I was). I was smoking pot in order to **function**. It wasn't an addiction. I've been to Narcotics Anonymous meetings, and there is a real wall of separation between cannabis smoking and the truly hard-core drugs. Then again, I kept telling myself I should quit, and then I began telling myself I wanted to quit, and then I was telling myself I **was** quitting. But I could never quite actually manage to quit.

At the same time, a funny thing happened. While attending a state school affectionately dubbed "Granola U" (after the legendary '70s hippy students who lived in chicken coops in the farmland around the university while attending school) and while pursuing a degree in English under such educators as an Indian Muslim (who insisted that *Coriolanus* was Shakespeare's greatest work), an atheistic civil rights vet with a sidewinding left eye (who prided himself on making people cry in class), and a Jewish-by-marriage creative writing prof (whose great claim to publication was being the wife of a Zen Rabbi who wrote a book on the fusion of Buddhism and Judaism), I nonetheless somehow managed to sit down for my first literature class next to the only practicing Christian (to my knowledge) in the entire program. What do you know? After a few weeks of enjoyable conversation before and after class, and after learning that I considered myself a "Christian," he invited me to visit his church.

His invitation probably saved my life. It without question saved my soul.

The congregation was a little conservative Calvinist church plant that met in a rented Masonic lodge. It was the first time in my life that I can remember hearing the Gospel preached directly **from the text of Scripture**. The pastor was preaching through the Book of Galatians, chapter by chapter. As St. Paul talked, so he preached about sin, about grace, and about the two meeting together for the life of the world in the cross of Jesus.

So it came to pass that I was in church, not for the first time, stoned high to paranoia and preparing to call my mental slavery to cannabis "**sin**" during the corporate confession in the liturgy. Not for the last time, I pleaded with all my heart and mind and soul for God not just to forgive me for my addiction-like use of it, but please, please, please, please, please free me **from it**. I was held captive by my own flesh and could not free myself. My sin was before me every morning, noon, and night. And **that** was when I first met Ozymandias.

Charm Is Deceptive and Beauty Is Fleeting

"Ozymandias" (1818) is a poem written by Percy Bysshe Shelley, the husband of the woman who authored *Frankenstein*. One morning at church I found it nestled inside the front bulletin cover, a space where the pastor regularly printed some tidbit from culture or literature that was thematically connected to what he would be preaching that day. It's a short poem, as precise as it is beautiful. It goes a little something like this:

> I met a traveler from an antique land
> Who said: "Two vast and trunkless legs of stone
> Stand in the dessert. Near them on the sand,
> Half sunk, a shattered visage lies, whose frown,
> And wrinkled lip, and sneer of cold command,
> Tell that its sculptor well those passions read
> Which yet survive, stamped on these lifeless things. . . .

And on the pedestal these words appear:
'My name is Ozymandias, king of kings:
Look on my works, ye Mighty, and despair!'
Nothing beside remains. Round the decay
Of that colossal wreck, boundless and bare
The stones and level sands stretch far away."

Can you see it? There is a peddler with his carts and mules wandering without direction through endless, deserted sands. The scalding gusts blow at the scarf draped around his head and loosens his cloak so it billows behind him. But then all stops. He stands alone, silent, in a holy grotto, some mystic, pagan shrine seemingly undisturbed by the fouling winds. But it **has** been disturbed. Not even this sanctuary has hidden itself from **time**.

At its center is less than half a man, his stone knees and thighs pockmarked by long and ceaseless weathering. His torso has fallen, but who can say where? Perhaps it was hauled away by another peddler like himself, thinking to make a profit. Beside the broken monument lies the head, with one forsaken hand.

"*What is this strange, abandoned relic?*" the merchant asks himself, edging closer to wipe the residue of dust from its faded base. There, in strange Egyptian runes (which, of course, he has studied) he reads the mighty legacy: "Thou gazest on Ozymandias! Pharaoh of pharaohs and Emperor of All! Tremble at me, at my magnificence, and at all I have created. Be struck with awe at my supremacy. Bow even at my memory, for none has risen like me, and none shall again!"

That's it. All else is wasteland, sand, and dune. The only striking is the scalding of the sun, and the only trembling is the chuckle of laughter bubbling in the merchant's belly at the boast now turned by a decapitated stone scowl into the most comically ferocious of jokes. This Pharaoh of pharaohs, whomever he was, was a very unhappy looking sort!

"Poor chap," the peddler mutters. *"With breath alone I am so much more than you."*

As a young man struggling against the destructive storms and passions of the bizarre American experience, the words of the poem blew me away. Everything came rocketing home, congealing into one epic revelation of my own vanity breaking against the cliffs of futility. All my victories and all my failures stood as immortally irrelevant as a statue in the middle of the Sahara. A man doesn't need to wait for the Day of Judgment to learn the true value of mortality. We are **all** Ozymandiases. Not only do we all have the same end, but **more important**, we all also have the same terribly mistaken habit of thinking that by our efforts we can make the end to be something better. We think if we can only live, breathe, eat, drink, and work long enough and hard enough, then eventually we'll get everything to the place where what we have done will really, truly, actually matter.

Fame. Glory. Meaning. Who can blame us? Everything about this life looks as if it really does matter, as if our efforts on this planet **should** amount to something. Sure, life has some bumps, but isn't it obvious that with a little elbow grease we can smooth those out? There isn't one of us who doesn't need to eat three square meals a day, but who is going to argue if we find ways to make those meals taste better? We each need a little sleep, and we can't do it while standing, working, or keeping watch. So who wouldn't want a softer bed, a more stable lock for the door, or some way to cheaply and easily heat the home in winter or cool it in summer? What's wrong with trying to make the best we can of this material world?

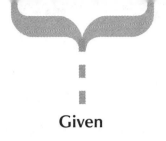

Given

Every good gift and every perfect gift is from above,

coming down from the Father of lights with whom there

is no variation or shadow due to change. (James 1:17)

Nothing. There is nothing inherently **evil** about a little filet mignon, an iPod, or a car new off the lot. **But**, there **is** something terribly, horribly wrong with all of them because sooner or later (and more often sooner) they're all going to **rot**, rust, get digested, get excreted, burn out, go out of fashion, and/or **fall apart**. Tables and chairs, pots and pans, shirts and shoes, everything that is anything in the world has the same cursed predicament of looking gorgeous and seeming as if it might just last forever, but never proving to be anything more than fading dust in reality. This goes not only for all the "stuff" we spend our lives trying so hard to make and own and keep and fix. Worse. Against all our incessant hopes, dreams, and lies, this goes for **you** and **me** too. Even if Ozymandias did really live and achieve the consummate height of all the demigod pharaohs put together, it still amounted to a silly attempt to cut down the largest tree in the forest with . . . with . . . a herring.

LIFE IN AMERICA

One of the most telling moments of my experience as a pastor was when I was called to visit the elderly mother of a parishioner. The lady, well into her eighties, was not a member of my congregation, and though she was raised as a mainline Protestant, she had not been to church for some thirty plus years. She was a lifelong smoker and as frail as a baby bird fallen out of the nest. I entered the shadowy hospital room, where she lay beneath the flickering blue of daytime TV cranked up way too loud, undergoing treatment for her growing inability to breathe. After introducing myself (and managing to get the melodrama turned down), the first words I was able to coax from this confused, meager, sickly person were "I just don't understand. **How did this happen?**"

"How did this happen?!" I wanted to cry out at her. "You've been sucking tar into your gravity-burdened mortal flesh for sixty years! You've done nothing but sit and stare at that box for the last twenty-five! I'd say mid-eighties is a darn fine run! Don't you know . . . **everyone dies**?" Of course, I did not speak so bluntly as my zeal desired, but I did devote the rest of my visit exclusively to this theme: (1) humans don't live forever; (2) this is God's own testimony to us that there is something desperately wrong afoot; and (3) that is the entire reason why He sent **Jesus**.

But this is just the thing about these latter days in our American wilderness. It is the reason fewer and fewer people are willing to darken the door of a church, much less give a hearing to the Good News about Jesus. Twenty-first-century civilized people do and spend everything in their power for the length of their entire lives working to convince ourselves that even if we don't live forever, we can live for a few moments as if we will and never have to face the consequences. "*It might happen to everyone else. But it will never happen to me.*"

And we're **good** at it. We're better at this than nearly anything else. Somewhere in our past, our cultural fathers, like peddlers traveling in the waste of a desert, came upon the grimace of Ozymandias. Unlike the peddler who laughed at the irony of it all, whatever philosophy our fathers held up to that point was simply incapable of handling the terror of that bleak visage. So instead they ran screaming from the grotto, sending us as a society hurtling headlong into an age of all-consuming dedication to hiding every and all decay from public view.

Our culture whispers, "Buy a new one. It's not your fault. Cover it with ketchup. So, there are a few rough spots? With the right pragmatic approach, with the proper mix of science, therapy, and effort, you can get the kinks worked out. If people must die, it can happen only when they're very old, and somewhere that most of us won't have to see (or smell) it. Death may not be our ideal, but at least it's still a long way off (which is almost as good as never), and maybe someone will cure it by the time you get there. In any case, either evolution or reincarnation (or maybe both) will take care of you after that. Just one thing is certain: whatever you might think about death, it is **not** a cosmic hex irrevocably placed on our species by any kind of 'almighty God.' By the time it comes knocking for you (which it probably won't anytime soon, **for sure** not tomorrow, so don't worry about it), it will all probably make sense anyway. By then you'll be 'ready' (whatever that means)."*

The only thing entirely certain is you're not ready now, not yet. The entire essence of American culture is bound up in that "not being ready," which amounts to hiding from the one fate we all most obviously share in common. Like children plugging their ears, squeezing their eyes shut, and shouting "nah nah nah!" we pile on the newer material and the next, better emotions, and the more real, more lasting fixes, pretending against all reason that death and decay aren't constantly staring us in the face. *Take two of these and call me in the morning. You'll feel better tomorrow.* Except that as many tomorrows come, they keep feeling exactly like today and maybe just a smidgeon worse.

We did not make a conscious choice for this pathology. We inherited it. But being the heir to something doesn't make it any less **yours**. Keeping moth and rust and thief out of mind has yet to make moth and rust and thief go away, but it does cost a boatload of money. To our society, that doesn't matter. We're far beyond reasoning with at this point. This madness is in our blood now. So what if an entire nation of people are committed to living beyond our means at the cost of any means possible? **The important thing is right now.**

We're running, but we're not running **toward** tomorrow. We're running **from** it. So we'll mortgage the farm for some more cheap electronics made in Shangri-La, or we'll sell the cells of murdered babies to invisible men who promise they will eventually use them to cure everything ever. We'll do this and more without thinking much about it because the entire *Sitz im Leben* of the American life is tyrannized by a mass hysteric case of collective, willful **ignorance**. Purposefully maintaining a corporate amnesia, we are neck deep in the narcissistic and naïve fourth rule every Christian ought to break as often as possible: the lie that you can find your best life **now**, which is to say, you can find God **in this world**. Or as Belinda Carlisle's 1987 hit proclaims, "Heaven is a place on earth."

Sitz im Leben

German for "situation in life," used to describe
the obsessions of any given era that the common
man is unable to see, even though they drive
his most important thoughts and choices.

THAT HEEL-GRABBING (QUIXOTIC) LITTLE KITSCH COLLECTOR

Once Mysticism and Rationalism had brought forth Pragmatism on the world, the doctors were surprised to see that grabbing at his ankle was a second child, smaller in stature but more beautiful in form. Named for the highest virtue both emotion and reason could imagine, even her brother and all his grand schemes can do little more than dote over her. Incestuously entwined around his arm whenever he is in public, he shows her off to everyone he meets, ever pointing out her companionship as the proof of his passion and wit. She is Pragmatism's goal, his meaning, his purpose of life, his reason for liberty, and the happiness he pursues. She is **Prosperity**, and she boasts of the name. She hides nothing of her attainments, always ready to fan her chic as she struts the walkway, the future queen of Pragmatism's impending reign.

> **Prosperity:** The belief that the way God feels about you is measured by how good your life is right now. Prosperity, then, is nothing more than worship of health, wealth, and wellness.

She has only one secret you are not allowed to know. It is her middle name. Against that knowledge both she and he guard, with all the tenacity of a pair of junkyard dogs. In a former age, it belonged to her great-great aunt, a queen in her own right, a queen and maybe even more. It was with hopes of such a return to glory that her parents named her so. But as Prosperity and Pragmatism came of age, they soon came to see that their parents may just as well have hung a dead, rotting chicken around her neck as an ornament as called her **that**. Some memories never seem to fade. After all, even in our decadent age, who would ever be so foolish as to fall in love with a girl whose middle name was **Mammon**?

Mammon: From a Greek word literally meaning "money" but in the New Testament embodying greed, unjust gain, and all manner of material gluttony. In the Middle Ages, the name Mammon was a symbol for all forms of idolatry, which is rooted in the coveting of the things of this world.

So they have hidden her secret and kept it well. Where Moralism, Mysticism, and Rationalism have certainly wreaked their havoc on society, not to mention on authentic Christian spirituality, they were never quite free within the confines of churches. For every Christian scholar whom Rationalism convinced to poo-poo scriptural inerrancy or the historicity of the Bible, there were five or more good men who sat in the pews and scoffed at the scoffer, refusing to allow such rubbish to be preached from their pulpits. But today, it is no longer so. Pragmatism and his lusty sister have all but waltzed into the churches. Pastors and laity alike looked up, noticed their fine clothing, and rushed to meet them. "Please, have a seat over here."

Soon, they both were seated on thrones before the assembly, every wish and whim of countless congregations submitted to their scrutiny and tested by their measurements.

"*It is simple,*" she said at her coronation. "*Have you received clear and present good living? Are you finding life in its fullest? Are you getting the best of all you wish, and are you getting it **now**? If not, then you have only one hope. You must ask my brother what you are doing wrong and obey his every word when he tells you what to do next.*"

The promise is as outlandish as it is foolish. It flies in the face of everything mankind has ever experienced in the annals of history, not to mention it is the near opposite of all the Christian Church has ever taught or believed about our present evil age (Galatians 1:3–5). But her beauty is stunning, next to which nothing can compare. Her allure is compelling, next to which all else seems bland. American civilization is built at least partially on an economic experiment that theorizes that by encouraging and escalating individualized human greed (the ability to "capitalize" on our interactions with our neighbors), we shall all wind up with a bigger, better deal in the end. How can churches raised in such a schoolyard not start to believe such thinking is God's own idea about Himself? So it is that, today, across all denominations and borders, a vast majority of American churches are driven not by sinful beggars in need, but by spiritually stuffed consumers who are looking for one more way to capitalize their already near perfect lives by taking a lazy bite out of Christianity.

It is the devil's same Lie, only spun with a new colored thread for Prosperity. If she came out and preached, "*You can find God in all the many material things of this world,*" most people would look at her like she was nuts. Of course, you can't find God in stuff. My iPhone is metal and plastic. If God exists, He is somewhere else, cheering me on and planning on how to help me get the next iPhone as soon as it comes out. Bald-faced lies never work so well as those that are half true. So Prosperity never blows her kisses and winks with open claims. She hides her middle name with all the wisdom Pragmatism can give her. But if you're listening carefully, even a well-camouflaged lie is still a far cry from the truth. Counterfeit dollars might fool the teen with her mom's credit card, but they'll never fool a bank teller who handles the real deal all day long. So Prosperity doesn't have to come out on national TV and say something as audacious as "*Give Jesus a try for forty days and see if he doesn't give you health, wealth, and purpose*" before you can know she's taken the lead in American Christianity. You can spot her rule even when she's playing it cool and saying nothing more than "*Hey! Look at me. Don't you want to be like me? Following Jesus is all about being like me.*" It's always the same promising, sultry tease that, against all odds and contrary to all of human history, you can find total, unlimited, safe, health, wealth, and positive energy right here, right now. You can live your dreams. You can make it last.

"*That's right. The Bible says so. You can do all things through God who strengthens you. You can even build a statue in the desert and have it last forever.*"

Dancing with the Devil

It should never be a surprise to Christians when we see the unbaptized chasing after the wind and trying to grasp oil in their hands. What other hope do the children of this age have than to get as much out of this life as possible? If you're as likely to die tomorrow as to live, why not eat, drink, and be merry? If you're to eat, drink, and be merry, why not eat and drink the best you possibly can?

Self-Satisfied, Bored, and Soon Dead

Woe to those who lie on beds of ivory . . . who sing idle songs to the sound of the harp . . . who drink wine in bowls and anoint themselves with the finest oils, but are not grieved over the ruin of Joseph! (Amos 6:4–6)

But what should surprise us—what should **upset** us and **vex** us—is to see a vast majority of American "Christian" churches preaching this same utopian quest as if an abundance of wealth in this life was the central message of Jesus and His Scriptures. Even the best secular PR agents in the world couldn't honestly spin that kind of message out of the man who taught His disciples that friendship with the world is enmity with God (James 4:4). Then again, it shouldn't have been possible for churches everywhere to embrace the notion that human beings will be justified on the Day of Judgment based on how much money they spend on pilgrimages to see the elbow joint bones of St. Ytevïan. It shouldn't have been possible for churches to claim the Holy Spirit's guidance as they burned a man at the stake for teaching Christianity should be based on accurate translations of the Bible. But, of course, those things have happened too.

{ **Prosperity's lie:** You can find God in this world. }

The lust for Prosperity does funny things to people, and churches are no different. Caught up in the desire to get closer to the good-looking girl on the dance floor, we imagine that once we get there, once people see us with her, then we'll be even better at winning friends. *"It's all for Jesus and His mission,"* we tell ourselves. But that's not the way Prosperity's dance goes. She doesn't let you lead. Once you're near her, you've got to match your saunter to her steps. If you grow tired and need a rest, she won't be following you off the floor. There's another sucker just as wide-eyed and eager as you to step into your place.

She's the dancing queen, and this is **her** dance. You are, at best, just another brick in her pyramid, another cog in her scheme. For even the best of us this means that once we get a taste of being near her on the dance floor, we'll do anything we can to stay on the floor as long as possible. If it means selling out an old conviction here or a cherished notion there, then so be it. With a few vague words about "the Spirit's leading" and "having a heart for Jesus," an entire congregation—heck, an entire church body—can willingly jettison their whole history and system of belief in hopes of being the one Prosperity smiles at next. Infatuated with dreams of a better experience in this life now, we forget why we are at the party in the first place. We forget we aren't here to fit in. We are here precisely because we **don't** fit in.

We are aliens and strangers (Ephesians 2:19). Our clothes will never match. Our language will always be in a square dialect. If ever we look down and see we've started dancing the same way everyone else is dancing, wearing the same threads everyone else is wearing, and saying the same things everyone else is saying, then we've done anything but become all things to all people (1 Corinthians 9:22). We've become nothing to no one but ourselves, a shadow cast by the image of the world, when we were supposed to be a city of light set high on a hill (Matthew 5:14).

How to Know If You're a Heretic

Falling prey to popular deception and false teaching is nothing new in the history of the Church. The New Testament is flush with warnings that the name "brother" or "pastor" or "Christian" does not guarantee immunity from the devil's Lie (Galatians 2:4; Romans 16:17). The question then is how to know if and when the leaven Jesus warned His disciples about has become the very thing making your favorite spiritual bread taste so very good.

One of the easiest tests for your soul food is to take a moment and listen to the culture around you. If what you're hearing in your church is the same thing you're hearing on TV or reading in the latest book recommended by O magazine, then chances are something is amiss. The next thing to do is take those same teachings and compare them to what Christians have said over the last two thousand years. If you then find that the "Church" teachings you're hearing have never been taught by any other Christians ever before, then it's high time to start questioning their authenticity as "Christian." Sometimes when the shoe fits, it means you shouldn't even think about wearing it.

For example, in the early decades of the Church, as Christianity spread, the old, pagan mystery religions started to experience a decline in popularity. One of the ways they looked to drum up new business was by borrowing the veneer of Christianity and using it to camouflage their older core teachings, especially the teachings inherited from Greek philosophy. Even before the last apostle died, there were innovative "denominations" staking a claim for alternate versions of Christianity in the spiritual marketplace. But these new teachings did far more than simply steal away a few unwitting members from the local congregations. They also converted **pastors**. With the help of those pastors, they soon were converting entire congregations.

After a few hundred years of this, one of the most industrious of these innovative teachers had grown incredibly popular. His name was Arius. With a knack for writing catchy tunes, he taught "because God is an immovable object" (a popular tenet of Greek philosophy), "**therefore,**

Jesus, the man, cannot be that same God." Jesus was "like" God, or Jesus was the "Son of God." But he was not **actually** God.

By the time the Council of Nicaea met to discuss this teaching in AD 325, the majority of representatives were already convinced that Arius was right. It is nothing short of miraculous that the same council wound up condemning both Arius and his teaching. The outcome is a testimony to the ancient Church's love of Scripture. It was by carefully studying **all** of the Word, together, that the vast majority of Christians at the council had their faith in Jesus' divinity restored. But the real point here is to see that the reason Arius's teaching spread so quickly and with such strength was because it wasn't just any old idea. It was based on one of the most common and popular assumptions of the culture, painted with a loose and flaky Christian coating.

Culture: The capacity of humans to inhabit a common experience as a civilization, often embodied most clearly through shared symbols and the arts.

Several hundred years later, the Church met another similar problem. The decline of the old Roman Empire was answered by the new economy of medieval feudalism. The emperor reigning in conjunction with a senate gradually gave way to the king, who ruled over all the land by God's design or by "divine right." It was during this same period that social decline and difficulties within the churches were answered by the claim that God also wanted only one man to sit in rule over His Church.

In tandem with the development of medieval hegemony, we also see, for the first time, the "Christian" teaching of papal rule over the entire Church of Christ on earth.

During the Reformation, yet another new idea sprang straight out of the cultural winds and into the churches. For the first time in fifteen hundred years of Christian history, it was popularly taught that Jesus Christ is *not* present **bodily** in the Lord's Supper. There were a large number of would-be radical reformers who rejected the older teaching that the bread in Holy Communion *is* Jesus' body. Few teachers were as adept at arguing this as a man named John Calvin. He and his followers summed the whole argument up with the catchy quip "The finite cannot contain the infinite." That is, according to our knowledge of **material** like bread, wine, or water, it is impossible for such things to contain the almighty God's sovereign glory. It is obvious to human reason that material cannot create or effect the **spiritual**. The growing Enlightenment and its popular assumption that everything can be explained by human reason enhanced that it was only reasonable to say this. *When one breaks open the bread of Communion, there is no blood inside. See! Obviously, it can't be Jesus' body.*

These are not the only false teachings in the history of the Church, but the point is when false teaching arises, it often is accompanied by two facts. First, it is totally new. Scripture might be used to support it, but Scripture was never used to support it before. Second, it mimics the philosophy and culture of whatever popular assumptions are held by the world at the time. Once again, Scripture might be used to support it, but Scripture is not the actual foundation of the idea. For that foundational idea, we look to whatever happens to be the currently held "common" sense.

Today, our age is tossing another entirely new teaching into the mix: the belief that success, wellness, and growth are the real proof of the Holy Spirit's activity among us. This is the teaching of Prosperity.

CG Stands for Charles Grandison

But Prosperity always has a problem in the Christian Church. Once preachers have begun to promise "success" as the proof of God's will, then Christians, congregations, or denominations who can't find success have only one alternative: to believe they are missing out on God. In order to find God, then success must then be manufactured, often at any cost.

When you want to dance with the girl at the heart of the American party, the first order of business is to make sure you stop looking like the biggest sore thumb in the house. It's then that Pragmatism sidles up next to you and whispers, *"No one is going to hang out with you if you dress funny, talk like a fool, and dance to your own beat. I'm her brother. Trust me, I know. Listen, if you want to dance with Prosperity, then you must wear what the world wears, talk like the worlds talks, and do what the world does."*

So, off churches go in search of the world's most popular, best-selling ideas.

We look for the successes that "God is blessing," and then we take them home and try to make them our own. We baptize any idea that looks like it works with whatever Christian frosting we can mix up, throwing in a few dashes of Bible verses here and there, but always testing it by the same immutable standard of measure: does it get more bodies in the pews (or in newly installed, stadium-style cushioned seats)? It's no secret that this style of Prosperity-driven theology has been leading American churches by the nose for a long time. In fact, most of its most recent adherents are very proud of it. They even commonly call this application of the principles of capitalism to church "the Church **Growth** Movement."

> **The Church Growth Movement:**
> A philosophical movement within evangelical Christianity that emphasizes sociological study of target populations and organizational efficiency as primary means of effective missionary work.

Not everyone in this CGM always teaches the same things. Many of its adherents mean very well and desire to be faithful. But Prosperity doesn't really give a rip about intentions. She only cares if you're chasing her, and she knows that once you start really trying her dance, you soon won't have time for much of anything else.

It all starts with a tease. *"Picture it. Imagine how beautiful the Church could be if only all the congregations and Christians would get their acts together and really do everything the way we're supposed to. What if we could get everyone to stop being hypocrites and work together to be the kind of Church God is leading us to be. Imagine if all the people were leading transformed, more fulfilled lives! If we were doing that, then we could probably complete in only a few years the entire mission Jesus left to us. Isn't that what Jesus would really want? For us to succeed at the mission He gave us?"*

That is step 1: envision the Church as a popular girl (just like Prosperity always is). Step 2 is to ask Pragmatism what reasonable steps can be taken to get the makeover really going. Once this (1) vision and (2) plan are in place, step 3 is to do what all entrepreneurs must do: put your vision and business plan to the test by entering the market.

In the market, only two words matter: boom and bust. Boom is the mark of the Spirit's Church. Bust is the unforgivable sin. Over the years, the Church Growth Movement has morphed into many shapes and sizes, but its center has never changed. The styles keep shifting faster than the sand. Enough tomes filled with metaphysical theories to make even Thomas Aquinas blush have come off the presses. But the innovative dogma has remained the same: if the church is growing, it proves that it is Spirit-driven and alive. So if we want it to be alive and Spirit-driven, we certainly better find a way to make it grow. The true churches are the ones always prospering more and more, **and** prospering with people whose personal Prosperity is also on the up and up. Up and up and more and more. Congregations consuming religious consumers all together searching for consumption as the one proof God is on our side. *"They will know we are Christians by* *our wellness.*" The only heresy is anything that might cause your life or your congregation to go into a **recession**.

Most church growth principles are little more than warmed over American business tactics (which doesn't make them evil in themselves), but applying these tactics to the life of the Christian Church has had a rather devastating effect on a market unprepared to be a market. In a twenty-first-century culture that glorifies Prosperity, churches that are the most innovative at preaching versions of Christian*ish* Prosperity are often able to fulfill their vision of growth. With the itching ears of our age already finely tuned to be tickled by anything justifying their consumer lifestyle, men like Donald McGavran, Robert Schuller, Rick Warren, and Bill Hybels watched their franchises explode like the "church" versions of Starbucks and Walmart. But what has gone unseen are the countless smaller congregations that found themselves unable to compete. Going to seminars sold by the same conglomerate congregations, pastors and people rush home to their failing church businesses and apply the tactics themselves. But for the majority, this only hastens their demise by ensuring their storefront church is only offering a cheap imitation of the real deal being sold up the street at the superchurch. The more congregations close their doors, the more pastors and denominations believe they need to apply more principles to try to stem the bleeding.

Worse, religious consumers willing to buy a product promising personal Prosperity in their relationship with God only stick around if the product really delivers. The dirty little secret of the Church Growth Movement is that its rise to ideological fame and fortune has presided over one of the greatest backslides in **church attendance** in recorded history. Once individual lives find that they can't keep up with Prosperity's dance, they drift away. After shopping at the low-price superstore long enough and having the cheaply made plastic religion fall apart for the umpteenth time, they eventually lose the desire to go shopping at all.

Perhaps still more amazing is that this pattern of burning out American pews didn't just start in the 1980s (as its proponents often claim). The Church Growth Movement is the tail end of a theological wind that has been emptying American churches in the name of "the Gospel" for over 150 years. Its true pioneer's name has long been set on the sidelines (right next to Ozymandias). But during the American era of the Reconstruction after the Civil War, he was **the** prophetic voice of leadership anointed to usher in the Spirit's outpouring of growth and blessing upon all the churches of the world. A mastermind, he saw far ahead of his time how Prosperity could be forced upon churches by harnessing logic to engineer the right kind of tool for enticing the sinner into taking God for a test-drive. That perfect tool he called the "revival," and with it he convinced American Christianity it was experiencing a Second Great Awakening. It was a fire lit in the harvest fields that has been burning them over ever since, a fire lit with the match that was the preaching and theology of Charles Grandison Finney.

Revivalism: A philosophical movement arising in eighteenth- and nineteenth-century Protestantism that believed an increase in spiritual interest and renewed life could be achieved in all churches through the introduction of so-called "new measures."

THE OLD "NEW" MEASURES

The life and work of Charles Finney was prolific enough that volumes could be (and have been) dedicated to him. But his enduring legacy to Christianity is the belief that one can increase the number of conversions to Christ by learning how to intentionally manipulate unsuspecting religious consumers. He believed, taught, and practiced that if the Church was serious about evangelizing the world, then the real mission was to learn how to harness human motivations and use

them to drive individuals to commit their lives to Jesus. Once the act of the will had been sold, the born-again believer would leave behind any false motivations through obedient discipleship. But up to that point, until a man committed himself to God, God's Word was certainly not the moving force in evangelism. It was salesmanship. To make the sale, anything that could move the unconverted closer to contact with the revival was fair game. According to Finney, in any given context those factors might change, but true faithfulness meant whatever "new measures" would work needed to be adopted as swiftly as possible.

For Finney, the "new measures" usually meant catchier music, more entertaining and practical preaching, and an emphasis on the great blessings received from the Christian life. Amazingly, as much as innovations and technology have since morphed our world, the more the context has changed, the more Finney's "new measures" have remained the brand, spanking same. If anything has actually been amped up in the transition from classic revivalism to the postmodern CGM (besides the guitars), it is only the preposterous upper limits of the prosperity promises being made in Jesus' name. It was shameful enough for Finney to introduce his crass capitalizing approach to a most holy and ancient faith, but the depravity of Finney 2.0 seems to know no bounds.

American Christianity appears oblivious to the history and evolution. Drunk on the effects of the countless, carefully designed, canned, fresh, "out of the box," manipulated mystical experiences, skepticism melts away. Laid bare, we believe (and pay for) whatever is sold next. Whatever the newer, better guarantee, this time with these principles, this plan is the one final method-strategy-vision-program-DNA-you-name-it-rigamarole that will answer all your needs to find God **in this world**. Whether it's with a three-car garage or the superpower to cast out demons and heal diseases, the promise itself is only the frosting. The cake is Prosperity.

But according to the actual history books, the Second Great Awakening was no real awakening at all. American religious life was not particularly weak or failing before the revivals, nor was it particularly strong or successful after them. Nor was the Awakening known for being expressly pious or sanctified. One historian friendly to the movement noted that if you took away the worship, there would still be enough excitement to attract plenty of young people.[5] Meanwhile, it was commonly quipped that as many souls were **conceived** as saved at camp meetings. Several states banned the sale of liquor within five miles of such meetings due to perpetual rises in drunkenness during the events.

What the Awakening did achieve was the transfer of large numbers of Christians from more traditional denominations to newer, revival-oriented bodies that sprang in the bull market for new measures.[6] This left embedded forever in the spiritual DNA of American religious consumers the hunger for sensationalism as the key to finding God. Finney himself made no qualms about it: "The object is to get up an excitement, and bring the people out. . . . I do not mean to say that [these] measures are pious, or right, but only that they are wise, in the sense that they are the . . . means to the end. . . . The object of our measures is to gain attention, and **you *must have* something *new*** [to do that]."[7]

5.   Roger Finke and Rodney Stark, *The Churching of America* (New Brunswick, NJ: Rutgers University Press, 2005), 99.

6.   Finke and Stark's *The Churching of America* is a fascinating assessment of American Churchianity, and its section on the Second Great Awakening is eye-opening on this point. In short, the Second Great Awakening birthed several versions of the Methodist and Baptist churches, but not without first emptying the pews of the Congregationalists, Episcopalians, and Presbyterians. (See figure 3.1, p. 56.)

7.   Charles Grandison Finney, *Lectures on Revivals of Religion*. (New York: Leavitt, Lord & Co., 1835), 167–68. Emphasis mine.

"Religion is the work of man," he said in the same work. "It is something for man to do." Then he went on, "[But] there are so many things to lead their minds off from religion . . . that it is necessary to raise an excitement among them."[8] Today, there is no clearer example of this heritage than the very old battle over the new measure *par excellence*, ironically still being called "new" even after 250 years. It's merely gone out and picked up an even newer and more exciting word for the word *new*: "contemporary."

PRAISE AND LITURGY

It has been said the one who defines the terms always wins the debate, and this can certainly be seen with the rise of the contemporary Christian music movement. One doesn't need to look at the lyrics of every song and hymn side by side or weigh the merits of guitar versus organ to get to the heart of the debate. If you really want to know what all the fuss is about, you just need to listen to the terms chosen for the debate and then ask yourself, "**Who** *chose those terms?*" and "*Why did they choose* **those** *terms?*"

The idea that a group of people who sing out of a hymnal with an organ is not "contemporary" (which literally means "happening right now") is only slightly more jaundiced than claiming that singing catchy songs designed to spur the emotions isn't one of the most strongly entrenched "traditions" in American worship, dating all the way back to Finney himself. The real question of the contemporary versus traditional debate has never been "Can churches use forms and traditions in the present time in order to praise and worship God?" Who would argue with that? So why the *contemporary* versus *traditional* labels? Because those who started the debate framed the debate with those words in order to sell their trust in Prosperity-driven worship without ever having to mention her name.

From its very start, Finney's strategic revivalism had to be sold to groups of Christians who were resistant to it. Like any good

---

8.   *Lectures on Revivals*, 9.

salesman, Finney answered their skepticism by putting the best possible construction on his product. For Finney, the phrase "new measures" was the right kind of spin to capture all the cultural power of the age of Industrial Revolution and scientific discovery. In the same way, more recently the phrase *contemporary worship* has been introduced, not to describe what the movement actually is, but to sell the movement as the kind of up-to-date, prosperous "style" that every postmodern person likes to think of himself as naturally inhabiting. *Contemporary* is a positive word, intended to build a positive image. What could be more **practical** than *contemporary*? What could be more **beneficial** than *praise*?

Meanwhile, the other "style" is decried with dogmatic sounding words like *traditional* (ideas we get from dead people) and *liturgy* (no one really knows what that word means, but it sounds old and stagnant so it can't be good). These words are intended to build a negative image, the picture of an awkward, dusty building full of gray-haired, boring people. Such words can only describe backward places, trapped in "maintenance" mode ministries (negative), and adamantly opposed to being "mission-minded" (positive). What could be **less Spirit-filled** than *tradition*? What could be **less meaningful** than *liturgy*? *Praise* we can sell. *Lament*, not so much. With the terms predefined to favor the selling of one "style" over the other, the real debate is kept far out of sight. What is the real debate? It is whether the planned emotional manipulation of unsuspecting worshipers is the Holy Spirit's model for evangelism and "doing" Church, or whether it is a diabolical error intended to rip the free grace of justification right out of the heart of the Evangelical churches. Is that thing we call "contemporary worship" just traditional worship, only not so boring because it is now set to guitar, or is it a new tradition of radicalism that is more exciting precisely because it makes room for the worship of our own fleshly passions? Is it just another "style," or is it the cultural *Sitz im Leben* of capitalism manifesting itself as a spirituality and selling itself as counterfeit Christianity? Is it just some "new measures" for doing what we've always done, or is it a whole new song and dance sung to the tune of Prosperity? From where I'm sitting, the centuries-long history of the movement and its reliance on Prosperity's language to define the debate out of existence, so that the debate is never allowed to take place, speaks volumes on the real state of the predicament. Without even knowing it, the vast majority of American churches are following lockstep in Finney's tradition of using innovations in excitement to manufacture predetermined outcomes that are then used as "proof" of the Holy Spirit's presence. The belief that this act of man will make Christianity more prosperous in the present age is all but swallowed wholesale, without so much as a glance at the ingredients list. Meanwhile, despite all the claims, none of the ideas are actually cutting edge. None of it is outside the box. It is the same, tired movement that was emptying churches 250 years ago, repeating the same, tired lie that the secret to unleashing the power of God's Spirit in the present age is a matter of enticing the churches to measure all things, starting with worship, by their proximity to Prosperity.

Weeds That Eat You

What was sown among thorns, this is the one
who hears the word, but the cares of the world
and the deceitfulness of riches choke the word,
and it proves unfruitful. (Matthew 13:22)

What happens when individual Christians believe this lie? If all we have is praise, then what happens when it is no longer a time to live but a time to die (Ecclesiastes 3:2)? How will you weep, mourn, and wail while always on the up and up (James 4:9)? The threat of contemporary revivalism is not the use of guitars or amplifiers, but the hidden assumption of its history, the root of a movement to "change" the Church

in order to make it more possible to find proof of God by pointing to positive experiences we are having **right now**. Jesus and His cross are not enough. Promises made about the Last Day don't draw crowds the way promises about the present do.

THE LAW OF PROSPERITY

How many times can a person try one more time to believe in Prosperity as the rule for measuring Christianity? How long until the whole thing starts to look like a giant sham, a pyramid scheme prospering the preacher but never the preached? Find an atheist who used to be a Christian and ask him how many times he tried to **feel** God before he gave up. Then ask yourself, *"What was his faith actually in? The historical resurrection of Jesus or Finney's new measures?"* Who really let him down? God or the promises of Prosperity?

{ **Prosperity** is the worship of Mammon. }

But what happens when the **right now** promises don't come true? It was bad enough when being a Christian meant one had to be morally perfect, striving to self-justify through working hard at the Ten Commandments. But when the law of "love your neighbor as yourself" is replaced with the law of "find success, happiness, and a healthy physique," Christians wind up trying to shoulder a burden no human being can bear. If one wants to keep calling himself "Christian," he has no choice but to begin down the road of lying to himself. Putting prosperity on credit, he can feel and look like the man the preacher says he's supposed to be, but he only winds up in debt, just as American consumer culture planned all along. His wife must push and prod and pull and diet to stave off the perishing of her physical beauty, while also holding down her own full-time, successful career **and** raising two (three at most) handsome, talented, college-bound, morally presentable (which mainly means **successful**) children. Her anorexic tendencies and the constant friction in the marriage may be the same thing experienced by everyone else in America, but shudder the thought that the people at church should ever know! Together, they pretend with all their might to be the Joneses, little aware that the Joneses are two steps from divorce, are self-medicating in their own hidden ways, just sprang bail for Johnny, and took the family vacation out of state in order to keep Julie's need for an abortion quiet.

There is no guilt like the guilt of **failure**. It is one thing to see the world around you constantly chasing a bigger, better tomorrow, filled with meat and drink and vacations in the sun. It is another thing altogether to believe the lie that this is Christianity. To be sure, Christianity does teach that God plans to give to every person in the world ultimate abundance in and through Jesus Christ. But Jesus Christ was very, very clear about what that means. He said, "My [prosperity] is **not of this world**" (John 18:36). This world is filled with all manner of wars and rumors of wars (Matthew 24:6), where moth and rust destroy and where thieves break in and steal (Matthew 6:19), where charm

137

is deceptive and beauty is fleeting (Proverbs 31:30), where the pursuit of prosperity is a snare filled with senseless, harmful desires that threaten to plunge you into ruin (1 Timothy 6:9), a wide and easy path filled with plenty of growth but leading only to destruction (Matthew 7:13).

Against this sandy land where storms will come and blow, authentic Christianity stands firm as a house built on bedrock. This world and all its decay, rot, and anti-prosperity cannot touch it because it cannot touch Jesus. Jesus Christ is risen, and **He** is the treasure kept in heaven for **you**. This Good News of the Gospel is the promise that God does not expect you to find abundance (or even happiness) in this dying world. Christian contentment is knowing that both to be brought low and to abound are godly for the sake of Christ, for the sake of His cross, and for the sake of His atoning blood. Both to face hunger and to face plenty will harm the body eventually, but neither of them can touch the soul kept safe in Christ. Christianity has never budged from this truth because Christianity is not about **this world**.

More than this it is the special blessing of Christianity when, for the sake of the name of Christ, one endures weaknesses, insults, hardships, persecutions, and calamities over and above the normal trials and pains of human life on a sinful planet (1 Peter 2:20). Christian faith is the belief that all your sicknesses, poverties, and catastrophes are only the tip of the iceberg, reflecting the much deeper problem you carry buried beneath your skin-deep appearance: your sin.

Through all of it, the only thing God requires you to feel is a repentant awareness of needing to be saved from it.

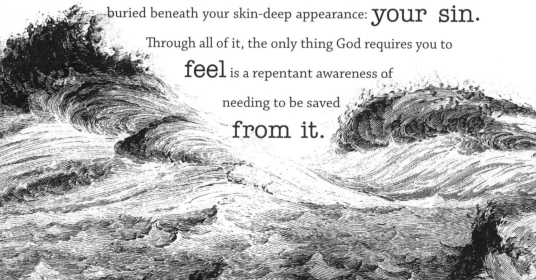

Authenticity Suffers

In this you rejoice, though now for a little while,
if necessary, you have been grieved by various trials,
so that the tested genuineness of your faith—more
precious than gold that perishes though it is tested
by fire—may be found to result in praise and glory
and honor at the revelation of Jesus Christ. (1 Peter 1:6–7)

To combat this inherited evil dwelling in you, God also insists that you experience a little water slapped in your face, along with the regular taste of a bit of bread and wine on your lips. About these experiences He speaks to you and tells you that they are of Christ. He says these words and signs are His imputation, His binding of your death, debt, and failures to the cross of Jesus, and the great converse grafting of Jesus' resurrected health, eternal wealth, and divine prosperity into you . . . **through faith alone**. You don't see Him, but you **believe** in Him (1 Peter 1:8). His mind is your mind (1 Corinthians 2:16). His future is your future (2 Timothy 2:11). He is safe (1 Peter 1:4), immortal (1 Timothy 1:17), imperishable (1 Corinthians 15:54), having conquered death once, never to die again (Romans 6:9), having overcome this perishing world (John 16:33), having prospered (Matthew 28:6) in the true, God-given way (John 14:6), *for you* (1 John 4:4).

This is the theology (the knowledge of God) through the cross of Jesus, unleashed upon the entire world through the Church that is the assembling of sinners bound to promises of Last Day righteousness received **now** through **faith alone**. It is a holy spirituality that is all about the promises of God's words. It is never as tantalizing to the flesh as the lies of Prosperity, but then again it's not a lie either. As truth, you can build on it with every confidence. Pure **Christ**ianity is astronomically more freeing than all the hopes and expectations and constant failings of this present evil age.

GOD'S MEASURES

I did not stop smoking pot the day I met Ozymandias. True conversion to Christianity is never easy, nor fast. Even once the spirit is made willing by the regenerating words of Christ, the flesh remains weak so long as we sojourn in this world (Matthew 26:41). By daily contrition and repentance a Christian must be renewed through the drowning and dying of the sins and evil lusts that again and again creep out of us in attempts to drag us back down into the ways of the world from which we are redeemed. The new man who comes forth to live before God by faith in the righteousness of Christ learns that on this side of the war there is no victory the likes of which Prosperity sings.

> So I find it to be a law that when I want to do right, evil lies close at hand . . . the law of sin that dwells in my members. (Romans 7:21, 23b)

In the war waged against one's own soul, sanctification's most certain fruit is an ever-growing awareness that for every sin you manage to leave behind, you find six more, all worse than the first, that you didn't even know you were harboring within. Stopping the hands from evil is the easy part. The heart is where the fight marks the real battleground. Thankfully, it is God, not you, who fights with all the weapons of His spiritual Word against the sin living in you. There, the more He wins, the more you will also see the scars of your internal leprosy and inbred reprobation. There He fights with His light against your darkness to reveal to you just how truly you are a poor, miserable sinner. But He does not leave you naked, pitiable, and blind. He also preaches to you the deep, deep love of Jesus, whose blood is your white clothing, whose mercy is your great honor, and whose Word becomes your new, eternal sight.

Getting away from my mental dependence on marijuana took a long time and a great amount of Gospel. At last, it was not the dangers and sinful self-destruction that brought about the change, nor was it a visionary moment of superpowered reversal. It was **forgiveness**. Forgiveness preached, forgiveness confessed, forgiveness sung, and forgiveness **bestowed** over all my tears and failed attempts propelled me one day to wake with my self-destructive habit far enough behind me that it hasn't entrapped me again. But I make no mistake: my sin is not gone, nor will it be this side of the Last Day. Nor do I believe for a moment that I came closer to God by segregating myself from one addictive corner of this world. It was because God had **already come close to me**, just as I am, that He was able to bring His success in doing the one thing we in the world need most—we need to be killed. He killed me, and He raised me in the person of His Son. Right now. Already. By **faith alone**.

All human attempts to realize the victory of Jesus as something we can act on right now, every other measure we dream up for doing the work of His religion, amounts to the activity of dogs returning to their vomit (2 Peter 2:22). Our greed fights back, seeking to idolize the present world by worshiping it rather than its Creator (Romans 1:25). God has said these things are not Him, nor are they a way to know what He thinks about you (Matthew 12:39). Even without the catastrophe of sin messing it all up, the created world is entirely limited, set in its course, unable to do one whit more than He created it to do. Building churches by any and all means possible is not building the Church. All of our experiences, all of our studies, all of our sociology and strategy, every new or old measure and excitement, every single thing in this world cannot bring an unbeliever to Christ. **Only Christ can bring a man to Christ**, and Christ has **spoken** about how He plans to do that.

The Moment God Killed You

> In Him also you were circumcised . . .
> by the circumcision of Christ, having been buried
> with Him in baptism, in which you were also
> raised with Him through faith in the powerful
> working of God. (Colossians 2:11–12)

Do you want to find God now? Do you want to know how He feels about you now? Do you want an answer untouched by the sands of time and undiminished by our greedy attempts to build heaven out of this halfway hell? Then believe His words: I baptize you (1 Peter 3:21). Take, eat. Take, drink. I am here (1 Corinthians 10:16). I am the Word made flesh (John 6:55). I am the source of living water (John 4:10). I am the bread from heaven (John 6:51). I am your root, your portal, your rebirth (John 15:1; 10:9; 11:25). **That** is how God feels about you. Buried and raised with Jesus, where He has said you are buried and raised with Him, the Father now believes you **are** Jesus. Better, He **promises** it (Galatians 4:28). Even though the entire world is ranting and raving that right now you sure don't look like God's Son, that you are weak, flawed, mortal, and broken, against all of these fanatical lies God your Father has lifted up the cross of Jesus. There this world is inverted on its cursed, decaying head. There death is life. There weakness is strength. There affliction is prosperity.

"I thirst!" the Creator of water said (John 19:28), and with those words He mocked Prosperity. "Man shall not live by bread alone," He laughed (Matthew 4:4). "I have food to eat that you do not know about" (John 4:32). A few weeks later He was chilling on the shores of Galilee grilling fish (John 21:9). Shortly after that He ascended to the right hand of God, leaving His apostles the commission not to conquer the world, but to preach that He already had (1 John 2:14).

No matter how big you build your barns, you can only eat your bread today. The secret of Christian contentment is that tomorrow we do not eat here at all. Tomorrow we dine in paradise. Imagine all the personal torment that might have been spared Ozymandias if he had believed that. He could have still ruled the world, and he could have still built a statue. But there's a good chance he would have learned not to sneer, not because he'd found Prosperity, but because he'd become content to believe that you cannot find God in this world. In this world, Jesus sends His Word to **find you**.

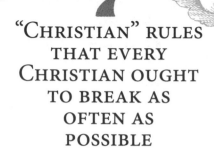

"CHRISTIAN" RULES THAT EVERY CHRISTIAN OUGHT TO BREAK AS OFTEN AS POSSIBLE

Never #4

Never follow a rule because it benefits you **now** (and if it mentions "abundance," run screaming from the room).

The Fourth Rule to be **BROKEN**

Prosperity.

You can find God in this world: the worship of mammon.

Never follow a rule that has to start over
(again and again . . . and again . . .) again.

Tiger and the Terrible, Horrible, No Good, Very Bad Word

I once met a man whose name was Tiger (and no, he didn't play golf). I was only a few weeks into my second call as a parish pastor, having been set down by the Spirit almost as far from my San Diego roots as I could get without leaving the continent, smack in the middle of the vast urban settled concrete tundra of greater Philadelphia. Part of the call included working as an aide to a local mission society called Philadelphia Lutheran Ministries, founded to reach out to inner-city immigrant communities. Tiger came from one of these communities (Korean), but he was attending one of our small churches (think "fifteen people of European descent, a building, and no pastor").

The first time I met Tiger, he was in an impassioned conversation with our executive director about his plans for helping the congregation turn their little ship around. But like so many zealous Christians throughout history, his zeal got the better of him. As I listened, a great deal of things came clear for me, because in only four words he managed to sum up the single most slippery false teaching of our age, which just so also happens to be the fifth rule every Christian ought to break as often as humanly possible.

"My family and I play music for worship," he said. *"If we can just get the people in the congregation to find God's presence in my family's music, then the congregation will certainly grow."*

Forget the debates about music. That's not even where I'm going. Forget all the arguments about style and culture and context. Forget worship and praise and liturgy and song. Skip all of it and go to the root. Four deadly words: **"If . . . we . . . can . . . just . . ."**

Of all the spins the devil puts on his original Lie, this one remains the most subtle. "IfWeCanJust" doesn't care about denominational labels or barriers. IfWeCanJust is not a respecter of doctrines or traditions or the lack thereof. IfWeCanJust doesn't shoot flaming arrows. It uses a scoped sniper rifle with a silencer. If the Church is a body, then IfWeCanJust is a cancer quietly taking over cells and using them to destroy the system from within, but all without sending symptoms or pain to the mind. With its four seemingly harmless words, IfWeCanJust bypasses all our defense systems and goes straight for the jugular of one of the most important teachings of the Bible: **ecclesiology**. Now, I know I just about lost you there. I broke a major rule of being cool and writing about spirituality. I said a fifty-cent theological word. That wasn't any ol' two-bit term. I dropped the mother lode. The E-bomb. Justin Timberlake knows the meaning of "justified,"[9] and while Christopher Walken may not have had a fever for it, he certainly got the general drift of "communion."[10] But nobody—and I mean **nobody**—is comfortable rollin' with **ecclesiology** in their crew. Try it at your next prayer breakfast. Pull your friend aside and tell him you're worried about his ecclesiology. "Oh, no. Doc's got me on a prescription for that, I think."

But here's the thing: **everybody** is into ecclesiology. Big time. We just never call it that. We call it all sorts of other things from "fellowshiping" or "discipling" to "small groups" or "strategic planning." Sometimes we call it *"we've never done it that way before"* or *"this is the way we've always done it."* In other circles you might even hear it as *"I can be a Christian even if I don't do that."* In its one million ways of going unsaid, ecclesiology is the art of talking about the things we believe make the churches to be part of *the* Church. Literally, the word just means "words about" (*logia*) "the Church" (*ecclesia*). It's a humdinger fancy way of saying "churchology," or what we know to be true about the Church.

---

9.   Made famous by his rise with the boy band NSYNC, Justin Timberlake survived the band's breakup to become a solo sensation with his debut album. The title? *Justified*.

10.   An American stage and screen actor with a serious pedigree, perhaps most famous to the under-forty crowd for getting a little overexcited about Will Ferrell's talent with a cowbell, Christopher Walken also starred in a 1989 made-for-TV movie about being abducted by aliens. Though something of a step-down from his 1985 stint as arch villain in the James Bond semiclassic *A View to a Kill*, the "true story" docudrama abduction left his unique face permanently imprinted on at least one eleven-year-old's memory. The title of the movie? *Communion*.

Ecclesiology: The stuff that makes a church into "the Church," that is, the things that make any gathering of people into the assembling of God's people. A lack of this "knowledge of the Church" is the root of the fifth rule that all Christians ought to break.

Ecclesiology may be too old school for most people, but churchology is a hot ticket. It's selling books quicker than hot cross buns. It's spawning superstars and Web sites and one-hit wonders faster than the Billboard Top 100. It's the talk of the conference circuit, a blitzkrieg of missiology, mission mindedness, missional missioning, and "doing church." It's been the  talk of the town for a long while now, in part because many faithful Christians just genuinely want to be faithful in what they do, and in part because everyone who is in the know about how the Church is doing in America knows it is glaringly obvious we are entirely messed up. Secularism is rising. Attendance is dropping. Kids are leaving. Something is desperately wrong. Intuitively, our best thinkers and leaders all know churchology sits at the center of it all.

Because of this, churchology has become like an ongoing string of episodes on *Unsolved Mysteries*, with everyone watching and hoping to be the mastermind who figures it all out and claims the reward. No doubt, for most of us the reward would be to see the Church prosper. But there's a lot of money being made in the meantime. This week a pastor with a recently grown following pops up and claims, *"Eureka!*

I've found it!" He sells books about how he made his congregation work, tours the conference circuit, and watches as the fame of his success bolsters the numbers of his congregation even further. But then, after everyone else has taken his theory home and put it to work, it doesn't fix the problems. Secularism still rises. Attendance still goes down. Kids still leave. So the next week another pops up with a more newfangled twist on cracking the churchology code.

But the more I've read these books and listened to these teachers, the more it becomes clear that we're no closer to cracking the code than when we started. In fact, if our words mean anything, we're in the exact same place. Guru after guru is just shouting the same answer over and over again. We change the catchphrase, but the meaning stays the same. "The answer is Christian fellowship!" Wait, no . . . that didn't work. "The answer is Christian community!" Wait, no . . . that didn't work either. "The answer is *communitas*!" Um . . . "Don't ask questions! We need to change. It's time to reboot! We have to repackage! We need to re-imagine! The Church will die if we don't rethink!" When that doesn't work, there's hardly a breath lost before we're back at the drawing board, buying the next hot book, looking to the latest young, hip pastor, trusting him that this time his rehashed version of "really, really (for real this time), innovation" will get things going.

But the premise never changes. It's like we're a big corporate pit bull with our jaw locked on what we think is a tasty bone. We think if we just chew hard enough and shake long enough, we'll prove our dominance and get something good out of it. The problem is that we don't have a bone at all. We have a lead pipe painted with hallucinogenic, ultratoxic paint. We keep saying we are going to do some "out of the box" churchology brainstorming, but we never get out of the box of our failing foundation. We start every single answer with the assumption

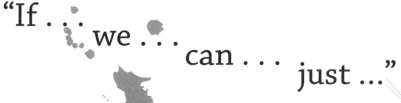

"If . . . we . . . can . . . just . . ."

IfWeCanJust: The belief that God's blessings
for the Church can be received by us only after we
have first done (*you fill in the blank*). IfWeCanJust,
then, is nothing more than worship of ecclesiology,
that is, the worship of our efforts to be Church.

LYCANTHROP(CHURCH)OLOGY
AND THE RISE OF THE W(H)ERECHURCH

IfWeCanJust (*fill in the blank*), then we will see God moving
in the Church. It's the fifth rule not only every Christian but every
congregation and every denomination ought to be absolutely on the ball
about breaking as often as possible.

We're not breaking it, and it shows. It started like a habit on the
side, something a few of us were doing in a dark alley on Friday nights.
But now we're hooked. Now we're selling it on the street corners and
putting it in our children's food. It wasn't supposed to hurt anything. It
was supposed to make things better. It was supposed to be our next great
step in Christendom, in mission, in being **the** Church. But the signs of
long-term drug use are showing. Far worse than one last dance with Mary
Jane, we keep trying to kill the pain of our addiction by taking higher and
higher concentrations of the inebriant. We are convinced the problem
isn't the drug, only the mixture of what it's been cut with. IfWeCanJust
find a purer source. IfWeCanJust get the recipe perfect, then we'd finally
keep the fifth rule and manage to **find God in our efforts to be
the Church**.

Denominations keep bankrupting. Churches keep closing.
Faith keeps dying, most especially faith in the Church.

"I don't have to go to church to be a Christian." "Church is just
for hypocrites and religious people." "Do you know how many wars
and social problems have been caused by the Church?"

Such comments could be called out for their extremism or their lack of factuality, but the bigger problem is their confusion. What is "the Church"? An organization? A club? A bunch of people? A building? Nobody knows, but we keep throwing the word *Church* around anyway. "The Church is dying. The Church needs to change. Church is boring. Church is a waste of time. The Church needs a new roof. That person was never Churched. Jesus never wanted to start a Church. The Church used to do this. The Church needs to do that."

Once upon a time, in keeping with the language of the apostles, it was common for Christians to refer to the Church as their "Mother" (Galatians 4:6; 1 Peter 5:13; Revelation 12:1–6, 13–17). No longer. American Christians today, though we're not quite sure what the Church is, are far more likely to see the Church as some doting old crazy lady to whom we are unfortunately related in some extended-family kind of way. She might be able to show up at family gatherings and tell the same five stories over and over again to anyone unlucky enough to sit by her, but most of us secretly think it would be best if we just bit the bullet and penned her up in a nursing home. At least then we could live off the sale of her estate for a few years.

But it's worse than that. In recent years many of us have become convinced that the problem is not only that she is old and a little dotty. The problem is that she is sick. We're not sure how, and we're not sure why, but we're sure that it is true. If she wasn't sick, then she wouldn't look so old and feeble. She'd be young and spry and buxom. But here we are, stuck with this nutty old bat whom, everyone calls "Church," and we can't quite bring ourselves to believe it. Most of us still believe that the Church is out there somewhere; we just don't know where she is or how to find her. Where did the Church go? No one knows.

It is as if this old woman before us once was the Church, but then underwent some ungodly transformation into a lower life form. It is like she was bitten by some ancient, mythological monster whose venom turned her into a grotesque version of itself. As a result, she has become the W(h)ereChurch, a half-breed mistake of creation that Jesus never really intended to be, a dilapidated shadow of the real Church that once was.

The W(h)ereChurch: A horrific beast of a religious community, the grotesque shell of what once was probably the true Church, but now has become only something people call "Church." Beneath its sickness, the true Church has vanished, and now it is our job to find her!

Although we are not quite certain how any of this happened, most of us don't think too deeply on it. Rather, we focus our energies on the hope that it is not too late. "If we can just reverse the effects," we tell ourselves, "then before the Church vanishes altogether, we might be able to bring her back to her true form." But to find this answer, we must learn from her (not by listening to her, of course—that would be ludicrous!) through the trial and error of study. Somewhere deep within her sick present state, there might lie some hint or clue as to how to make her into the real Church again.

So, like hypochondriacs with a projection problem, we bring in doctors of every stripe to tell us how to fix her. Some of us even go to medical school ourselves. But one way or another, almost all of us get into the business of diagnosing what's wrong with "the Church," taking measurements, trying little home remedies, observing the outcomes. In prodding and pricking and watching her every response, we may just find the answer, the antidote will give us the Church as we always knew she ought to be.

We may still shy away from fifty-cent theological words like "ecclesiology," but we're on a quest for true, real, "authentic" knowledge of the Church. Some still hold out hope that by finding such knowledge, they can revive a true, real, "authentic" denomination, but many more would be happy if they could only find a true, real, "authentic" congregation. Still more believe that they improve their odds by searching for a true, real, "authentic" small group. But we are all trying desperately to discover the right churchology, a silver bullet that will turn that long-toothed, wrinkly hag back into the kind of woman we won't be embarrassed to show off on our arm.

IfWeCanJust hunt down and administer the proper cure . . .

But then the batty old woman starts to fight back! No sooner do we draw blood samples and administer a few remedies than she reacts like a cornered junkyard dog. This, of course, only further confirms our suspicions about her illness. We bring out the medical belts and strap her down, ignoring her protests. More tests. More trials. We pump remedy after remedy into her. Scars and fatigue begin to show, not only from the disease, but also from the side effects of our potential cures. It doesn't matter. Nothing can deter us. Without our medicines, she will only get worse anyway. "It's for the good," we tell ourselves. "The problem is that we just haven't committed ourselves to trying hard enough. We haven't thought out-of-the-box radically enough. Eventually, the law of averages means that we must stumble onto something eventually, some right combination of factors, some right calculation of answers."

IfWeCanJust find it . . .

It's a silver bullet we're looking for, so we cast aside our injector and begin testing metal shot on the struggling, horrid old woman. Mixing mathematical projections and best guesses with a little divination, our alchemical search for pure silver goes undaunted by the kicks and thrashes of what are clearly becoming the poor creature's death throes. "We're running out of time!" some of us scream. "Get more radical still!" others yell. "The innovations of our innovations must be more innovative than ever before," we all agree. "Yes! We must find and try never-before-seen-or-heard-of answers, or surely the little that is left of the Church will perish."

IfWeCanJust . . .

It is a long and storied tradition. It is the only real tradition of American Christianity: the perpetual quest for pure and perfect Church, the hunt for the truly Spirit-filled assembly of people that we can point to and say, "See! That is God's people." And we believe more firmly than any doctrine that this "Church" can be found only on the other side of our renovations to whatever the current "Church" is.

The lie behind it all is founded on two basic assumptions. The first assumption is that the gnarled, slightly cranky old woman bearing her crosses before us is not the Church that Jesus intended her to be, but has instead become the W(h)ereChurch, some half-leftover shell of the real Church, sickened and dilapidated until we can barely be certain the Holy Spirit is in her at all. The second assumption is that Jesus has surely left it up to us to fix her.

After over several hundred years of repeating our experiments on the foundation of these two assumptions, we have yet to lift the old woman up out of the rocking chair and present her a diva of the dance floor for all the world to see and long after. The only clear result of this manic tradition is that there are now fewer churches, fewer pews, and fewer people in them than when we first began. This, and the fact that we have ingrained into the assumptions of every new, smaller generation of Christians that the only hope for not getting smaller still is to pin our mother to the floor and unload another round of fool's silver point-blank into the dear old lady's chest.

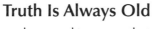

Truth Is Always Old

He gave the apostles . . . so that we may
no longer be children, tossed to and fro
by the waves and carried about by every
wind of doctrine, by human cunning,
by craftiness in deceitful schemes.
(Ephesians 4:11a, 14)

Now, I don't think for a moment that anyone really wants to kill
the Church. But I am convinced that the IfWeCanJust churchology
is a tradition of men doing just that. I have watched brother pastors
desperately consume every last trend, promising to remove the dross from
their ammo. I have listened to friends as they try to sell me on the latest,
greatest development in silver bullet production. I've read missional
how-to manuals that rival rocket science in their attempts to replicate a
theorem for the authentic apostolic silver bullet. I've read history books
detailing how the Anabaptists thought they'd found the silver bullet in
rejecting infant Baptism, how the Puritans thought they'd found the
silver bullet in casting off the hierarchies of the Church of England, how
the Revivalists thought they'd found the silver bullet in the application
of the new measures, how Pentecostalism thought they'd found the silver
bullet in the pouring out of ecstatic spiritual gifts, and how Liberationists
thought they'd found the silver bullet in helping disenfranchised people
groups, and how . . . and how . . . and how . . . IfWeCanJust . . .

Meanwhile, I have seen Punk Rock John and Emo Dan and
Scientific Sally and Genuine Barb all get caught in the crossfire. Seeking
authentic Christianity (which means seeking forgiveness), they only
found marauding mobs crusading left and right in an endless w(h)erehunt
for the answer to our mythical W(h)ereChurch. Eventually, most of
them came to believe the whole charade was a myth, a story told to keep
children in line or to convince the gullible to give their money away.
After a while, our pessimism regarding the current state of the Church
combined with our megalomaniac optimism regarding our ability to fix
it led to souls emptied by the constant experience of extreme letdown.

Whatever the "IfWeCanJust *fill in the blank*" was, they saw it filled enough times without the promised results until they gradually came to believe that the W(h)ereChurch didn't exist at all and that the old woman before them was only a hallucinating lunatic whom they were better off staying as far away from as possible.

HOOKED ON A RESTORING

Of all the examples of this highly American spiritual heritage, perhaps none is so crystal clear as the Restorationist movements of the nineteenth century. Strictly speaking, the Restorationists developed within the latter swells of the Second Great Awakening. The great excitements generated by Finney's methodologies overflowed with an optimism that with the right combination of new measures and efforts, Protestant Christians might just manage to usher in the second coming of Jesus. But this super optimism about human abilities also combined with deep pessimism about whether or not this could take place within the confines of the current churches. The Restorationists asserted that the current churches weren't even Church at all. The "Church" people saw was only a shell left over by the death of the real thing. The real thing, unfortunately, failed.

Restorationism: A nineteenth-century movement of Christians who sought to bring back, or "restore," the Church of Jesus Christ, which they believed had ceased to exist. Instead of ending denominationalism (as they had hoped), they only further splintered the American spiritual landscape, giving rise to such new denominations as the Plymouth Brethren (1827) and the Disciples of Christ (1849).

How did the one Holy Church of Jesus die? W(h)ere did it go? The answer to that is buried in lost history. But one thing was for sure. The Church was gone, and nothing could be more self-evident (or so the argument goes). Just read the Book of Acts and compare it to what you see. Christians today are nominal in their faith, culturally traipsing through lukewarm motions. Denominations are divided and built on traditions of men or disputes over minor points of doctrine. Is that what Jesus wanted? Clearly not! Where is the missionary Spirit of Pentecost? Where's the Kingdom's power? Where are the signs and wonders? Why don't our young men prophesy and our old men dream dreams? See? That settles it. We don't know who dropped the ball (and we aren't exactly confident of what the ball looks like either), but one thing is certain above all: there is a ball, and it is up to **us** to get the ball back. IfWeCanJust . . . **start** . . . **over** . . . then we'll get it right this time.

Restorationism gave rise to such new church bodies as the Plymouth Brethren, the Disciples of Christ, and the Churches of Christ.[11] Other groups such as the Seventh-day Adventists and Mormons lay their roots in the same assumption. The Church that Jesus started failed, so it is up to us to bring it back. In this way, Restorationism is the single shared tradition of Americanized Christianity, the belief that we, over here in this corner, by getting back to "IfWeCanJust (you fill in the blank)," are turning ourselves into the Church Jesus always wanted us to be.

This need is ingrained in our habits like a theological DNA, a hyperobsession with starting over. Again and again, with all the hindsight of an amnesiac, we declare that everything that came after the apostles but before us has obviously failed . . . **but**! *We will be the ones to get it right.* **IfWeCanJust.**

We haven't. To be sure, we have built countless new denominations. We have seen the rise of countless new congregations. More new churches have been started in the United States (both denominations and congregations) than anywhere else in the world. American Christianity is a patchwork quilt of official statuses and associations. But the kingdom of God?

---

11.   F. E. Mayer, *The Religious Bodies of America* (St. Louis: Concordia Publishing House, 1954), 351–52.

The millennium? The city on a hill? These things neither Restorationists nor their spiritual heirs have ever achieved. Silver bullet churchology has amassed a fabulous pedigree of indefatigability in splintering, dividing, secting, redefining, reenvisioning, starting fresh, starting new, and starting over, but we have yet to be satisfied with the results. Even if one generation seems content, their children soon prove the only thing they have received from their parents is a discontent with the current state of the Church. So they, too, rise up and decide, "The Church has clearly failed. We must fix it! It is time to start over! (Again.)"

We can do it . . .

IfWeCanJust not make the same mistakes . . .
IfWeCanJust get a clean strategy . . .
IfWeCanJust get away from the past . . . Then!
Then we will finally see the one Holy Protestant
and Acts 2 Church. Then!

Then all the world will see it too!

Yes, the road behind us has been paved with many fallen comrades and catastrophes, with fortunes spent and hours drained, with heresies invented and faith lost . . . but . . . maybe . . . IfWeCanJust start over one more time (just one more time!), then this time we just might get it right.

We never do. But that doesn't matter. There is only one thing we are totally certain of. One thing is beyond any shadow of a doubt: there is a silver bullet out there somewhere, and eventually we are going to find it. With it, we will leapfrog back to the apostolic age. We will revitalize the future by applying the perfect biblical principle. We will find success in this holy tradition/mission of questing for the cure to the W(h)ereChurch. The existence of the silver bullet dare not be questioned any more than a medieval monk ought question the Roman papacy.

Well, I'm questioning it. How many times will we start over before we start to wonder why all this starting over always looks exactly the same, produces the same results, and leaves us (or our children) with the conviction that our only hope is starting over (again)? Why does the patchwork quilt look more like a blanket knit out of one (really, really ugly) skein of yarn? Why does all of the out-of-the-box thinking stay inside the box of thinking the Church should look like Prosperity, that the path of Prosperity will be found through Pragmatic study, that Pragmatic study will result in reasonable (Rationalism) principles (Moralism), that will result in the perfect Church experience (Mysticism), and that it's up to us to make it all happen right now?

Maybe we've, like, totally got the wrong idea, dude.

ALWAYS RECYCLE YOUR LEAD BULLETS: THE THREEFOLD PATH OF FAILED CHURCHOLOGY

The problem goes even deeper. Protestant Evangelicals (and my own Lutheran tradition with them) are not the only ones on the hunt for the W(h)ereChurch. There are other major players in Christendom. Protestant silversmiths prefer to pretend these others aren't on the hunt, but they are no less engaged in the great game of churchology than we are. Yet while we Protestants search for the silver bullet, the Roman and the Eastern churches believe they already possess it. Long ago they found and dogmatized their alchemical recipes for true silver. Whether or not these claims are valid or whether our sister churches have been drinking too much water from those old Roman aqueducts lined with lead is something most Evangelicals (me included) would quickly rise to debate. But what if, on closer inspection, we find that our protesting churchology has amounted to little more than melting down scraps of metal pirated from those same aqueducts?

What if all of our "new" recipes are nothing more than a fuzzy copy of the old answers we claim killed the Church in the first place? Wouldn't it be a stark irony if we found we were cooking with nothing more than a generic brand of the pope's original recipe? What if the only difference between Protestant brand silver bullets and the Roman Catholic Church version is that we're crafting silver BBs, whereas the papacy long ago decided this w(h)erehunt required nothing less than .45 caliber shot? If we are authentically, radically engaged on the quest for "deep Church," then it should disturb us to no end if, in our search for the silver bullet, we find ourselves offering up watered-down versions of Roman Catholicism.

If for all our boasting about rethinking and renewing we are only rubbing the tarnish off a mirror full of cracks, how long until our hands get cut and start to bleed? If the same mirror reveals that all our churching is nothing more than the Walmart version of Rome's original Restoration Hardware, then the question really must be begged, are we actually, authentically, the real, true Church at all? If the Reformation didn't fix us, then who or what are we? What in heaven's name (literally) do we think we're doing reinventing anything? If the ancient traditions already found the heavy duty answers we're looking so hard for, and all our visioning cannot come up with anything better than cheap knockoffs and copies, then shouldn't we all be heading back to the ancient communions like rats abandoning a sinking ship?

The trends are showing significant numbers of the present generation doing just that. Those who are not driven to atheism or Buddhism by their college experiences are showing themselves radically content to take a little swim across the Tiber (to Rome) or the Bosphorus (to Constantinople) w(h)ere, at least, no one is pretending churchology is still an open question. There they aren't claiming to have finally found the silver bullet every other week. Even if they have the wrong bullet, at least they are going to stick with it. Believing "BecauseWeHave" is more comforting than constantly returning to **IfWeCanJust**.

162

This is exactly what has happened. I am no superscholar, and I don't claim to have seen everything under the sun, but from what I have seen, every attempt by modern Protestant missiology to rediscover the right churchology can be boiled down to putting our hopes in one of three essential elements. Like alchemists trying to turn lead into silver, Evangelical churchologists of every stripe are mixing and matching varying levels of these three ingredients, sometimes more of one, sometimes less of another, but always the same concepts. We believe IfWeCanJust stumble on the right combination of the three, then all our lead bullets will be magically transformed into pure silver. But the closer we get to a workable solution, the more we mimic the churchology of Roman Catholicism.

THE FIRST PATH: THE IDOLATRY OF ORDER

The first ingredient is **structure**. This is the ingredient most w(h)erehunting alchemists are aware that they are looking for. After all, the w(h)erehunt is the search for authentic Church, and what is Church if it's not an organization? And what is an organization if it's not a structure, an institution, some official way of making Christianity **work**? IfWeCanJust **find the right structure** for our church government, then the mission can really get done! Rome believes they have this already: their definition of the rock on which Christianity is founded is the hierarchy of apostolic succession under the key-holding hands of the occupant of St. Peter's seat in Rome. That is, the **pope** is the guarantee the Roman churches are the one, true "Catholic" Church.

Further east, the seat of Peter has been subtracted from the equation, but the "Orthodox" are still quite content to rest their confidence in a genealogy that traces the **laying on of hands** from bishop to bishop in an unbroken line stretching all the way back to the original Twelve. Even semi-self-respecting Protestants such as the Anglicans find this idea persuasive, seeing the structure of an unbroken **succession of bishops**, priests, and deacons as the **essential** thing about Christ's Church. Calvin and his Reformed would disagree, but not without still putting their hope in the right way of organizing. For them, the presbytery with its degrees of ruling and teaching elders is the one God-required government the churches need in order to be truly blessed. "But no," quoth the Congregationalists, "it is **congregational independence** God requires." "Nay," comes the Baptists' repartee, "the individual is given **soul liberty**!" Yeah and forsooth, the search goes on: it is the **voters assembly**; it is the voters assembly and **women's suffrage**; it's everyone a **minister**; it's everyone a **missionary**; it's a **mission statement**; it's **vision casting**; it's **small groups**; it's **house churches**; it's **policy based**; it's **Spirit–led**; it's **virtual**; it's **fractal**; it's **organic**. Oh? None of these finally fixed everything after you tried them? Well, IfWeCanJust start over one more time, then surely we'll find the structure that does.

Every group and structure mentioned above has proponents who claim their particular structure is the one required by the Bible and the only one God will bless. The real dilemma is that not one of them actually "works," at least not in the way IfWeCanJust wants them to. Not one of them has ushered in the golden age. Not one of them prevents the threat of false doctrine or human tyranny. Not one of them has the power to stop liars whose consciences are seared. No matter how many times the new structure fails, no matter how many types of structures we try out, history shows that within a generation or two, the structure is usually in shambles, being abused, and needing to be saved, often from itself. Every time we put our hope in the promise of "IfWeCanJust find the right structure, then we can really do Church right," we put our hope in an out-and-out lie.

164

The Second Path:
The Idolatry of Worship

Whether it's ancient hierarchies or a big youth program, no structure alone delivers the silver bullet. That second ingredient that must be added to the recipe is the right **liturgy**. By liturgy, I don't mean traditional worship. I mean what Tiger was talking about at the start of this chapter. I mean **the way we worship**. I mean planned, corporate, human **prayer**. I mean what we as men and women do in God's general direction whenever we gather together.

The problem is that worship, whether old or new, cultured or kitsched, traditional or contemporized, by itself has no power whatsoever to save the churches. Even the very best liturgies are in some way human inventions. The most faithful prayer in the world, insofar as it moves in the direction **from us to God**, is still a human work. But that hasn't stopped w(h)crehunting churchologists from insisting that IfWeCanJust **change the liturgy**, perfect it, get it right, bring it back, take it forward, **then**! Then the churches will at last become the Church God wants them to be.

Rome has already perfected this art too. The **sacrifice of the Mass**, authorized by the papal See, including its re-presentation of Christ as a new (but not bloody) sacrifice by the priest to God the Father, is the central Christian way to merit forgiveness from God. For Rome, the Mass isn't *a* way to worship. It is *the* right way. It is the real way to entice the Spirit to come down out of heaven and (literally) infuse the churches with His grace.

But just because Rome messed up worship doesn't mean that we can't fix it! IfWeCanJust **get rid of all the Catholic stuff** and start from scratch, just us and our Bibles, certainly we can come up with worship the way God wants it. When the Reformation first hit the ground, some groups said, "If it's not in the Bible, then we won't use it. Only the Psalms. No instruments!" You can see how long hope in that silver bullet lasted by visiting your nearest church some Sunday. Someone eventually noticed that getting rid of instruments hadn't really fixed anything and suggested, "Well, maybe IfWeCanJust **use some instruments** but only with the Psalms, then our people will get more inspired by the words. Then our churches will be more alive." But it wasn't long before someone else was saying, "I like all these instruments just fine, but do all the tunes and words have to be so melancholy? Maybe IfWeCanJust get the **music to sound more uplifting**, then our churches will really take off." Another says, "Hey, have you heard about all these new measures that everyone is using? They're really bringing in the crowds. You can even see signs of the Spirit's presence among them. Maybe IfWeCanJust **make the music more catchy**, then some of these visitors might stick around."

It keeps going. "That's the ticket! Why stick with all these dead letter prayers anyway? The Spirit is life. We need **prayers from the heart** and sermons that aren't written. Surely, that will make a difference." "Yeah, and why should only the pastor pray and preach? Surely, IfWeCanJust get **everyone to participate in worship**, then we'll see the churches really grow." "Hey, how about letting the **youth lead worship**?" "Why can't **women preach**?" "You know, this is the age of entertainment. We can't expect people to understand anything unless we **present it in drama**. Jesus taught in parables after all." "Whoa . . . did you notice that this amp goes to 11?"

Wham, bang, boom. We have even more churches, more divisions, more styles, more sects, more buildings, and more liturgical variation than you can shake a kaleidoscope at. There's a faux silver thread running through the entire development, and it is a mad optimism in the ability of our music and prayers to be the essence of the Church, to make us real Church. Yet not once in all the constant updating of worship experiences does abundance flow out over the churches. "Maybe the problem is all these denominations and their worship traditions," someone says. "Maybe IfWeCanJust **be plain 'Christian'** then we'd really see things get going." But wait a minute, now we're back to structure again. At the same time, every single one of these many liturgical traditions claim that they are Christian too. So which one(s) really is/are it? What way of worship will really help us be the true Church? Where can I find a congregation that has an authentic conduit to God's Spirit?

Behold, the W(h)ereChurch! Our silver bullet recipe is still incomplete. There must be one more ingredient to add to the mix. That third ingredient is **person**.

THE THIRD PATH:
THE IDOLATRY OF THE LEADER

"Here's the deal, brother. Our preacher is kind of boring, and you can bet that in the end this lack of **charisma** is keeping people away."

"Really? Our preacher preaches just fine, but, I'll be honest with you, he's not very **sociable**. I'm pretty confident it's kept the membership from really committing to discipleship."

"How interesting. Our preacher is so friendly that he never gets any of his work done. If only our seminaries taught **administration** and **leadership skills**, then I'd bet we wouldn't see all the problems we see now."

"I hear that. But you know, even with good leadership skills, your preacher can't really lead without a **Spirit-anointed vision**. We used to have that problem at my congregation too. It's just not biblical, you know. You need the Spirit to bless your decisions. So we sent our pastor to visioning training. He learned how to discern God's will for our community through Spirit-led prayer and demographic studies. Would you believe we've googolplexed in size since then, and we have lots of young families joining now?"

"Wait a minute. You still have elderly and sick people? Our preacher is a true apostle of Word and faith. He's anointed by the Spirit with a double portion. No one ever gets sick anymore, after they've given their **seed offerings** and learned the **law of attraction**. I'm sure your preacher could get anointed. Maybe if he came to one of our outpourings, then your congregation wouldn't still be stuck on the first rung of salvation, but could also receive all the **blessings of healing** that Jesus promised. The more we receive the Spirit's latter rain, the closer we are to completing the Great Commission and seeing the kingdom of God come."

"That's just stupid. You mean you are still waiting for the Kingdom? And you think that snake-oil salesman who calls herself an apostle can be trusted? Don't you know that Jesus gave the Keys of the Kingdom to Peter? If you want to really, truly be Church, then you need to bag all that hocus-pocus and find **the one person** Jesus told you to listen to if you ever hope to receive His Spirit. You need a preacher with both **charisma** and **history** on his side. You need **a priest** who has been consecrated by **the pope**."

Structure, liturgy, and person. When you break down the myriad of churchologies panhandling their mission of starting over and over again and again, they always come back to this same pattern of man-centered blunder. IfWeCanJust find the right way to **organize**. IfWeCanJust find the right way to **worship**. IfWeCanJust find the right **person** to bring the two together, to stand in front and convince us that our way is the authentic way, **then** we will be God's assembly. Then we will be the real Church! **IfWeCanJust . . .**

But here's the raw deal. This means no matter how often or well we reorganize, update the worship experience, or apply the latest leadership techniques, we will get the same results as every start-over protesting generation before us. WeWillJust end up with the latest rendition of mini-pope 2.0, hawking a wannabe Mass remix, while insisting that this latest attempt at "doing" Church is the way God has always really wanted it to be. Is the only real problem that the churches a generation before us didn't have people quite as awesome as we are? Do we really think that all our melting down of the lead of "starting over" in a quest for silver will finish in anything other than the same disappointment of mediocrity, passing on to our children the same addiction to rejecting the last reboot in favor of their own?

As another generation walks down the same threefold path to fail, some of the most consistent among us will notice this, abandon the protest, and join up with the stasis of leadership, structure, and worship frozen to a chair in the Vatican. A few others will gamble on the same cards dealt by the hands laid on in Constantinople. Others will follow their hunt for authentic worship straight out of Christianity and into eastern religions. Still more will seek out an authentic godly life under the prophetic leadership of Muhammad or Joseph Smith. Yet more will give up official religion altogether, deciding that secular philosophies offer them a far more reasonable explanation of the ordering of the universe. Structure, worship, and person will play central roles in all of these new quests. So will Moralism, Mysticism, and Rationalism. But the common thread in every case will be that the method for seeking God will still be starting over with the recycled belief that if you can't find God in **this** assembly of people, then maybe you can find Him in **that one**.

ECCLESIOLOGICAL PORNOGRAPHY

It is like a young man who has watched too many movies growing up so that now he is on a quest for the perfect bride. He believes she will meet every expectation set by every beautiful woman he has ever seen on the screen. From party to party and club to club he seeks and searches, finding countless women who are themselves on the quest to be the most beautiful woman in the world, in order to have their emotions won by a man just like him.

But after the first night's stand and a few follow-up phone calls (and maybe an argument or two), he starts to notice her flaws. He sees the flabby spots and the wrinkles already forming beside her eyes. Her roots haven't been dyed often enough, and one of her acrylic nails is broken. Her breath smells after she eats garlic, and she expects him to get out of bed and shower before she'll hug him in the morning. Next thing you know, he's back at the parties and clubs, once more searching for the immaculate woman he expects to find out there somewhere. He hardly knows he is doing it. He thinks he is looking for love. He believes he is searching for the perfect romance. But the problem is that he isn't looking for love of any kind. He is not looking for a real woman at all. He is looking for **pornography**.

It's a hush-hush part of living in American culture, but the porn industry is more than just a multibillion dollar cash cow viewed by nerds and pubescents on the Internet. For decades, promoters of pornography have systematically transformed the sexual assumptions of nearly everyone in our civilization (even those who aren't watching it). Our definitions of beauty and love have been dramatically altered. Mainstream movies and television mimic the pornographic style of eliciting sexual excitement in the viewer. The behaviors and dress considered acceptable today would have caused riots even sixty years ago. Clothing styles that used to be worn by hookers are sported by fifth graders at school. Virtue is far passed being under assault by this enemy, which many churches are extremely reticent even to acknowledge. Virtue has already been abandoned.

This impact of porn on the lives of Christian churches, marriages, and young people is hard to overestimate, but the point here is the way that porn works to destroy the romantic dreams of a young man looking for his lifelong love is the same way silver bullet churchology works to undermine faith in God and His Church. Porn begins to poison a young man by showing him an image of a woman who surpasses all his wildest dreams. Then, it shows him another. Then, it shows him another. Again and again, it lifts up a newer, better, more recent, more enhanced picture of what his romantic (sexual) life **could** be until, without realizing it, he begins to believe it **should** be that way. Without even knowing it, he begins comparing every woman he meets to the (entirely unrealistic) fantasy images he believes in. The end result is that he can never be content in any relationship with a real woman. He finds himself moving from one to another, casting longing eyes about him, even while out in public with the woman he is momentarily semi-committed to. No matter who she is, she is never able to live up to the image he believes she must be, not because she is a failure or unlovely, but because he is addicted to women who don't exist.

Heat-Seeking Hearts Don't Help Us

They have eyes full of adultery, insatiable for sin. They entice unsteady souls. They have hearts trained in greed. Accursed children! (2 Peter 2:14)

Silver bullet churchology works the same way. Just as pornography feeds young men and women falsely perfected images of impossibly idealized sexuality until they cannot find contentment in any real relationship, so also trying to compel God's blessings into the Church through "IfWeCanJust" theology preaches a falsely perfected vision of an impossibly idealized "Church" until no congregation can live up to its expectations. The manipulated images of "what the Church ought to be" in the end only teach us not to love the Church as she really is, but instead to lust after a Church that can never be. As a result we treat our congregations the way young women are being trained to treat themselves. We try to squeeze our "Church" into a tighter dress, thinking this might better turn the eyes of visitors who glance our way. We put fake eyelashes on her and paint her lipstick a brighter red. Those with the means fork over vast amounts of budget to purchase the latest enhancements and tucks. We hire fitness trainers to put her on a workout regimen. We hire consultants to help us airbrush the pictures we take of her. They encourage us not to let any of our old convictions get in the way of going further. "You need to lower her bodice even more," they say. "That is what the young men today are looking for. You can't expect anyone to take interest in her if she's not at least willing to go to second base on the first date."

Just like the effects of porn on young men, the average American Christian is only further trained to expect from the Church something that she is not. Like the young man clicking from image to image on the Internet, the Christian begins to hop from congregation to congregation, the rush of new experience lasting only so long. By doing all we can to dandy up our "Church" in order to attract some visitors, the other end result is that we ourselves begin to fall prey to our own propaganda. After paying an escort model to stand beside us in public, we've expected her to fall in love with us, cook our meals, do our dishes, and rear our children. She laughs, takes the money, and goes on to the next guy, while we are left sitting beside the same decrepit W(h)ereChurch. Forget that two thousand years of Christians were comforted in her arms, calling her Mother. Forget that she has always been imperfect because she has always been made up of sinners. Forget that her true beauty has always been the hidden faith of a gentle and quiet spirit, steadfast in comfort, graceful in blemishes, wise in age, and in God's sight very precious. Forget all that. Today, expecting her to be a trophy wife, having wasted our last pennies on plastic surgery, and insisting that she play the harlot for anyone who happens to drop by, the only thing we've gained is a spirituality that excels in training Christians to worship their covetousness.

{ **IfWeCanJust** is the worship of covetousness. }

The effects of decades of this churchological porn on American Christian churches will not just go away. The new measurement of what ideal "Church" ought to be will be deeply ingrained in the culture of churchgoers and pastors everywhere for a long time to come. The stakes have been raised, and they cannot be brought back down again. The result is **not** a Christendom steadfast in commitment to the Word. The result is **not** a Christianity steadfastly aware that Church is a life together bearing with the weaknesses and burdens of others. The result is **not** Christians steadfastly believing we are a congregation of sinners assembling for the purpose of receiving communal forgiveness. The result **is** a reciprocating trend of disappointment, church shopping, denomination hopping, spiritual frustration, and eventual religious impotence.

What we once found beautiful we now call average, at best. What once could make the blood race now stifles and bores. What once was beyond fulfilling we can only call incomplete. New converts, committed laity, and pastors alike, we are hungering for a church that does not exist. So strong are our expectations that many of us have no problem dating the prettiest church we can find, even if she never mentions Jesus or His cross at all. Even there, as soon as politics show themselves infecting the institution or whenever the pastor isn't quite as entertaining as he once was or the day when the worship doesn't quite get the tingle going like it used to, the lust we've learned to hope in wakes up, and we begin casting hungry eyes elsewhere.

But with every disappointment, with every love lost, more and more church shoppers only visit and never join any of the churches at all. To this shortage of commitment, the cry goes up that we must start over. We must renew our vision. We must think out of the box even further. We must seek more radical forms of change. Like any young man recently broken up with his latest fling, we try to medicate our heartbreak by looking at even more **porn**.

IfWeCanJust.

Driving a Stake through Silver Bullet Churchology

No matter how many times our humanity fails the task of perfecting the churches, nothing can cure an addict who refuses to admit he has a problem. Addiction to the silver bullet presses forward, never dissuaded by the constant turnover of clientele nor the manifold closing of congregations nor the clear loss of doctrinal integrity behind it all. The addiction insists all these things are caused by the W(h)ereChurch rather than by our attempts to cure her.

Pastors are far from immune to this addiction. They know even better than most just how harsh members and visitors alike can be in judging the churches. How we function, how we sing, and how we are shepherded are all put under intense scrutiny and pressure by every casual visitor who strolls in to take us for a test-drive. Pastors know that while perfection may be impossible, it won't stop people from using perfection as their criteria for judging the congregation anyway. While this ought to spur faithful preachers to call out this covetousness as the idolatry it is, more often we are driven to try and preach, structure, and worship our way into it.

So we read books on leadership. We revamp the liturgies. We consolidate power so we can be even more proficient at both. Sometimes it works, and a mini golden age descends on the parish (which usually lasts until that pastor leaves or retires). Other times, the people's view of perfection clashes with the pastor's view. The people liked more traditional praises. The people trusted democracy to preserve them from false teaching. The people miss the old version of house pastor, who drops by on summer afternoons for gab and sweet tea. One can still find these mini bronze ages scattered throughout the American landscape too. But they also tend to last just until a new pastor walks in the door.

On both sides of the aisle, there is still a giant golden cow smiling down over the entire thing, a perfectionism of expectations forced on us by the belief that "we can find God in ourselves as we try to be the Church." Hearing God has a people, we have believed we can find God **in** those people. In our institutions, our leaders, and our praises. In **us**. We look for God in the individual persons and groups who assemble around anything and call it "Church." But we also keep noticing these people are a bunch of dead bones. *"Aren't these dead bones supposed to live?"* we ask. So we sit and bang the bones together like sticks until they break, one after another.

{ **IfWeCanJust's lie:** We can find God in our efforts to be the Church. }

The history of Christianity is flush with attempts at trying to fan the smoldering wick into flame, which only succeed in snuffing it out. From bouts with supererogatory monasticism to total sanctification movements and latter-day rain outpourings, from restoration to restoration **ad nauseam**, Christianity's affairs with varied institutions, liturgies, and prophets of every stripe are a storied search for perfection in the people who make up the churches. Whether we are looking for a way to justify individual hearts and lives or to justify what we can accomplish together as a community, there is an incessant belief that there must be a trick to it. It is an addiction to the belief that there is some hidden bit of knowledge we just haven't thought up or found yet. It is obvious something is wrong, but we can never quite put our finger on what it is, because we can only come at it with the assumption that it is up to us to find it and fix it, when it is **us** that is the problem.

What if the church(es) aren't supposed to be perfect in any way apart from faith in Christ? What if putting our hope in structures, songs, and men to lead them are not the answer but the things getting in the way? What if we're straining out gnats but swallowing camels? What if we wrote "if we can only change **x**" into its mathematical equivalent as [Jesus + x = Christianity]? What if we do the math and see [Jesus + x = Christianity] resolves to [x = Christianity – Jesus]?

What if Jesus has no intention of building a visible kingdom in this world? What if hoping for what you see doesn't create saving faith? What if it actually **kills** it? What if the most important thing in Acts 2 is the words of the sermon that was preached?

Turn It Down

Take away from Me the noise of your songs;
to the melody of your harps I will not listen.
But let justice roll down like waters, and righteousness
like an ever-flowing stream. (Amos 5:23–24)

What if you aren't supposed to find God in the churches? What if God doesn't care about either voters assemblies or apostolic successions? What if God hates our music? What if the last place God wants you to look for Him is in the personality of any man who is not Jesus?

What if the Church isn't an organization at all? What if she isn't about human rituals so much as divine promises? What if she doesn't need a leader so much as pure preaching? What if the churches are not gatherings of people in whom you find God, but the people gathered together because God has found them, called them, elected them, **is gathering** them with the spiritual working of His Word alone? What if the congregating of the saints happens only because God sends His Gospel and gifts to be rightly preached and given in that place? What if the true unity of the Church only needs this doctrine of the Gospel and giving of the Sacraments? What if all human traditions, all rites, all ceremonies, and institutions of men cannot add or detract from this reality? What if salvation is Jesus' work? What if His one Holy Church will continue forever, no matter what we do or don't do?

Does the fact that there will always be many hypocrites and liars within the Church(es) in this life mean it isn't really the Church anymore? Or is it possible God's Word is **God's** Word and is not affected by reason or the institutions or commandments of men? What if God sent twelve men into the world with one command: If you forgive the sins of anyone, they are forgiven. Baptize them into My name. Teach them My words. Trust Me on this one. In this, I am with you always, **especially when it doesn't look like it** (John 20:23; Matthew 28:16–20; Colossians 3:3).

What
if the silver bullet
is realizing there is no silver bullet?

AUTHENTICITY IS FOR POSERS

In the continued warfare of start-over churchology, the American churches press on and on until faith becomes the casualty. Bouncing from congregation to congregation, seeking whichever community's most recent visible fad tickles the fancy, most people eventually grow weary of club hopping. A person can take only so many "this time it will work" attempts. Some eyes drift to the exotic images of Rome and Eastern Orthodoxy. Others are pushed deeper into the ecstatic promises of Pentecostalism. But even rebaptisms can only be tried so many times before the secret things of the cults begin to have a greater appeal. If not the cults, why not Hinduism, Buddhism, or Islam—why not neo-paganism? They look pious enough, and at least they don't change every five years. When all else fails, God probably doesn't really exist anyway.

In espionage, unintended consequences are called blowback, the often violent, unplanned results suffered by a civil population due to the actions of their own government's military operations. We live in an age encountering tremendous blowback from the hunt for the W(h)ereChurch. Every new attempt, every church shopped, every latest fix guaranteed to work, every answer lifted up as the brand-new "authentic" path to real-deal communion with God becomes one more broken promise. Every broken promise takes one more second off a ticking time bomb of diabolical disappointment and doubt. Over and over again, each individual soul is thrust back into the hunt, back to starting over again (and again), back into wondering just what on earth is the matter with the churches or if the Church even exists at all.

Looking for God in All the Wrong Places

O foolish Galatians! Who has bewitched you? . . .

Let me ask you only this: Did you receive the Spirit

by works of the law or by hearing with faith? Are you

so foolish? Having begun by the Spirit, are you now

being perfected by the flesh? (Galatians 3:1a, 2–3)

Each time you look for God you just keep finding people. Sinful. Sinning. Sinner. People. This is happening because **you cannot find God in the churches**, not if by churches you mean the denominational structures or the individual people who

177

make them up. It is not in the people who make up God's assembly that God reveals Himself. It is in God's revealing of Himself that people are drawn together to be God's assembly. So, if we want to see more of that happen, then we need to take a good hard look **not** at all the varied assemblies described in the Book of Acts, but in **what** those assemblies assembled **around**. When we do, we will find one constant, complete, pure, and perfect answer, no silver bullet at all but a plain and slightly foolish preaching of God's Word about the death and resurrection of Jesus.

With all that's being said about the future of the Church, all the fear and mad attempts to stave off the apparent collapse of American Christianity, remember the Church's future has never been nor ever will be in the hands of men. This is the great riddle of the Church's history from day one: she lives! And she lives because **He lives**. "He is risen!" In Him, in simple childlike faith in Him, she has outlived the demise of ancient worlds, global transmigrations, and industrial revolutions. Are we so narcissistic as to believe that our age is so very different?

The Church will live on, and this will not be because "we men" discover a silver bullet to pin down w(h)ere the Church can become the dame of our dreams. She will live on because that is the will of God. If God desires the Gospel to be preached among our children, then it will happen as surely as the sun will rise tomorrow. So let us pray for it! We show a flabbergasting lack of faith in Jesus' ability to be our Savior when we laud visionary leaders who proclaim that without our adoption of this or that new technology, this or that strategy, this or that plan or opinion, then the Church shall surely perish.

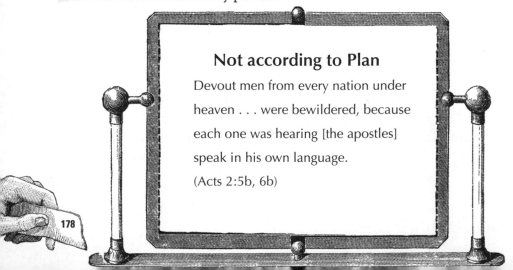

Not according to Plan

Devout men from every nation under heaven . . . were bewildered, because each one was hearing [the apostles] speak in his own language.

(Acts 2:5b, 6b)

"Change or die!" they cry. But the Word has never been concerned with human impediments, not even the impediment of language itself (Acts 2:11)! The word needs no achievements, revolutions, restorations, transformations, rights, principles, or dreams. **The Word is His own means.** This Word shall remain so long as Christ the eternal Preacher desires to preach it to us. The Church exists today the same way she existed before us and the same way she will exist tomorrow. **By His grace. Through faith.** Faith in the preached Word.

Perhaps part of the problem is the modern error of thinking this Word is nothing more than a religious message, an ideal, and it has become the Church's "job" to get unbelievers to accept it. But Scripture shows us a Word of God that is eternally more than a bit of spiritual information. It is divine essence, filled with the power to pluck up and break down, to destroy and overthrow, to build and plant and create (Jeremiah 1:9). And to **save**. Man's words can never do this. God's Word **only** does this.

If there is something to marvel at, it is that this Word of God is placed on mortal man's lips, the treasure of eternal power set in jars of clay. This is the miracle of Christ's churchology. Wherever His Word is real, wherever it is believed on as pure, wherever it is honored, wherever it is praised, wherever men, women, and children think about the things it says, there the Church will always be—tangible, real, true. In such a list "authenticity" is suddenly little more than a tacky attempt to pretend to be real. The real Church has no need to talk about authenticity because insofar as she lives from and for this Word, she is always actual and concrete. She cannot be faked. She is the THEREChurch: there, where the Spirit communes the saints through the Word and the Sacraments. There, where everything that Jesus taught is given free rein to be true: pure, holy, and given "**for you**." There, where the essential structure, liturgy, and pastoral role remains the preaching of

"You are declared the Body of Christ. Take it. Eat it. Believe it!"

To deny this is to deny God's ability to tell the truth. We should not call God a liar on the evidence that we are liars ourselves. The world will never see the righteousness of faith by looking at the assembly of sinners who believe in it. The object of faith is never the believer nor the believers, but the One in whom we have believed.

When such faith believes Jesus' promise that the Church is His work that He will accomplish through the weak folly of preaching His death and resurrection, the harsh spin cycle of starting over is broken. Jesus' Church never starts over because Jesus' Church can never quit. Jesus' Church can never quit because Jesus' Church never **tries**. The true Church never **does**. The true Church is **done to**.

All the congregating in the countless organizations with their myriad litanies overseen by a bunch of schmucks are worth nothing if they cannot preach this pure foolishness that "you" are alive now and forever because you are already dead, judged, buried, and raised in Christ. There is no starting this over. There is only believing it is true because Jesus continues to preach to you that it is. It is an unbreakable structure, a divine authority, a pure worship to hear Jesus speak through the lips of sinners, "I forgive you."

Church Done for You

The life and death of the churches, regardless of their denominations, individuals, pasts, presents, or futures, all depend on being **the** Church. The churches will always be weak, sick, and fragile. But the authority with which God Himself preaches in their midst is anything but weak. He preaches that His Church is strong, sound, and unbreakable because He is unbreakable, because His Word is sound, because His resurrection is strong enough for all mankind. As churches we live by faith that we are this Church for Jesus' sake. The churchology that we are Church because of Him must be our unshakable faith. "I believe in the Holy Spirit. I believe in the one, holy, catholic, and apostolic Church."

Here is your redemption. Here is your saving, world-judging, paradise-ushering Lord. He enters even now with every authority in heaven and earth, with promises to wash you and teach you so you remember through faith what ought never be forgotten: you have no need to start over. "Be still, and know that I am God" (Psalm 46:10).

> ## Done Already
>
> He saved us, not because of works done by us in righteousness, but according to His own mercy, by the washing of regeneration and renewal of the Holy Spirit, whom He poured out on us richly through Jesus Christ our Savior, so that being justified by His grace we might become heirs according to the hope of eternal life. The saying is trustworthy, and I want you to insist on these things, so that those who have believed in God may be careful to devote themselves to good works. These things are excellent and profitable for people. (Titus 3:5–8)

This is the lonely way of the Bible's churchology. It stands against traditions of men at every angle. Like a little ship caught up in a perfect storm, the hope is not in the passengers but in the pilot.

It has often appeared in ages before our own that the Church was done for. But the hindsight of history has shown us again and again that the most grievous mortal wounds in the churches were ever those self-inflicted by people arrogant enough to think it was their task to save the Church by fixing it. For far too long this has been the one human tradition shared by all American denominations. We are far too unified in our too high opinion of our own thoughts, doings, speakings, nervous anxieties, and arrogant laxities. In all these, we pay tribute only to the world. In all this, we harbor only a secret disbelief in Jesus' ability to "Church" us. Looking for God in our ability to make ourselves stronger/better/faster/more Church is doing Christianity as if Jesus is not actually present, which means as if Jesus is not actually God.

"With might of ours can naught be done, Soon were our loss effected" (*LSB* 656:2). But **our God is a consuming fire** (Deuteronomy 4:24). If He preaches that the holiness and perfection of His Church must be believed in, must be grasped by faith the same way His resurrection is grasped by faith, then this Church truly and actually exists. If He preaches, **"You are My Church** by nothing more than the merit of My words about Me and My cross," then that is an unbreakable and undying reality shared with all believers as we are dispersed throughout the world, not in order to conquer it, but in order to wait for that great day when we shall all be gathered again from the ends of the earth to celebrate with all the faithful the marriage feast of the Lamb in His kingdom, which has no end. Wherever this Gospel of Jesus' death and resurrection is given away for the free forgiveness of sin, wherever His Sacraments are still there to mark a people set apart for Himself, there is the pillar and foundation of the truth. There is Christ. Always. With all authority in heaven and earth.

No Need to Hunt

Then if anyone says to you, "Look, here is the Christ!" or "There He is!" do not believe it.

(Matthew 24:23)

You will never find God in the churches because you will never find God in people. But you are the Church because in Christ, God has found you. The Father laid on Jesus the iniquities of us all.

To be sure, we ought to organize the churches in whatever manner best keeps us from forgetting that. If the needs or effectiveness of the structure change from time to time or place to place, it is neither the end nor the future of the Church. It is the present.

To be sure, we ought to seek for ways to let the Word of Christ dwell in us richly, teaching and singing songs that proclaim the excellencies of what Christ has done (Colossians 3:16). We must hear the pure words of forgiveness, baptize the repentant, and feast on the Supper. If the rhythm of organs or pianos, strings or horns lifts up this Word with melodies that move our hearts, there is no sin in it. But if the pipes become too expensive or the electricity goes out, then there is nothing wrong with singing **a cappella**, so long as we never make the mistake of thinking the tunes themselves are the future or the past. They are the present.

To be sure, the one who desires the office of preacher desires a noble task (1 Timothy 3:1). He must be able to teach, be an honorable man, and be well versed in what ought to be preached. If he's also a human, then thank the Lord your salvation does not actually rest on him but on Christ, and thank Christ that His Word is simple enough even a child can confess it. That is the point. That is why it always works. But the man who preaches it is neither the past nor the future. He is the present.

The Church's one foundation is Jesus Christ, her Lord. He is the past and the future and the present (Hebrews 13:8). This Gospel will never be as glamorous as the hunt for a silver bullet to perfect life in the present evil age, because this Word will always be preaching about a cross, a death, and our iniquities that caused it. But it is only in this cross that we also hear the promise of something worth more than silver or gold—an eternal, empty tomb.

This is the only churchology that can never be broken because it is the only churchology not dependent on you. You don't even have to start over to believe it. It's been the same answer yesterday, today, and forever.

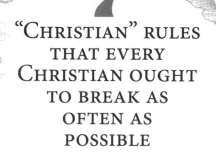

7

"CHRISTIAN" RULES THAT EVERY CHRISTIAN OUGHT TO BREAK AS OFTEN AS POSSIBLE

Never #5

Never follow a rule that has to start over (again and again . . . and again . . .) again.

The Fifth Rule to be **BROKEN**

IfWeCanJust Churchology.

You can find God in churches: the worship of spirituality.

NEVER
#6

Never follow
a rule that
doesn't like
rules.

Sin and the Final Fantasy

Tidus gripped his glassy sword rimmed with blue fire, staring in horror out over the coastline as he sprinted up the cliff side pathway. Beside him hurried Yuna, her mahogany hair dancing on the heavy winds. He had to protect her at any cost. She was his only hope: the world's only hope.

Reaching the pinnacle, he and the others steeled themselves, spreading out in formation. All of this was so new to him, nothing like his life had been before the nightmare vision, which shook his memories and ripped the life he thought he had lived entirely away from him. None of it mattered now. The breakers were growing more violent by the second, and the enormous tidal threat was nearly upon them. Whatever monstrous creature was hidden within that watery monsoon had to be enormous. What could one young woman and a few companions hope to do to stop it from annihilating the village below them? They weren't ready yet. Luna hadn't even come close to finishing her quest to find the final Aeon. Without that, they didn't have a chance.

There was no choice now. Now was when the beast was before them. Now was the moment of reckoning. Now was time to do battle with Sin.

In 2001, video game developer Square released one of the most anticipated games in the history of console gaming: *Final Fantasy X*. The franchise of *Final Fantasy* had begun as a minor league release for the 8-bit Nintendo Entertainment System back in 1987, but had spawned multiple lines of games for nearly every console system, not to mention "manga" comics, novels, toys, cartoons, miniseries, and rumors of a full-length, entirely computer-rendered feature film. *Final Fantasy X* marked the next gigantic step in production, a transition from the scrolling backdrops of yore to truly three-dimensional graphics now made possible by the explosive advances in gaming technology. But it was more than just the giant update in style that caught my imagination as I settled back in my

basement apartment to play
through the game over a two-week
spring break at Seminary. More than anything, I was curious
to discover what kind of theology might be buried in a game
that was bold enough to name its antagonistic enemy "Sin."

Like almost all forms of media that tell a story, many games
and game worlds have a theology. One way or another, game developers
build a spirituality into their game worlds. It's part of creating a realistic
fantasy. In most cases these "religions" are an inventive spinoff of
paganism, rooted in some idea about many gods and their connections
to the world. Some games don't even bother to hide it, pilfering their
ideas directly from old European mythologies. Others are more subtle,
merging elements of Christianity (such as cathedrals filled with stained
glass) with anything from Far Eastern philosophy to make–believe
systems of magic. But in all my years of casually observing the religious
fetish of the gaming world, never once had I come across a game willing
to engage such a core concept of Christianity as sin.

As I might have expected, *Final Fantasy X* presented a fairly
disappointing rendition. The use of the word turned out to be little
more than a cherry picked term, tossed in to give a spiritualish feel
to the story, but without any real meaning. "Sin" was just a big
monster that threatened to destroy the world every generation
or so. Whenever it rose up, it needed to be defeated so the world
could go back to peace for a while. Although the defeat required the
self-sacrifice of a specially trained "summoner," it was still pretty
disappointing. It was more like sacrificing a virgin by throwing her
into a volcano than any real kind of Christian atonement. I can only
imagine how cool it would have been if the Sin-beast had been more

than a big, nasty meanie, but instead a creature created by the expression of all human evil combined, a monstrous, ever-present threat feeding off our hatreds. Just as cool would have been a sacrifice that didn't merely placate the creature, but truly defeated it through sacrificial death.

Atonement

Atonement is the power of creating justice by exchanging one penalty for another, "an eye for an eye, and a tooth for a tooth." It is the belief that an evil once done can be "bought back" by substituting an equal or stronger good. In Christianity, this describes the ransom that Jesus Christ paid, nailing the debt of our sins to the cross.

All the elements of the potential story were there, but they were mishmashed and confused. In the end, there is no atonement at all. The band of heroes just decides to kick Sin in the teeth really hard. But then, for little apparent reason, their hero has to die anyway (or disappear or time warp away). It was truly bizarre. Yet, the more I thought about it, the more I realized how unreasonable it was of me to expect the makers of *Final Fantasy X* to create a sin-monster symbolizing real sin and its defeat. I mean, when even most of modern Christianity can't be bothered with getting sin right, why should we expect game makers who have no vested interest to do any better?

In fact, the more I thought about it, the more I realized that *Final Fantasy* got "sin" exactly right, at least as modern people have come to believe in it. There's a lot of ex-Christian baggage still floating around American culture. Christian*ish* terms and ideas, even "Jesus," are still a part of pop culture, only with totally undefined or changed meanings. This Christianity-haunted Western civilization still believes in sin. Sin is something you're not supposed to do. It is a bad thing or a set of bad things, which can sometimes be really nasty, but are just as likely an arbitrary judgment from old, dead white people who were dumber and more bigoted than we are today. Either way, big or small, right or wrong, hateful or helpful, if *Final Fantasy* is any indicator, "sin" is always, always, always something **outside** of us.

IDOL ADDICTION

This is not the way the Bible defines sin. The Bible talks about sin as more than a few honest mistakes or some of those stupider things you didn't really intend to do when you were young. Sin is a disease. It is the universal tendency of humans to prefer self-serving actions and speak self-serving words because we are constantly thinking self-serving thoughts **so that** we can get the most we can for ourselves in any given moment or circumstance of life. The result is that we end up harming other people, at the very least on a daily basis, and often while being entirely ignorant of it. You know: war, famine, and poverty. No one person makes those things happen. **We** make those things happen. We do it with our habit of creating "hurt" in the process of working with all our might to benefit ourselves.

Far from some holy "to do" list foisted upon us by mean spirited religious people of bygone ages, sin is the Bible's way of describing the inbred human need to do evil because we believe it will help us get more good for ourselves. God made countless good things when He created the world, but almost all of them can be twisted into foundations on which to build little chapels of self-trust, self-hope, or self-love. These are personalized idols, "stuff" in which the semblance of self-sufficiency, safety, and control can be worshiped in the form of whatever we feel we need most at the moment. Rather than receiving God's gifts with thanks, we misuse them in the worst possible manner: to replace Him!

The Bad Guy Inside

For I know that nothing good dwells in me, that is, in my flesh. For I have the desire to do what is right, but not the ability to carry it out. (Romans 7:18)

This habitual use of stuff for convincing ourselves everything is just fine is far worse than a giant monster who wants to eat the planet, which we could beat up by kicking its teeth in. Idolatry is a far more dangerous enemy because it is a need we have **inside** of us. We are **addicted** to it.

The dictionary definition of an addict is a person who can't stop doing something. Drug addicts can't stop using illicit (and harmful) chemicals to generate feelings of escape. Along with the physical addiction a body develops to the use of certain drugs, the mind relies on these feelings as coping mechanisms for dealing with the countless pains of life on a fallen planet. While the human condition of sin is a little more subtle than illicit drug use, the way it works is not very different. In fact, doing evil in the pursuit of my own good is by far the most potent of all addictions.

Most of us only do a little evil at a time, something on the side, only when we feel we really have to. But just like the drug addict, we also do it to get a feeling—the feeling of escape, the feeling of being in control. In order to flee from the in-breaking of helplessness or dependency that so often comes with life, we start using the things we come into contact with for our own benefit. In a hungering lurch from one moment of frustration to the next, by thought, word, and deed, with countless personal little battles going on all day, every day, day after day, we wage a war against everything and everyone in order to gain and keep a personal impression of stability and control. We call it independence, freedom, self-sufficiency. But it is much more than that. It is rebellion, mutiny, and anarchy.

We are addicted to the need for personal control, unable to stop ourselves from traveling deeper and deeper into self-will. With a little help from carefully selected friends, we prop one another up in a self-imposed ignorance, shouting down any hint of the reality that we are not actually in control at all. We are bent and keep trying to straighten ourselves by telling one another that "bent" is really "straight." We are curved terribly inward and cannot justify ourselves because we keep insisting justification will come by turning further inward still. We are blind but cannot see our blindness because we keep shouting, "I can see just fine!"

This is the true final fantasy of sin, the belief that if you can gain enough control of enough of the right things, then you can force everything else in life to go the way you want it to. So, what really matters is not what you call "sin," whether it is a giant monster or all the things you think other people shouldn't be allowed to do. What really matters is that by nature you believe it is up to you to drive the things you think are evil out of your life by any means possible. According to the wisdom of our age, there are no holds barred in this quest. There is only you and your need to make everything just fine or to convince yourself that it will be soon.

This is the highest possible good, that you be able to live your life in anyway that you see fit. It is also the real definition of sin and the sixth rule every Christian ought to break as often as humanly possible. The belief that it is God's deepest wish for you to live your life however you want is the lie that "You can find God in **Freedom**." It is the arrogance of thinking that the purest religion is no religion, that the truest spirituality is to be a law all unto yourself.

> **Freedom:** The belief that God's will for you is that you choose your will for yourself, that His strongest presence is found in His absence, that His only law is that you become a law unto yourself. Freedom, then, is nothing more than the worship of lawlessness.

FEAR JUNKIES AND TRUST WINOS

Dependent, weak, and out of control, we add up our countless individual needs to be laws unto ourselves into one vast culture of co-dependent, mass hallucination, high on white lies, hoarded stuff, and hurt people. But don't worry. As long as we don't believe it, we can get on pretty well (at least until we die) pretending all of the bad stuff isn't really true, or at least it certainly has nothing to do with **me**. At the very least, it's everyone else's problem. Meanwhile, there is a whole wide world of stuff and people out there to use in any way **I** can for keeping **me** convinced of just that fact.

At any moment where a lack of control rears its beastly head, rather than being still and believing God is in control, we cast about for anything in our vast pantheon of stuff and forge it into a refuge, a god of momentary personal stability. We craft these gods from bank accounts and careers, hobbies and family, eating, dieting, drinking, teetotaling, shopping, saving, sex, spending, being entertained, finding a cure—it doesn't matter. We worship anything promising to give us the momentary high of happiness. Those moments are gifts from God, but we wield them as illusions for staving off the painful withdrawal symptoms we keep experiencing as creatures cursed with lives lived in a constant state of dying. Refusing to believe it, we fight back by offering up to these idols hard work, dedication, and devotion, even prayers (as modern people, we call them "worries"). But we are only addicts, day-by-day avoiding the intervening reality that we are not in control by hiding behind anything helping us cover reality with the illusion of something better.

It never works for long. As with the use of any other drug, sinners cannot get high on the same dosage of the same idol for very long. The more you look to the same substance for the same result, the more you build up a tolerance, which weakens the positive effects. The lies that we tell ourselves in order to believe we are managing the danger of sin can only stave off the hard reality for so long. Whatever fills our need for hope, trust, and control in this moment, whatever might get you spiritually "high" today, it is never quite enough to keep the high going tomorrow. With time and use the immunity grows, and gradually we become numb to the effects of false promises. It is never long after we've put our trust into one lie before we need to look for another, to seek out a new idol in order to get the same spiritual results we've grown to expect.

Soon after you thought you'd found the one thing that would make you happy, you are back looking elsewhere for something with more potency or more quantity, a new idol to worship that can take the game to a new level altogether. As if we needed it, the world is also filled with messengers cheering us on in this binge of self-dependency. "Just do it!" "Just understand it!" "Just feel it!" "Just own it!" Even "Just believe it!" is very popular, so long as "it" is anything other than "they put Him to death by hanging Him on a tree, and God raised Him from the dead on the third day." Any hope. Any dream. Any faith. Anything good enough to give you that little boost, to keep your spirits high just a little bit longer, these are the things to seek, to serve, to love, to trust.

Rather than telling a different story, many versions of Christianity have joined the fray as just one more way to feed the addiction. With the Bible open in his hand, one preacher or another tells you Christianity is God's way for you to get control of your life. After all, "For freedom Christ has set [you] free" (Galatians 5:1). Ripping a few verses like these out of their context, good-looking men and women who are obviously in total control of their own lives cheer on your discontent with the present.

Desperately addicted sinners that we are, we latch onto their proffered lies like a junkie starving for a fix. We don't care what the lie is cut with. We just need to believe something. "God would never want you to be unhappy!" That one will justify all sorts of selfish decisions, hands down. "God is moving you from glory into glory!" That one will get you through a few hard times, so long as there is a chance of still winning in the end. "Christianity is all about love, and love means enjoying life and living it to the full!" Anybody with an itch can scratch it with that one.

Thinking about all of this objectively is just as much a threat to our control as not finding a new fix. To realize our spirituality amounts to nothing more than bouncing from high to high, idol to idol, lie to lie, only to be disappointed with the side effects and built-up tolerance every time, would be as depressing as an alcoholic realizing he can't quit drinking even if he wants to. Rather than do that, much like the alcoholic, we develop a coping mechanism we wield with great efficiency. The alcoholic learns denial. The Christian idol worshiper learns to **forget**.

Much in the way drunkenness deteriorates the mind, idol addiction begins to put holes in the memory. For Christians who get caught up in such preaching, this means not only do they learn to forget all their failed spiritual highs, but also bits of what should never be forgotten are shed in order to make room for yet more highs. Bits of Christian history and tradition become to us no more than another family heirloom that might be pawned at the shop in order to buy the next drink. Piece by piece, it all begins to disappear in a forever-search for the perfect rush, the one we are praying won't be gone when we wake up hungover tomorrow.

Then, without even knowing it, too busy chasing escape to have seen the last chance pass, it is no longer only the traditions of men that go missing from our personal versions of Christianity. Hungry for a new fix and unable to find it from all the same old experiences, we are ready to listen when someone says, "You don't need to go to Church to worship God. You need to find God in a way that's right for you."

That's right! we think. *I'll give that a try.* But this is no simple herb to smoke in your religious pipe. This is a rock that needs to be melted down and shoved straight into your veins. The high it brings is exhilarating, and its freedom is like nothing you've ever felt before. By now, all the old heirlooms have already been sold, but it's not such a big deal if we have to start skipping meals in order to pay for this fix. Goodness! You wish everyone could believe this, so you start handing out samples to all your Christian friends. "I'm just minoring in the minors," you tell them. "But I'll always remember to major in the majors."

Making Room for Fail

When the unclean spirit . . . comes, it finds the house empty, swept, and put in order. Then it goes and brings with it seven other spirits more evil than itself, and they enter and dwell there, and the last state of that person is worse than the first. (Matthew 12:43–45)

But it's already too late. Hooked on the crack cocaine of idol worship and shooting up higher and higher doses of your own personal religion, you are already set adrift in a self-medicated spiritual drug trip, with nothing but your short-term memory and hunger for the next high as your guide. Your house is swept so clean it becomes a playground for any spirit or wind of teaching that breezes by. By the time you notice that there are Hindus and Buddhists, liberal Imams and Rabbis all shooting up the same beliefs with you, it doesn't disturb you. In fact, they help stave off the immunity that is already building up. "All people in all religions are just worshiping the same God in a way that is right for them," they say.

"Yeah!" you realize. "That's right! How was I so blind before as to think my religion was the only one that could find God? Jesus couldn't have possibly ever taught something as closed minded and legalistic as that!"

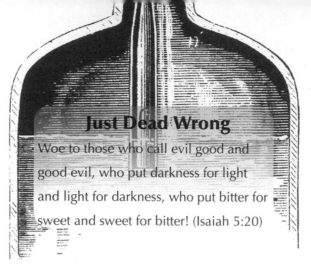

Just Dead Wrong

Woe to those who call evil good and good evil, who put darkness for light and light for darkness, who put bitter for sweet and sweet for bitter! (Isaiah 5:20)

With this vague "God" as your idol and your dreams as your justification, **You** have every excuse for doing everything and anything **You** want, even if it means calling good "evil" and calling evil "good." If talking about the big, bad sin monster outside of **You** helps maintain the charade, then **You** will talk about it. If that fairy tale loses its potency, then **You** will exchange it for another. What matters is that **You** keep believing that whatever the problem is, it is a problem outside of **You**, a problem that, with the right set of idols, **You** can defeat because **You** are in control after all. **You** are a law all to yourself.

By any means possible, whatever it takes, this "Freedom!" has a nice ring to it. It is highly palatable to the American taste buds, and it sells by the metric ton, especially to Christians. Bottled, canned, or kegged, it is one of the favorite beverages served by all manner of denominations and associations. Conservative and liberal, contemporary and traditional alike, there is no style of Christianity safe from the temptation to sip sweet cocktails blended with the "Freedom!" base. With a nectary promise, "Freedom!" is an easy sell to people from every corner of personal taste precisely because "Freedom!" is the flavor of **your own personal taste**. Who wouldn't fall in love with a drink like that?

Can't you just see the commercial? A young man pops open an aluminum can with a "fizz!" and takes a good, long guzzle before turning to the camera with a smile to say, *"Freedom! It tastes so good."*

*Because God would never want you to do anything against your will. Because God is not a tyrant. Because **God is love**! That means God wants you to be free. He wants you to find yourself, to express yourself. He made you just the way you are! And anyone who stands in the way of that, well, that person stands in the way of God.*

Caught up in the pure potency of a beverage tailor-made just for **You**, few notice that in the dregs at the bottom of the glass floats a leaven no wary Christian would willingly ingest. "Letting the Spirit lead" and "Not putting God in a box" work up such a nice, warm buzz, without immediately apparent side effects, it is easy enough to ignore any warnings on the label. With a few more sips of "We'll just change the style, but not the substance" and "Let's celebrate diversity," we start taking deeper swigs. By the time we're singing, "The Spirit blows wherever He wills!" at the top of our lungs, no one notices the next song on the jukebox is "There are many paths to God." If anyone vaguely remembers having not liked that song in the past, the inebriation of Freedom takes care of any inhibitions when it finally comes on. After all, the alternative would be to stop drinking and go home. This is a grand party, and no one else is leaving.

But this party is headed for life in the gutter of narcissistic self-directed, self-reliant, self-obsessed self-fulfillment. Mindlessly caught in the rhythms, gradually strung out by the inebriation, Freedom is a blast to get hooked on, but it leaves you subject to the ever-shifting whims of whatever

Pragmatism, Prosperity, Rationalism, Mysticism, & Moralism happen to throw your way.

Digging through these spiritual dumpsters for your next meal, you mumble to yourself, "I don't have a problem. I'm totally in control." But you are not. You are merely lawless, and Lawlessness is not nearly so freeing as it at first seems. When Freedom becomes the law, it grows into a tyranny the likes of which few legalists have ever dreamed, a rule that will never stop until it has torn down every other rule in its path.

> Everyone who makes a practice of sinning also practices lawlessness; sin is lawlessness. (1 John 3:4)

MIXED DRINKS IN THE VALLEY OF THE SHADOW

The stream of Lawlessness is the channel that first cut the valley of the shadow of death. Sojourning Christianity once upon a time made a rule of shunning the waters drunk from this brook, even when all nations demanded that we kneel at its edge and sip its poisoned draughts. But then there came a day when Christians did kneel and drink, and they noticed that the waters did not taste nearly so putrid as they looked. The drink was invigorating. Intoxicating!

Soon, some decided to follow the stream north, to look for an even purer source. At the head of the valley they discovered gorgeous falls cascading down from unseen heights.

"The waters of Freedom!" cried one of them. "See how they come from the mountaintops above. There is no doubt the waters are even more pure, more potent, up there. If we press onward, there is little doubt we can reach the pinnacle. We can leave the shadows of the valley behind. There, we can quench our every thirst with the very source of purest Freedom!"

"Quick!" another shouted. "Shed your constraints! Set aside anything you carry that might hinder you. You must let nothing stand in your way. Every binding, every rule, every boundary, and every limitation must be left behind. By any means possible, climb. Fear not! God will provide the places to grip once you have shown you are committed."

Reveling on the freedom drunk from the falls, wetting their heads beneath its icy blast, the travelers put their hands to the rock face and began to climb by whatever paths they discovered. At first it was thrilling. Dreams of what lay far ahead excited the senses. But as they came higher, the going got tougher. Handholds became harder to come by. Glancing down, some grew dizzy and unable to find another hold for going up, but neither was there a safe way to go back. Yet others still saw a way ahead, but far from the freedom of choosing their own path, they could choose only the path set before them, and that at terrible cost.

On the climb to total freedom, it is not long before cuts and scrapes mar the skin. Muscles grow tired, and bodies become heavy. No matter how you try, you cannot shed the weight of past traditions and rules fast enough. Friends who can go no farther must be left behind. Every misstep carries threats of gravest consequence, a total fall to the rocky shoals. Other revelers who come near you with kind words only do so to grab the ledge you were reaching for. Still more call from below that the way you are going is a dead end up.

"Ignore them! Press on!" calls the preacher. "It is only a test! Those others are Pharisees who cannot understand the Spirit. They are trapped in legalism. Claims of danger are merely their interpretations. They block your path because of their jealousy and hypocrisy. They say the Scriptures forbid that foothold you need to take? Remember, the letter is death. The Spirit is life! Plunge your head beneath the falls and gulp down another draught of freedom. That will get you over these disconcerting opinions of others. They can't know what God really wants for you after all. It is up to you to find that."

But the more you struggle to climb, the more you feel the weight of this Lawlessness. It does not feel like Freedom at all. It feels like a giant shackle around your neck, forcing you forward even when you'd rather climb back down, offering you no foothold, binding your heart, and enslaving your mind. Being a law unto yourself has bound you to a path you cannot leave.

Meanwhile, far down in the valley, another group of those grown drunk on the waters of the stream followed it southward until eventually they came upon a mere, a vast lake where countless others lounged in seeming comfort and relaxation. There were no scrapes and bruises here! As they kneeled to drink yet more of the bubbling pool, a preacher mingled among them. No one knew where he came from, but he was a cheery host. Though slightly aging, he wore a robe of brilliantly self-satisfied confidence. With his goblet sure in hand, casually stooping to refill his drink from the pool, he encourages all who come within earshot to gorge themselves on the lightly carbonated mix.

"Forget climbing to pure Freedom!" he preaches with strange glee. "Here is where the most potent Freedom ferments. Come! Drink deep and long. You will see. Who needs the mountain heights? This valley is not so bad once you satiate yourself. It is God's will for you to embrace Freedom in this vale, to transform this place by the liberation of your heart and the progress of your mind. Judge no others in how they revel. Only let your own desires lead you, and you will make a heaven of this earth. Change your clothing and traditions if you like, or don't, or wear none at all. It doesn't matter. This is love. This is open-mindedness. Others cannot know what God really wants for you, after all. It is up to you to find that."

With more soft and pretty words, a chorus of songs rise about him, carried by those who lounge. Their melodies laugh at all questions of truth. Their harmonies reduce all spirituality and talk about God to more preaching of Freedom. "Learn the unforced rhythms of grace." "Take life as it is, for life is what you make of it." "God wouldn't have created you like that if He didn't want you to be that way." "Follow your heart, and never let anyone tell you what is right for you, for only you can decide that."

Sometimes the songs will mention Jesus, remembering Him briefly like a long lost but well-loved founder, a visionary—the first pioneer of libertarian religiosity. But Jesus' actual words? His "doctrines"? Any meanings He wanted us to believe no matter what? Such concerns are long vanished, not nearly so tantalizing as the Freedom that is preached in His name.

High and low, in mountain and valley, with varied styles and endless new songs, the message of the revelers remains the same. Climb the mountain any way you see fit. Enjoy life in the valley any way you see fit. Find happiness for yourself any way you see fit. It is not drunkenness. It is "Freedom!" Fret not over what taking such liberties for yourself might mean to others. It is your needs that matter most after all.

And That's That

Whether partying at the waterfall of legalistic Lawlessness or wallowing beside the mere "Gospel" reduced to countless revelers dancing around the sinkhole of American spirituality, the entire oasis is a valley of dry bones. Painted with a pretty veneer of Christian*ishness*, cocktails personalized to taste like what you're looking for are served from the stream of "whatever is right for you." But for all the spices added to the mix, the aftertaste at the bottom of the glass always remains the same. Sanctimoniously spilling liberty on the faces of anyone who enters, it is called **grand diversity**, but it is nothing more than a great faith in the power of rebellion, preached (of course) **in Jesus' name**.

Once freedom has supplanted tradition, in time the only tradition remaining will be that **no tradition is sacred**. Where does it end? After rebellion has rebelled so long that no man-made traditions are left to rebel against, what can a rebellious soul do next? After everything you can find has been torn down in the name of Jesus, what happens when you find that the next thing cramping your spiritual style is the place where Scripture says . . . **that**? You know, **that** one thing you are really bothered by Scripture saying, that one thing you only bring up when you're with other people who agree with you in doubting it.

Once the addiction has been harbored and lauded, once the habit has moved from casual smoking to the rock-bottom emptiness of hardcore hallucinations, once the heirlooms are all gone and appetite for real food has vanished, what kind of religious devotion can remain to the trustworthiness of Scripture? What happens to the freedom-seeking soul, having learned to believe that all this Lawlessness "is" Christianity, when he glances over the fence and notices that his atheist friends believe all the same things? What happens when it looks both familiar and yet even more enlightened still? What happens when he realizes that the only difference between atheism and lawless Christianity is that the atheist is more honest about what he really believes? What happens when he sees that while lawless Christianity might say that it believes God exists, it certainly acts as if it does not?

{ **Freedom's lie:** You can't really find God. }

When the rubber of "finding God in Freedom" meets the road of "believing in an almighty God," only one of the two can be left standing. A truly almighty God must be GOD enough to create goodness in such a way that it never changes, even if we happen to think it should. Everything an almighty God ever decided to say would, by definition, be the absolute and necessary truth. Such almightiness could not even be shifted by our myriad individual abilities to misunderstand Him. Such a God's truth would be so true that it could even break through human misunderstanding and leave in its wake actual, authentic trueness.

Such an almighty God is ruinous to the worship of Freedom. Such a God makes it impossible to say things like, "*The God I believe in would never say that.*" An almighty God would say whatever He decided to say, and then **that** would be what He expected us to believe. Far more important than whatever **that** happens to be, whether it is a prohibition against wearing blue jeans (there isn't one) or a prohibition against ordaining women (there is one), if there is a God who is an actual GOD, then that God has the power to speak in such a way that when He says **that**, **that** will be **that**, no matter how we might feel about it.

What kind of almighty God exists but has no ability to deliver words that can be trusted? What kind of almighty God would make the only **truth** whatever **truth you** choose to believe in? This kind of god-thing, whatever else it is, is not almighty. It is powerless and meaningless. When Christians claim the Freedom to not believe what the Christian God has said in Scripture, even though we might call it "Christian freedom," we have only managed to arrive at a practical atheism, a godless Christianity. We can boast all we want about how glorious this Freedom is, but it is a drug-induced denial, an attempt to say God is real while living as though He (or she or it) is not. We can preach till we're blue in the face about how freedom to find our own way makes God so much greater than all those people with closed minds can possibly see, but this doesn't change the fact that a "God" without the power to say **that** (whatever **that** is) is no God at all.

Building in Vain

The wisest of women builds her house,

but folly with her own hands tears it down.

(Proverbs 14:1)

Pretty as we might shine up this personalized religion, polishing it with makeup and a new pair of shoes, it can never amount to anything more than a spiritualizing of our inherited addiction to rebellion. It is a religion of self-destruction, like a foolish woman who revels in drunkenness while she tears down her own house. Once the freedom to mutiny has become the only unquestionable truth, it must follow its mutinous course, gradually removing everything and anything that stands in its way, piece by piece, stone by stone, until supports and beams vanish and only an empty shell remains. "Oh? **That?** You don't really need to believe **that** to be a Christian." In fair weather no one notices. But when the storm blows, the house has only one choice: to fall with a great crash (Matthew 7:27).

Christianity has endured and outlasted every kind of human kingdom and philosophy history has ever thrown at it, largely because Christian Scripture contains words with meanings that never change. It doesn't matter the culture or time, the Bible remains the same words. It holds no secrets, no **new** information, no hidden truths that haven't been known from the beginning of the earliest Church. It is a rock, a lack of freedom to change what we believe. This slavery to the mind of Christ is why Christianity has endured and why it will endure to the end of time (1 Corinthians 1:10).

But it hardly means there are not times, places, kingdoms, and philosophies where the churches have seen the Word overthrown in their midst, only to vanish like a passing rain shower. Wherever such death has occurred, it has always been within those churches where the Word of God first lost its authority to say **that**. Rarely, if ever, has violence been able to destroy the Church. When Christians are murdered for their refusal to give up **that** bit of God's Word, it is a witness that only grows the faith of others stronger. The more one tries to stamp out Christianity with the sword, the more it pops up. But once Christianity's enemies are allowed to take up the place of teaching in the Church's midst, they inevitably lead the people to exchange the truth of God for a lie, and so Christianity is destroyed from within. When false teachers are given the leisure and license to tinker with the insides of the Church in the name of Freedom, then it is only a matter of time before the day comes when no one remembers the Word of the Lord at all, and all that remains is a "God" without any power to say **this** or to say **that** for certain, whatever this or that might be.

I Hate Tradition on Principle

The effect of all such unbridled worship of Freedom becomes most apparent in those who benefit most from the firm ground of traditions: the children. Ironically, it has been in order to better reach the young that "the freedom to get rid of the rules" has been sold to countless congregations and denominations over the last half-century as the one unassailable golden rule of youth ministry. It is claimed that in order to reach the young, we must imitate their world, speak their language, do what they do, and think what they think, which means jettisoning anything of the past not part of the context they are being sold at the mall and on YouTube. Teaching them to embrace a culture of the past is out. The only true rule is that by the systematic shedding of all rules and connection points with previous generations shall the next generation be able to learn the faith. If anything is difficult, strange, or boring, it is anathema. What matters is keeping their attention, and nothing grabs attention like breaking all the rules.

The results couldn't be more disastrous. The Church in America is in a total crisis. Far from keeping our young, we've entirely lost them. It is a painful fact to admit, but a careful glance around any local congregation on a Sunday morning will make it plain. The faith once for all delivered to the saints has simply not been passed down to a super-majority of the upcoming generations, those very children who grew up under the super-tradition of getting rid of traditions.

There is an old wives' tale told around the baptismal font to justify the consciences of guilty mothers and Sunday School teachers, a poo-pooing of this stark news with the insistence that once these drifting children have their own kids and a mortgage, then they will inevitably trickle back into the pews as well (or at least into the stadium seating at the Church of What's Happenin' Now down the street). It's a lovely little myth. After all, "Train up a child in the way he should go; even when he is old he will not depart from it" (Proverbs 22:6). The problem is that if we take a closer look at the way we have trained them, we find this is precisely what has happened **already**.

Forget the fact that the current generation is not having kids. Forget they're already paying mortgages as they cohabit in "friends with benefits" partnerships. Even without these problematic trends, the dilemma remains that the reason people under forty are sleeping in on Sunday (or getting up to do any number of other wonderfully fulfilling hobbies instead of **going to Church**), is precisely because they've embraced the way we've trained them to go. They believe confidently in the spirituality of Freedom. Ask any one of them, and you will quickly learn their deepest conviction is that people need to do what is right for them. *"To each his own."* If you need to tell a few lies or want to enjoy sex without marriage, *"that's all good."* There is just one thing you cannot do, and that is to suggest that what someone else is doing is spiritually wrong. In a generation as self-centered and amoral as the day is long, the one unquestionable morality is that everyone must be free to worship God in any way right for them . . . which is precisely why you do not need to go to Church. *"That's not my style."*

It turns out the children have been listening to everything we say, and we've taught them only too well. They are practicing freedom to the full by staying at home on Sunday morning. Taught that "the Gospel" means the freedom to follow your dreams and ignore any stuffy warnings of the past that happen to cramp your spiritual style, those who have drifted away have done so because they have taken the lessons to heart. Why sing songs about wanting to find God in my life when I can just go out and do it? Why put money in a plate for some spirituality club to spend on who knows what when I can spend it on the things that make me feel fulfilled? Why bind myself to an old tradition when I can worship freedom just fine all by myself? Why waste a perfectly good Sunday morning listening to some blowhard chide me about how his style of freedom is better than mine, when the real Jesus just wanted me to love people and be happy?

The Supernature of Insignificance

Complete my joy by being of the same mind, having the same love, being in full accord and of one mind. Do nothing from selfish ambition or conceit, but in humility count others more significant than yourselves. (Philippians 2:2–3)

The Church of any era before our own would have had no trouble calling this glorious new religiosity exactly what it is—spiritualized **immaturity**. The die-hard commitment to pleasing **Me**, the zealous insistence on exerting my will, the undying passion for doing what I want, these are the religious equivalent of the stalled out, lazy, dysfunctional mentality of high school **senioritis**. That today's leading churches and theologians are rarely decrying it, more often boasting of it, preaching it as the next great dream, and lathering it on yet more children, only exhibits just how drunk on the love of ourselves we have become.

The worship of FREEDOM eventually becomes the worship of LICENTIOUSNESS.

Fostering spiritual adolescence has never been our stated goal, but it has been the implied message, whether proclaimed by a pastor as he boasts about his freedom to wear blue jeans and play lead guitar or by a woman as she boasts about her freedom to don a stole and a rainbow-colored miter. To the sound of the band or the sound of the organ, children across the board are learning there is only one tradition that really matters: the tradition of doing what **Me** wants. Once upon a time, Christianity was the pursuit of adulthood in Christ, maturity in Spirit, gray hair, and the wisdom of **we**. Now, adults and children alike are taught Church is the place where we get to do whatever we want and say that it is in the name of God. If a preacher dares suggest chocolate milk and donuts for dinner isn't helping us (much worse if he suggests the milk is rank, warm, and chunky), then no one doubts we are free to harp and moan like infants, demanding he change his tone and stomping our feet until he makes room for the kind of preaching we prefer, or we're free to leave (and take our offerings with us). Heaven knows there are plenty of congregations out there more than willing to sell us the religion we'd prefer to believe.

Man-made or divine, from Scripture or from history, nothing is sacred once mixed with the cocktail of freedom. Lawlessness brings with it the spiritual gift of immediate and total authority. There is no such thing as a higher level of faithfulness to pursue, no possibility of finding actual **true** growth, no such thing as objective maturity. There is what I like, what I want, and what you ought to let me have. It is the virtue of chaos, the belief that Christian freedom means we allow everything and condemn nothing. "*Judge not!*" after all. It is the super-rule of having no rules, the supertradition of antitradition, and it washes away all other rules and traditions in its flow.

Whatever else anyone has to say, they cannot assail the firm belief in
Christian freedom and your soul's liberty.

"Humility" is knowing that **truth** can never really be known.

"Mercy" is looking the other way when your friend is active in what those old, legalistic people would dare to call sin.

"Wisdom" is knowing that all those **traditions** and **doctrines** that were here before you were most likely made up by ignorant, totally bigoted people and don't really have a point anyway.

There is no question **You** will do a better job. That is what freedom means: "*I can do a better job.*" It is the only virtue left, the final moral absolute, and the reason why so many of our pews and stadium seats are empty. Once believed firmly, the license to do whatever you see fit and justify it by slapping God's name on the back is the best reason of all never again to darken the door of an actual **church**.

THINGS JESUS THINKS ARE COOL

The transition is usually seamless, made without much notice or fanfare. What begins as the stripping away of a few traditions becomes the only sacred tradition: the power to get rid of traditions in the name of Freedom. Like a snowball rolling down a hill, over time it picks up mass and speed, knocking off one tradition after another until nothing remains but the Freedom to do whatever we want. By the time the next generation stands on the precipice of a bridge leading out of the faith of Christianity, they cannot tell the difference between one side and the other, much less remember the path they took to get there.

They do remember Jesus probably would have wanted them to step out in faith and take a risk. They know somewhere He said something like, "You hypocrites! You have traditions!" When a dear friend of yours across the way challenges you, "You only believe **that** is true because the Bible says so, and the Bible is just a tradition of men," it isn't so hard to agree and walk across that bridge without looking back. With every step it collapses behind, leaving no choice but to continue on, come what may.

Voiding the Unavoidable

For the sake of your tradition you have made void the word of God. You hypocrites! Well did Isaiah prophesy of you, when he said: "This people honors Me with their lips, but their heart is far from Me; in vain do they worship Me, teaching as doctrines the commandments of men." (Matthew 15:6b–9)

But contrary to popular opinion and much misquoting of Matthew 15:6, Jesus loves tradition. He likes rules. He thinks they are awesome. In fact, He created them. Rules are the way God designed the world to work, and tradition is the way God created for passing on knowledge from one generation to another. When He built the world, He programmed humanity so that we use traditions to help our children remember what we ourselves (and our fathers before us) have learned.

Receiving the past is part of what makes us who we are. It forms us as something bigger than ourselves. It helps us grow on a foundation raised above isolation and ignorance, and it aids us in passing on what we learn to those who come after us. The handing down of statements, beliefs, legends, customs, and information from generation to generation is exactly what Dr. Luther once pointed out God wants all Christians to do when he wrote, "God solemnly commands in Deuteronomy 6:6–8 that we should always meditate on His precepts, sitting, walking, standing, lying down, and rising. We should have them before our eyes and in our hands as a constant mark and sign" (Large Catechism, Longer Preface 14).

God Created Tradition

Receiving the past is part of what makes us who we
are. It forms us as something bigger than ourselves.
It helps us grow on a foundation raised above
isolation and ignorance and aids us in passing
on what we learn to those who come after us.

The entire reason Jesus condemns the Pharisees in Matthew 15 is not because they have traditions, but because they had the **wrong** tradition. They had a tradition of ignoring what the Word of God actually said. That kind of thing always got Jesus a little heated, because the entire reason Jesus came to earth was to restore to humanity the **right** traditions—**His** traditions—starting with the tradition of **believing God's every last word**.

Jesus wants Christians, Christian families, and Christian churches to believe and pass on every word of Scripture as entirely, totally, and necessarily true. He wants us to hand on from generation to generation all the statements, beliefs, customs, and information He established while He was still with us. But this means not only keeping the Bible on our shelves but also reading the Bible with the belief that Christians in every generation between Jesus and us have believed the same eternal truth we will find there.

This means even words of mere men, even man-made traditions of those Christians who have come before us, if they contain and communicate the words of God, are something more than "mere traditions" that we are free to ignore. We should never place them on the same level as Holy Scripture, but neither should we despise them just because they aren't our own personal thoughts. From songs and books to prayers that share what Christians have always believed, listening to our brothers and sisters of ages past is what it means to be surrounded by a great cloud of witnesse (Hebrews 12:1). These confessions and consolations from our brethr pass on the Word of God through man-made traditions. This is a thing! This is what Jesus commanded us to do.

God built us so we benefit from the past, whether as family, community, or society. Since He has also given us His Holy Word as the source of truth and redemption, if we are not creating traditions to pass that Word on, to benefit those who come after us, one has to wonder how much we really care for that Word at all. We certainly spare no effort creating traditions for passing on everything from politics to baseball. Neither adding to its substance nor subtracting from what it says, it is the obligation of the Church in every age to say to all ages afterward, "Yes! Your God says **that**. And don't you dare forget it!"

The Word of God is God's own established and normal way of passing Himself forward in human history by means of the lips that confess His name, His marvelous acts, and the promises of what He will yet do. The idea that God would humiliate Himself in such a way as to be carried by the guttural grunts of sinners like you and me is at once amazingly unbelievable and scandalously offensive. But our inability to understand how sound waves might carry the Spirit of God from human soul to human soul will not stop the almighty God from doing it, especially when He has said **that** is what He is determined to do.

Real, Ultimate Power

For I am not ashamed of the gospel,

for it is the power of God for salvation to

everyone who believes. (Romans 1:16a)

The Early Church knew this well. From the Day of Pentecost onward, the God-breathed words of the apostles were the center of the newly forming Christian community. As the specially chosen ambassadors of Christ, sent by the commission of the risen Lord, years before the texts of the Bible were brought together in one place, they handed on Jesus' traditions among Jews and Gentiles alike. Baptism into the name of the Father, Son, and Holy Spirit was passed on by word of mouth, included with a little water, as the promise that Jesus' resurrection from the dead is now your resurrection too (Romans 6:3–5). A meal of bread and wine was handed down with these words: "This My body," "This is My blood," enacting Jesus' new testament, His own holy custom for proclaiming His death until He returns and delivering to you participation in that victory through faith (1 Corinthians 11:23–26). Equally as important, though often disparaged in our age of freedom worship, Jesus also gave "the **keys of the kingdom of heaven**" (Matthew 16:19; cf. 18:18; John 20:22–23) to the Church and to those called by Him through the Church to the noble task of overseer, to speak the simple, eternal words "I forgive you" because our sin has been taken away from us by Jesus, who now bears it in our place.

This threefold custom created by Jesus is not set against the Scriptures. They are what the Scriptures were written to drive home. When the men who founded the New Testament churches on these traditions started putting pen to paper, it is little wonder that wherever their letters were found, the churches began the tradition of saving and copying them. As soon as St. Paul had written, "I commend you because you . . . maintain the **traditions** even as I **delivered** them to you. . . . For I **received** from the Lord what I also **delivered** to you" (1 Corinthians 11:2, 23), the manuscripts began to be collected, cherished, copied again, and dispersed throughout the whole Mediterranean world. The *codex*, or the book, was developed during this time by Christians so all these holy writings could be kept together in one single place. From this tradition, that is from this faithful handing down of the writings of the apostles, we today still receive the statements of Scripture as the foundation of the apostles and prophets, Christ Jesus Himself being the cornerstone (Ephesians 2:20). More important even than the fact that these documents hold a pedigree that is the envy of all studies in ancient literature, the words written in them are the traditions of the one man who is **God**. They are the promise-giving ministry of the one perfect human, given to serve His perfection to the rest of imperfect humanity by passing down Himself from one generation to the next, guaranteed by the promised power of His Holy Spirit.

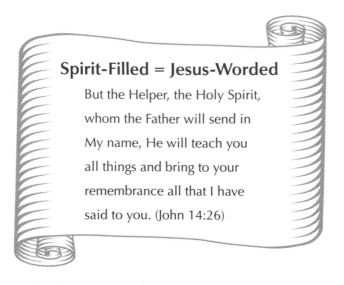

Spirit-Filled = Jesus-Worded

But the Helper, the Holy Spirit, whom the Father will send in My name, He will teach you all things and bring to your remembrance all that I have said to you. (John 14:26)

It is holy history like this that shows why the tradition of overthrowing traditions is a dangerous habit. Like an addiction, the one who practices it never knows where to stop. In our age, entire churches proudly sell the name "Christian," while with the same breath undoing every holy spiritual doctrine and teaching of Scripture. With rantings of *"Be free in the Gospel!"* they shout down calls to order that might slow the destruction of everything from the past. *"You're a Pharisee!"* becomes a card played to trump any dialogue that might lead to the need for repentance and a return to what was lost.

I am astonished that you are so quickly deserting Him who called you in the grace of Christ and are turning to a different gospel—not that there is another one, but there are some who trouble you and want to distort the gospel of Christ.

(Galatians 1:6–7)

With many half-truths, Freedom makes void the Word of God by lifting up Lawlessness as **another gospel**, a gospel that is no Gospel at all. As St. Paul lamented in his Letter to the Galatians, it is astonishing that Christians in the name of Christ can be so foolish as to distort His Word, grace, and gift of freedom from the penalties of sin into a tool for pursuing the selfish ends of our fleshly desires.

Love Knows a Bounds

These are the times in which we live, last days in which seemingly pious teachers rise up from our own midst in order to tickle our ears with sweet deceptions (2 Peter 2:1). "Do not worry about such an old-fashioned idea as pure doctrine," they say. "Such concerns are misguided. To focus on such things only divides us. We live in an age where we know better now. It is love and freedom that unite us. After all, since we're all sinners, none of us can perfectly understand Scripture anyway. Better if we just trust in the Spirit and leave it to God."

The next step may be years, even generations, in coming, but once the seed is sown, it will come. "Yes, Scripture is God's Word," they will say. "But it is also man's word. The prophets and apostles were sinners just like you and me. That is why we must admit the Bible does have mistakes and errors in it, things we no longer need to believe. But that's okay! We have God's Spirit to lead us, and He blows wherever He wills, which we are convinced is over there, in this direction . . ."

Both of these teachings are the same grossly impious lie. Both make the audaciously terrifying assumption that Christ's perfection is not quite enough to handle and overcome our human imperfection. The words can seem loving and soft on the ears. But when drawing a straight line, a small mistake at the start becomes a great misdirection in the end. So also a little leavenous lie will eventually leaven the entire lump of faith.

"Therefore," Dr. Luther reminds us, "doctrine and life should be distinguished as sharply as possible."

Doctrine belongs to God, not to us. . . . Therefore we cannot give up or change even one dot of it (Matt. 5:18). . . . A curse on a love that is observed at the expense of the doctrine of faith, to which everything must yield—love, an apostle, an angel from heaven, etc.! . . . One doctrine is all doctrines and all are one, so that when one is lost all are eventually lost. . . . It belongs to love to bear everything and to yield to everyone. On the other hand, it belongs to faith to bear nothing whatever and to yield to no one.[12]

Therefore, as I often warn you, doctrine must be carefully distinguished from life. Doctrine is heaven; life is earth. In life there is sin, error, uncleanness, and misery. . . . Here love should condone, tolerate, be deceived, trust, hope, and endure all things (1 Cor. 13:7); here the forgiveness of sins should have complete sway, provided that sin and error are not defended. . . . Therefore there is no comparison at all between doctrine and life. "One dot" of doctrine is worth more than "heaven and earth" (Matt. 5:18); therefore we do not permit the slightest offense against it.[13]

Better Than Bread Alone

The rules of the LORD are true, and righteous altogether. More to be desired are they than gold, even much fine gold. (Psalm 19:9b–10a)

Pure doctrine is not from us, but from God, and it is so sinless, so spotless, and so clean that even we cannot ruin it. Even carried upon the lips of sinful men and women, it is still Christ at work to save us.

---

12. Luther's Works 27:37–38.
13. Luther's Works 27:41.

Our individual understandings may never reach perfection, but neither does our ignorance have the power to steal Christ's perfection from His meaning-filled words. One of the greatest arrogances of our age is the idea that since we each have the ability to misunderstand what God is saying, this therefore means that God can't really have the ability to say it (or at least that He never meant **that** part we think He couldn't possibly mean), mainly because it gets in the way of the lawless **freedom** we want to exercise for our own benefit.

This is pride, claiming grace as an excuse to sin all the more. In the name of being loved by God, we insist He loves us so much He could never let us really know Him, nor His will for us. Once the churches of Christianity have compromised to this point, we are more than meaningless. Then all we have, truly, are the traditions of men and not a whit more.

To say "we all believe in Jesus so the other things do not matter" does not lift Jesus up. It casts Him down because it casts His teaching down. It replaces Him with a man-made tradition of hating tradition, under which no single word of His is safe. Once it has begun, one by one all the truths of Scripture will be rendered void, one by one relegated to the truthiness of the world and placed on the smorgasbord of half-believed religiosities until we welcome any false gospel with open arms but decry the scandal of the real Gospel's particularity as the greatest possible offense. By then, Jesus' crucifixion will have been quietly moved further and further from the center, an afterthought brought out on holidays as a nice story to remind us why we ought to be spiritual people and enjoy our freedom, until at last it is entirely gone with no one left who is religious enough to even notice.

Against this folly, St. Paul cries to us from the depths of our history, "I say it again: If anyone is preaching to you a gospel contrary to the one you **received**, let him be accursed" (Galatians 1:9).

Alas, too many of us have already forgotten how to hear. "Yes," we say, "but that is only your interpretation."

"No Law" Is No Gospel

You are no longer strangers and aliens,
but you are fellow citizens with the saints
and members of the household of God,
built on the foundation of the apostles
and prophets, Christ Jesus Himself being
the cornerstone. (Ephesians 2:19–20)

The sixth rule every Christian ought to break as often as possible is that "You find God in **Freedom**." As a rule, it is an assault against the very existence of truth. It strikes at the foundation of Christianity by undermining the power of Jesus Christ to speak to us with any real meaning in anything He says. Against this, the first thing we ought to learn from Genesis 1 (if we still believe any of it) is not what the length of its six days is, but the fact that when God spoke into the chaos of nothing, His Word created everything it said. His Word has more than the power to **mean** something. It has the power to **be** something. And it was **good**! John the apostle wrote in his Gospel that Jesus Christ is that Word, spoken into the chaos of our sin addiction in order to make us **good** again, to free us from our freedom-worshiping rebellion (John 1:1–18). He works by speaking, and what He has spoken always endures. When He speaks, it means He has done it.

So, when He says you are free from the consequences of your lawlessness by the power of what He has done on the cross—that is, by dying and rising from the dead—that Word as it comes near you is more than a mere idea about Jesus. It is the very mind of God, binding you to Jesus so that He is in your heart through faith. When you confess this same word, this is not your opinion, but the Holy Spirit on your very lips (Romans 10:8–9).

We may love the darkness, but God is a light shining into our valley, which we are simply not evil enough to overcome, much less silence. He is risen! It is true. At Pentecost, when the Spirit came, not in the earthquake nor in the wind nor in the fire, but in the solitary voice of St. Peter preaching with those Keys, even the curse of human babbling and miscommunication was no hindrance at all to the Spirit-filled Word. Human language is no obstacle to God. Still preached by sinful men and heard by sinful people today, Jesus still accomplishes a sinless purpose that can be as little divorced from His gift of **the knowledge of the truth** as it can be fused with latter-day ludicrous claims to personally receive special revelations straight from God (Titus 1:1).

Faith Believes in Something Specific

Jesus answered him, "If anyone loves Me, he will keep My word, and My Father will love him, and We will come to him and make Our home with him." (John 14:23)

From the beginning, sin has always been the pursuit of lawlessness (1 John 3:4), and lawlessness has always been the pursuit of personal authority (Genesis 3:5). All lies have always been a spin on the same Lie. Whether pointing you to your heart or your hands, your mind or the world, your spirituality or your personal freedom, *"Did God really say?"* is always near the root of The Lie's telling (Genesis 3:1). We are addicted to hearing it. But that hardly makes it fitting for Christianity to relax into its viperlike jaws as if Christ has achieved nothing more for us than a vaguely pleasant hopefulness.

Shall we really believe Jesus died in our infirmities so we might now have the "wonderful" freedom to walk around happy about our ignorance, doubts, and unbeliefs? Jesus does not justify sin and unbelief by saying, "Hey, man. Don't worry about it. It's okay." Sin is **never** okay. Jesus justifies sinners by obliterating sin. He smashes it dead. He pierces it with nails and scours it with whips in the agony and bloody sweat of His own flesh. He does not excuse it. He **absolves** it. He does not redeem rebellion. In the forgiveness bought with His blood, He **forgives** rebellion so that in His words rebellion meets its doom. There can be no mistake. Jesus' advent into the world brought the reign of God **here**. He is God's present, active **King**, ruling with a sword more potent than any iron or steel (Ephesians 6:17; Revelation 1:16). This sword is His Word, and by this Word, which always does what it says, He **rules**. He **reigns**. When He ascended into heaven, He did not leave the Church—us—as orphans, uncertain of our Father's will or our fate (John 14:18). But by powerful and eternal declarations, His Holy Spirit proceeded through the mouths of those blessed apostles and proceeds onward still through our mouths today (Matthew 28:18–20). Every modern-day preacher who remains faithful to those first oracles, every postmodern Christian who opens his mouth to confess again what was said once and for all, carries our Lord's antidote to the rule of lawlessness, both the Law and the Gospel of God's strong Word.

You cannot find God in the absence of God. Jesus redeemed us not to chaos and discord but into **concordia**, a harmonious unity of mind and Spirit. When the Word creates our oneness, then we are one even as the Father and Son are one (John 17:22). Jesus' pure doctrine fuses us together, through faith, into His own pure death and resurrection. These foundational facts for our faith are His proof that He loathes the thought of abandoning His creation to subjection in futility and vanity. Fallen though we are, He refuses to leave us without the fantastic gift of total certainty about who He is, what He wants, what He has done, and what He plans to do next.

This is why true Christian freedom begins with believing that the King who bought us back from our sin will not tolerate our use of that freedom to further prop up our rebellion (1 Peter 2:16). There is no "Yes, I believe in Jesus, but He didn't really mean **that**." This root of all lies must be divorced from His kingdom as far as the east is from the west. Against it He sends the promise "Truly, truly I say to you!"

Both God's lawful design of the world and His unconquerable Gospel working to redeem the world are the **"truly that"** which God has said, regardless of whether we believe it or not. No jot or tittle is merely **truthy**. Not a bit is given so we might say, "Isn't that a nice story?" None of it is just traditions of men. It is the stronghold-shattering, doctrine-giving Word of the almighty God, which will demolish every lawless claim and, one way or another, pull out of our sinful mouths the sinless confession "Amen! Yes, yes, it is surely so!" For all these reasons and more, it is a pretty good idea never to follow a rule that doesn't like rules. The forever King **reigns**, real and present. Based on true judgment and pure justification, His **rule** shall have no end.

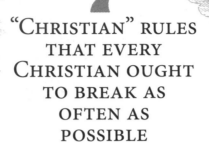

7

"CHRISTIAN" RULES THAT EVERY CHRISTIAN OUGHT TO BREAK AS OFTEN AS POSSIBLE

Never #6

Never follow a rule that doesn't like rules.

The Sixth Rule to be **BROKEN**

Freedom.

You can find God in **God's absence**:
the worship of Lawlessness.

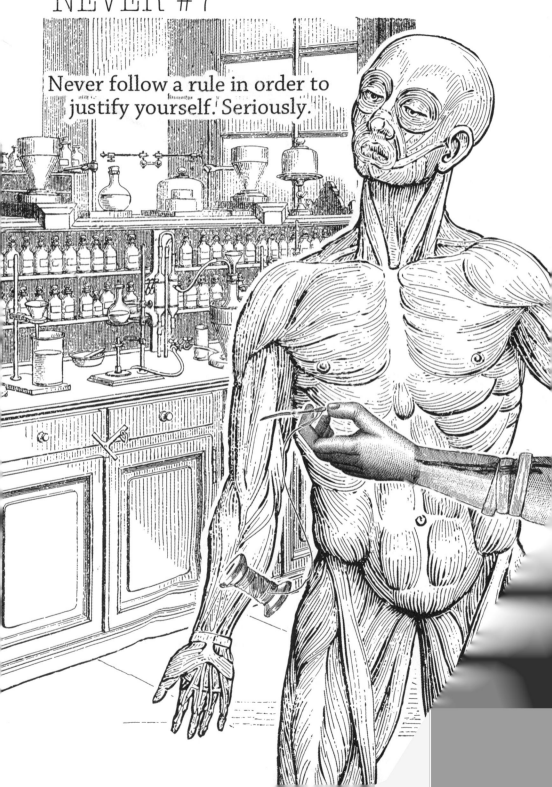

NEVER #7

Never follow a rule in order to justify yourself. Seriously.

THE FRUIT OF THAT FORBIDDEN TREE

His eyes opened. Darkness. Not darkness only. Sight, yet without light. Sight enough to remember despair, to recall the cause, to perceive the misfortune. He floats upon heavy swells, as if on the widest sea, but this is no sea of water. Casting his baleful gaze about he sees, spreading like flotsam upon the rolling tides, all his once mighty army. Now vanquished, they are each alike bathed in the ethereal tongues of a fiery gulf, a bottomless, rolling perdition. Each warrior's face bears confounded ruin. Each body is wrapped with molten chains, the marks of penal dismay. This is sight, but only sight enough to harbor woe, to know the realm of sorrow, to own a doleful shadow where rest can never dwell.

How unlike the kingdom for which they had warred! How unlike the bold companions he once knew them to be! Amidst floods and whirlwinds of sulfuric tempest, he turns himself with his great strength, which remains and feels to him yet undiminished. He then sees there beside him his captain, eyes also opened, but face grim and unseeing with the vacant thought of despair.

"Is it you, my friend?" he asks, through racking bouts of pain. "Are we yet ourselves in this most dire of exiles?"

"It is I," he speaks, his voice a bare whisper. "We are lost. By right of war and force of might, I see our fate. I fear, my Prince, nothing more shall our revolution e'er avail."

"What?!" he roars at his captain, vast and potent. His cry, though filled with power to shake the hills, flees into the void as a mist. "Speak never such cowardly words," he continues even so, yet now as tenderly to a child. "It is true that suffering we have found, and we have learned our potential weakness and seen our defeat. But do not submit to this deception. Do you not yet feel your faculties though through agony and pain? Can you not yet achieve every thought and deed that you once willed before?"

At this, looking about above the waves, he stretched wide his form, and ough burning suffocation bore down against his every muscle, by force of t he beat his wings and pulled himself up from amidst the blazing sea. ᴶ into the blackened sky in order to gaze down upon his host, the ungodly f all perdition yet pressing on his mighty shoulders, he spoke again,

but this time he did not merely speak.
He preached. He heralded his legion
with lyrics so sublime no heart or mind
might fail by to them to be stirred.

"Yeah! Farewell to happier fields
where joy forever dwells: hail horrors, hail
infernal world. Now this profoundest hell
receives its new possessor: I who bring a
mind not changed by place or time. I who can
make a heaven of hell, a hell of heaven. Here,
at least, we shall be free! Here we reign secure,
and I say to reign is worth ambition even though
trapped in hell: better to reign in hell than serve in
heav'n. What is more, shall we not rally arms and see
what yet may be regained?"

And so, the Archangel, born to bring the light, now
rallied all wicked guile to arms amid immortal darkness; "Who
shall yet believe, even after loss, that all these able legions,
whose exile emptied heav'n, can fail to reascend, self-raised, and
repossess their native seat? I say our better part remains! By work
in close design and fraud we shall still achieve what brute force effected
not. This infernal pit shall never hold us in bondage, nor this abyss long with
darkness cover us. My counsel will prevail: never think submission. War then!
War, open and understood, must be resolved!"

He spake: and to confirm his words, out flew
Millions of flaming swords, drawn from thighs
Of mighty Cherubim; the sudden blaze
Far round illumined hell: highly they raged
Against the Highest, and fierce with grasped arms
Clashed on their sounding shields the din of war,
Hurling defiance toward the vault of Heaven.[14]

---

14. From John Milton's *Paradise Lost*, Book I, 663–69. The entire section reflects and intentionally makes
     use of the language of Book I, 45–660.

Vainglory and the Self-Made Man

In *Paradise Lost*, John Milton paints Satan as the picture of everything the ideal person ought to aspire to be. He is confident, daring, resourceful, and powerful. He is well-spoken, clever, and talented. He is, in a word, a hero.

It's not that Milton wanted to convince the world that Lucifer isn't such a bad chap. Milton knew firsthand what the wages of sin meant, having gone blind the same year that his wife died in childbirth, his firstborn son following her six weeks later. (Two years later, his second wife and five-month-old daughter also died.) Milton was under no illusion about what the devil's tyranny means for our world. Yet Milton also knew the Bible. He knew that the devil's tyranny that caused such horrible things isn't finished yet. He knew that behind all the wars and rumors of wars and famines and disasters there is first an idea. A bad idea. A lie.

It's not that heroes are bad ideas. It's that the kind of heroes we most admire are bad ideas. It's that the things we think make one a hero reveals just how much we have believed this lie. When we put someone on a pedestal and worship them with our envy, it's not because he embodies all the traits of God. "Never say die!" "Make the best of every situation!" These are not the attributes of God. These are the traits of Satan.

This is what Milton set out to prove with his epic poem written in the tradition of Homer and Virgil. He set out to show how the natural human tendency is to measure all things by degrees of willfulness, power, and glory. So we come alongside the old evil foe, who has lost heaven itself in his attempt at revolution and is now buried in an abysmal lake of fire, tormented beyond imagination, with all his troops and warriors equally deglorified. But Satan has that fighting spirit any one of us wishes we could have. "If you have lemons, make lemonade!" "Pull yourself up by your bootstraps!" "Don't take 'no' for an answer!" Having forever lost the glory he had sought, knowing full well the mighty is far stronger than himself, Lucifer commits to "be all that he can be" **anyway**. The Prince of Demons "shows his mettle" by refusing to take even hell itself "sitting down." He can't win, and he knows it, but it doesn't matter. The present matters. The moment. He is the icon of perseverance, the embodiment of "sacrifice for the cause," the epitome of "staying the course."

So he rallies his fell army, and with guile and wise deception he ambushes frail mankind, taking whatever advantage he can get. While he does not succeed at pulling himself up, he nevertheless succeeds in tearing others down. His victory, "snatched from the jaws of defeat," is told with epic beauty in the final verses of Milton's poem as Adam and Eve take their solitary way, forever cast out of Paradise.

> They, looking back, all the eastern side beheld
> Of Paradise, so late their happy seat,
> Waved over by flaming brand; the gate
> With dreadful faces thronged and fiery arms;
> some natural tears they dropt, but wiped them soon;
> The world was all before them, where to choose
> Their place of rest, and Providence their guide:
> They, hand in hand, with wandering steps and slow,
> [From] Eden took their solitary way.[15]

The Christianity in us rightly weeps at this tragedy, but the humanity inside us sees in Satan exactly the kind of person each of us wishes we could be when the countless trials of life come barreling down: a winner. Each of us has a desire to change the world, to make it be the way we think it should be. We each want to find deep inside ourselves the will and power to refuse to let life be any other way. We may not wake up every morning wreathed with fiery-hell vengeance on our minds, but the groggy, bleary darkness of the alarm clock is hardly "Ode to Joy." From the first breath and the rub of the eyes, our next thoughts are about getting out of the hole and fixing whatever we find that needs to be fixed.

---

15.   From John Milton's *Paradise Lost*, Book XII, 641–49.

Whether it is the preventative maintenance of brushing teeth or the lofty goal of curing cancer, we throw ourselves into doing what needs to be done in order to make things as "right" in this broken world as we can possibly make them to be. We dream of finding the courage, wherewithal, and power to do something about anything that stands in our way, and to see it through to victory, no matter what the cost. On those who prove themselves most adept at overcoming, we lavish praise and honor. Those who show themselves masters of self-reliance and bearers of an indomitable spirit become the idols of every age.

"He overcame adversity." "She rose from the ashes." The clichés for describing our hunger for stories of the self-made hero are abundant, **and** each and every one are precise descriptions of Satan's finest attribute, the glory of self-reliance, so powerfully captured in John Milton's *Paradise Lost*. Lucifer "goes down in history" as the visionary leader who "against all odds" convinced man and woman, once perfect, to make the solitary choice to abandon their happy state and join him in his way of viewing the world, fusing his visionary definition of glory to their own hearts and minds forever.

To this day, despite all the horrors it has brought on us, despite the sickness and the death, the pain and suffering, the enmity and deception, we humans continue to idolize self-reliance as if it were somehow our one chance to find the source of every blessing. In our search for relief from the pain, in the effort to survive the risks of death, with self-reliance in our pride and that indomitable will to reach our dreams, the greatest asset we aspire to above all things remains the heroism of Satan's first arrogance. We wake up and notice the world isn't quite the way we'd like it to be, and like Satan, we drag ourselves out of bed and set off to change the lot of our existence.

If it takes another wrong to make a right, then so be it. Somehow, someway, we will put back together what has been broken in a way that it will never break again. Just as Satan hovered on his dark wings over his legions and preached to them one universal will to survive, so we speak and think of glory as the answer to our problems, despite all the evidence to the contrary. What else would any hero do? "A hero," after all, is what we call a man who has justified his own existence.

Seven Degrees of You

For the first six chapters of this book, we have explored a variety of spiritual lies, each one unique yet each one based on the same undercurrent of a theme. From the godlike qualities of reason to the search for gods in religiosity, from the temptress of Mysticism to her offspring, Pragmatism, we have peered into fallen man's terrible addiction to sin. We have analyzed our inbred (very bad) habit of taking the best things God has created and misusing them in the worst possible way: to justify ourselves.

In so doing, we have mapped out six faulty rules of counterfeit Christianity, which are actually subtle poisons, leaven kneaded into our knowledge of God (our theology). In the end these lies entirely warp Christian faith because the ever-Lie behind them is faith's antagonist. The core ever-Lie is the diametric opposite of fear, love, and trust in the true God. What is this ever-Lie? If we look back over our list of rules and carefully map them out, a pattern begins to emerge, a pattern that eventually reveals to us the original Lie behind them all.

NAME	IDOL	RULE
Mysticism	Emotion	You find God in your **heart**.
Moralism	Vocation	You find God in your **hands**.
Rationalism	Reason	You find God in your **mind**.
Prosperity	Material Things	You find God in the **world**.
Spirituality	Religion	You find God in the **churches**.
Lawlessness	Freedom	You find God in **God's absence**.

Do you see it? The final "Christian" rule every Christian ought to break as often as possible completes the pattern. Lurking within the other lies, it is the same assumption, the same rule Satan first invented, the rule that first caused the fall. It is the rule that kept Lucifer fighting on, even after he found himself hurled headlong like flaming lightning. It is the rule that gave him the inner strength to cast his eyes upward from bottomless perdition with the vow to ascend somehow, someway, by his own self-made efforts. Its **name** and its **idol** are the same: it is **you**; and your deception of you with false promises about you needs no other encouragement nor any other object of hope beyond the vacuous and willfully ignorant promise that somehow, someway, "**You** can find God."

> **The Ever-Lie:** The belief that you find God. The counterfeit "Christian" rule behind all other counterfeit "Christian" rules, then, is nothing more than worship of yourself.

This is the ever-Lie. It is the strategy Satan first used in his assault on Adam and Eve. When he asked, "Did God really say?" he implied the God they thought they knew was not the true God. That true God was somewhere else. To find Him, they would need to be like Him. So they ate, and so we died.

Satan's continued mastery over you requires that you never stop believing this, that it is up to you to figure out who God is, what He wants of you, and how you can get to Him. So the devil continues to preach this Lie in countless forms, all of which teach you success will come only through reliance on yourself. By keeping you reliant on yourself, he keeps you doubting God. Whether it is questioning God's existence or questioning what God has surely said, doubt keeps the field of play on Satan's home turf, where he always holds the advantage. Once you are not certain of God, once you believe God still needs to be found, once you cannot know surely what God has said, then only one option remains: finding truth or truthiness or wisdom or knowledge always must come back to reliance on **you**.

It is preached everywhere. "**You** be the judge." "**You** make the call." "**Your** heart, **your** hands, **your** mind, **your** stuff, **your** willingness, **your** belief." The adversary has no problem letting you have all these things and more so long as you remain faithful to his preaching that these are the things that really matter. They define you. You and they together are what really creates the meaning of the thing you call **you**.

I've always marveled at the favorite pastime/ quest of the post-1960s American middle class: the never-ending search for "self." One might think a mirror would do the trick, but who we actually are is not real what we're after. What we long for is who we want to be, what we might become, and the path to that being and becoming is the god you find . . . where Anywhere! . . . So long as it begins with **you**.

God did not create us with eyes to see our own faces. Therein lies a deeper truth, the real problem with the search for self and our endless quests for self-fulfillment. It is already a deception to believe we are not who God has made us to be. The place to find your identity is not within you but **without**. Your body is one giant, super hint. Your neighbors, your friends, your family—these are created revelations given to teach you who you are. Vocation is the identity God sets in front of your face, according to His design, to root you in a you that is not alone but defined by your relationship to others.

Of course, our vocations can also become idols when we put our trust in them to save us or believe we can save them from the effects of the fall. But under the reign of God in Christ, these vocations are redeemed. Heart, mind, body, world, religion, law—all these the risen King has restored. With His death and resurrection He justified all these things (including you!) in Himself. After such a marvelous reidentification of you as innocent, eternally alive, a child of God, the last thing He would do is send you off searching for **you** while you wait for His return. He says, "Sit right there, and I will tell you who you are! I know, because I made you. I redeemed you, and this is what I say you shall forever be."

The very notion of a quest for self abandons this good news, flipping everything over on its head and selling an eternal birthright for what amounts to a pot of porridge (Genesis 25:29–34). It uses creation as a means for clawing our way away from the God who gives creation to us. Like children trying to hide by squeezing their eyes shut, when we believe the lie that "You find God," we end up not with the promise of having a God but of **being one**. Therein lies the rub. We scratch and scramble to discover a way out of the sin of this world and into a world that is more like heaven, closer to the mark, a tighter picture of what we would have created if we'd gotten the chance to be God in the first place. We're clearly not gods, but we try till we're blue in the face anyway. Over and over again, we lift up the same broken attempts to set our world right, to line up the margins of our lives, to justify our existence.

EVERY WEED HAS A ROOT

She was raised in a broken home, and she still has the mental scars to prove it. The emotional bruises, which cause a constant pain, led her into a string of failed relationships. Sex and partying are her hope, but they fail her, leaving her lonelier than ever before. Yet one day she reads a book that promises her it doesn't have to be this way. The author has discovered the secret of life: through "positive thinking" the universe, a living god, will respond to the god within her and bring her all that she ever desired. And it was true! With meditation techniques and the centering of her soul, she succeeds in honing her emotions to a better transcendence, to a communion with the greater divinity. Every day, she is able to justify her world through the desires of her heart. She believes "you find God," and she is a master at it.

He started drinking in high school. At first it was just at parties, but by the time he dropped out of college his sophomore year, he was carrying a flask wherever he went. Broke and despairing, rock bottom hit him hard. But then one day a friend told him that it wasn't too late to discover his purpose in life. He only needed to learn how to look for it. And it was true! By learning the fivefold path to enlightenment, he was able to set all the right goals. He got cleaned up. He found work. He learned to worship and serve and be more like other good men. Soon, he was telling everyone he knew how they, too, could clean up their acts. After all, if he could do it, anyone could. With every new convert to his way, he justifies his world by the works of his hands. He believes that "you find God," and he is a master at it.

She had always been a Jesus Freak. She loved it. She adored singing praises to the Spirit and praying in front of the congregation. But she just didn't know how to handle her Biology 101 professor at State U. At first, she just argued with him. He only infuriated her by mocking her faith in God and her belief in a six-day creation before the whole class. The more she fought back, the more he seemed to win. The whole room kept chuckling at his sni jokes. Most of her classmates completely ignored her before and after class. Then, slowly, she started to realize that the professor had a point. He kept talking about the "facts," but all she ever had to go on was her personal experience, which can't be proven in a laboratory. All she had was her personal "values" and "faith." He had science. She began to question what she thought she knew so well. By the time she graduated with a degree in biochemistry, she was the one mocking Christians in the quad. "I used to think like you, before I learned faith is just something you believe, but science is about what is real." Now she devotes her life to what is certain. Perhaps, with only a few more solid answers, with a little more investigation, the whole thing might come together. One major breakthrough, and it all might make complete sense! With every next bit of research, with each newly designed experiment, she justifies her world with her mind. She believes that "you find God," and she is a master at it.

{ The Ever-Lie: You find God. }

I could tell a story about a preacher who justifies himself by his wealth or a story about a lady who justifies herself by handing out tracts promoting the American corporation she believes restored God's voice to earth in 1923 or a story about the punk rock kid who finally lined up the dots of life by believing there is no God at all. But all these vignettes are rooted in the same twist on the central backwards rule that dominates every human life on this planet with the deception "**You** find God." Every person you pass in the grocery store or see driving down the street could have their story plugged into the same equation. Every friend and every enemy carries in their nature the same adamantine chains marking us as broken spirits married to an abusive reliance on ourselves. Having once been caught in the vortex of "Did God really say?" we are now born into the choice to make ourselves the measure of finding out. We are ll heirs of the original sin.

Original sin: The inborn tendency of fallen humans to make ourselves the measure of all things. We lack true fear, love, and trust in God because we have placed true fear, love, and trust in ourselves.

The original sinner was Adam, the man created good but who, by listening to his deceived wife, **chose** to be evil (1 Timothy 2:14). Whether or not he knew the fullness of what that might mean at the time, he did know it meant choosing to go against God. That free choice that he made, to ally himself with the enemies of God, is no longer a choice you and I are given. As humans, there are many things in life we have power to choose or reject, but friendship with God is not one of them. Because of Adam's fall, because his being the father of our race is about more than a six-day history lesson, because he and his spirituality are literally the root of humanity, now all human beings who are conceived are born the worst kind of chips off the old block.

Death Is Always Earned

For the wages of sin is death, but the free gift of God is eternal life in Christ Jesus our Lord. (Romans 6:23)

We don't just do sin. We are fused **with** sin. That means we are born **without** original righteousness. The true fear of God and pure trust in Him as God do not naturally flow from our hearts. The opposite is true. Even the infant, from the first moment, is full of selfish passions and the inclination to believe he is the only important person in the world. This is not an action that the baby commits. This is an innate disease, **the** disease that is the primal cause of every death.

Are infants sinners?

Yes.

How do you know?

Because infants die.

This inheritance is truly sin. The Church Fathers called it **concupiscence**, and it is **more** truly sin than any of the actual sins you commit in your entire life. It is the **cause** of all those other sins. So horrific, so terrible is this sickness that it has no natural cure. It is the true contagion, a doomsday scenario, a virus so vicious the only way to cure it is to purge everything and anything corrupted by it.

 Concupiscence: The inherited disorientation of mankind, an innate tendency to desire what is evil rather than what is good.

Bizarrely, learning about this **concupiscence** of our nature is some of the most wonderful and helpful news Christianity has to offer. Too many Christians have been taught to spend their lives trying to cleanse their hearts from every last wicked thought and inclination. The new convert sees a few stones in his garden and begins digging them out. By the time he has discovered that three inches below the topsoil is nothing but slate and bedrock, his hands are slashed and bleeding, his breath is short, and he doesn't know where to go. "You need to pray about it," some preacher tells him. "You will find God, and He will help you when you're truly committed." It's a lie.

This is where the rubber of pure doctrine meets the road of life. The pure doctrine of original sin is great reassurance to the heart that has failed constantly and miserably in purging itself, because it teaches you to believe you've been trying to do the impossible. You were born with not only a few wicked habits on the surface, but with a deep-seated contempt for God Himself, a total inability to fear Him enough to do the right thing in every moment, a complete absence of trust in His ability to take care of you through every possible scenario. These chief defects of human nature, this corrupted disposition, while not good news in itself, can be very freeing to **believe** in. The sins of your heart, in any given moment, flow from your inbred disease of "animosity toward God," and the Gospel truth is that it is something you can do nothing about.

When you believe what the Scriptures say about your sin, say, that "None is righteous . . . no one seeks for God" (Romans 3:10–11), you can at last begin to understand why things are the way they are, and why you do all the things you do. This is a God-given knowledge of sin, a revelation His Spirit sends to jump-start our awareness of a need for saving faith by jump-starting our awareness of a need to be saved. We cannot know the magnitude of what Christ has done without first recognizing the full reality of the malady to which He is the antidote.

If we cannot confess that even all the best of our everything—works, emotions, purposes, plans—are all filthy rags, then it remains impossible for us also to believe God's own work and plan to save us from it. While defending our own pious thoughts and words and deeds, we play a charade, building up man-made excuses that have no power against the evil and death that plague us. So long as you insist on justifying your own existence, it remains impossible for you to receive God's justification of you by grace alone.

Some Christians quote verses such as 2 Corinthians 11:30 and Philippians 4:13, as if Paul were saying, "I will say I am weak, but I'm actually pretty sweet thanks to my newfound Jesus-power." But this is not what Paul is saying. Paul does not think that, thanks to Jesus, he is no longer weak. On the contrary, he confesses that, thanks to Jesus, he can boast of the fact that he is weak because his weakness no longer matters. It only highlights all the more what a great Savior Jesus is. A Christian does not have to pretend to always be strong. The longer he spends as a Christian, the deeper he becomes aware of the fact that he is a profound sinner (1 Timothy 1:15).

An Honest Confession

Against You, You only, have I sinned and done what is evil in Your sight, so that You may be justified in Your words and blameless in Your judgment. (Psalm 51:4)

When the Christian honestly assesses what is going on with his heart according to the Word of God, he finds that he doubts both the goodness and the wrath of God; we are bored by God's Word; we are angered by the fact that God does not rescue us from the curse of this world immediately; we consider God's allowance of afflictions a hateful thing; we abhor God's willingness to let wicked men prosper and good men suffer; we daily are stirred up by rage, lust, desire for glory, hunger for wealth, and countless other things like these. The Apology of the Augsburg Confession, one of the primary documents of the Reformation, says it this way:

Human nature has been delivered into slavery and is held captive by the devil. He fills human nature with a passionate desire for wicked opinions and errors. . . . Just as the devil cannot be conquered except by Christ's help, so we cannot free ourselves from this slavery by our own strength. World history shows how great and powerful the devil's kingdom is. The world is full of blasphemies against God and wicked opinions. The devil keeps all tied up many hypocrites who appear holy and who are wise and righteous in the world's eyes. . . . Since Christ was given to us to remove both these sins and these punishments and to destroy the devil's kingdom, sin, and death, **we will never be able to recognize Christ's benefits unless we understand our evils**. . . .

We know that [in this] we believe correctly, in harmony with the Church catholic of Christ. (Ap II 47–51)

Devout Christian faith does not hide from this sad fact of concupiscence. With St. Paul, we confess it, because the depth of our sin is equivalent to the depth of Christ's love (Luke 7:41–47). So we acknowledge these things to be present in every person, including **you**, not so we may embrace them, but so we may believe Christ has paid for them in full.

Now Another Righteousness

The true value of a Christian is not what you do, but who you are in Jesus.

With enough work, it is possible to appear to be a pretty good person. You can pursue honor and justice. You can make the right decision in the right moment most of the time. You can see what will help someone else and do it. This kind of goodness is easy to judge. The goodness of works is evident, and it doesn't matter if you are a Christian, a Jew, a Hindu, or a Wiccan. It is very possible to be a good person, because this kind of **good person** is about what you do. But this kind of goodness is not the only goodness there is. More important, it is not even the best kind of goodness there is. Not only is it weak, coming and going with the moment, but as much as we pursue it, we never seem capable of reaching it completely. This is because we're missing the better kind of goodness.

This better kind of goodness is not of this world. It is not the goodness of what one does, but the goodness of who one is. The source of this goodness is always the one true God **and** who He says you are in relation to Him. In the Garden of Eden, He created Adam and Eve perfectly good before they ever did anything. They were not good because of works, but because that was how God made them, how He spoke them into being. They were crafted by His voice, breathed into with His life, called the identity of His own image. Their goodness was first God's identification of them as good. All the other kind of good that they would ever do, even in a perfect world—the good of loving each other, being fruitful, and caring for creation perfectly—all of this flowed first from that original, passively **received** goodness.

Their vain jump into the fall turned all of this on its head. It wasn't just that Adam and Eve ate some pear that was off-limits. It was that they believed by eating this pear they would themselves become the source of their own newer, better goodness. "You will be like God," the serpent said (Genesis 3:5). It is as if he said, "You will be good **apart** from God. Knowing good and evil, you will identify yourselves as the good you make yourselves to be."

Just like that, with an attempt to be actively good on their own, they tried to justify what was already straight and in so doing bent it beyond recognition. Thinking the lesser good could make a better good than the best good (itself given freely!), they curved the eyes made for looking outward back in on themselves.

We have been broken in this self-absorbed, self-deification ever since. By turning our backs on the true goodness coming from God alone in order to pursue endless fool's goodnesses made by us, we became what all things without God must be—evil. Worse, being evil, we are now incapable of objectively admitting it. We instinctively know life on earth should be better than it is. But the best we can manage to do is scamper about like mad ants, trying desperately to re-create goodness out of anything we can lay our minds, hands, or hearts on. The problem is the goodness we **do** is still sinful, and the goodness we need to **receive** can never come from us. It never has, and it never will, because it is the original goodness that comes from God alone.

The result is the addiction we have explored in-depth in this book. Each in its own way, the six rules of the previous chapters teach us to take whatever goodness we do manage to make and immediately turn it into an idol. These rules of counterfeit Christianity teach us to believe with our self-made goodness we can restore ourselves and again have a goodness like God's. But the more we try to create ultimate goodness from ourselves, the more ultimately worthless we prove ourselves to be. It's not that there is no good in the world, or that you or I or anyone should stop doing the right thing. It's that when we do the right thing with the lesser, active goodness and then hold it up to God and say, "See, this goodness is like Yours," we are at best repeating the original problem. We are re-originating the original sin. The more we try to be the authors of goodness, the more we are trying to be God Himself. Trying to find God, we make "You will be like God" the goal of our every effort! Thinking we are climbing back up to truth, the first foothold we reach for is The Lie, which caused our fall in the first place.

Counterfeit Christianity always teaches the worship of yourself.

It is the essence of wickedness to believe wickedness can become goodness. This is why fallen man's natural religion is always a quest to lift himself off the earth and into heaven. This is also why it is always about as effective as trying to fly by pulling on your own bootstraps. The more you yank, the harder you squeeze your eyes shut to tap the strength within, the less you are able to see how the total failure of what you are actually doing is rooted in your false belief that you can do it. It is kind of like a beggar who is dressed in filthy rags but is convinced that with enough stitching and cleaning he can make those rags into a robe fit for a king. In exactly the same way, even the best human goodness, even goodness untainted by the wickedness of sin, still would not restore us to the original, perfect goodness. No **active** goodness of ours could ever do that because the perfect goodness we lost was never active to begin with. It was **passive**. It was **received**. It was a **gift** from the start. If it is ever to exist for us again, it must be a gift once more. Having self-identified ourselves with our sin in our fall, we must hear a word from outside of us, a word of God that reidentifies us with Him anew.

That Word He has given in Jesus. He says, "Yes, you are a sinner. But now, I say, I have redeemed you. You are Mine. Now, I say, I re-originate you good with **My** goodness."

This is the pure doctrine of forensic justification (or imputed righteousness), and it is pretty much the sweetest action thing in the entire world. Men and women of self-made evil need a better goodness to come to us from the outside and regenerate us. Like a man in cardiac arrest, we cannot make our own heart start to beat again. So God places a defibrillator on our chest, a shock that is a hero the world could never conceive of, a glory that is a cross the likes of which no poet ever dreamed. "Jesus of Nazareth . . . crucified under Pontius Pilate . . . dead . . . buried . . . and on the third day . . ." *Thump, thump.* There is a pulse, and the pulse is faith, not something you do, but something done already that, once heard, wakes you up to rise from the dead (Ephesians 5:14).

It is impossible to receive by doing. The heart's beating is not the electricity it needs to live but is **caused** by it. In the same way, the Christian life is not about trying to get close to God. The more you work to make yourself good for that purpose (which is ultimately for your own selfish sake and so not good at all!), the more you drive a wedge between yourself and the Creator, who never intended for you to be a source of goodness in the first place. It is a return to the original sin of hoping to be good apart from Him, the worst kind of sin, an attempt to be God. One of the first lessons taught in children's swim classes the world around is what to do in an emergency. When a swimmer gets a cramp and begins to drown, the lifeguard will dive in and pull the swimmer out. But in that saving act there is one thing the drowning swimmer must absolutely never do. Once the lifeguard has him, he must stop trying to swim. If he does not, if he thrashes about insisting he can somehow save himself, he will not only succeed in drowning but will drown the lifeguard too.

This is what the original sinner must learn to believe. Attempts to do good works are not the problem. The thrashing arms of the drowning swimmer are not the good things Christians do as people already saved by grace. The thrashing arms are the attempts to make those good things the

source of salvation, whether in whole or in part. Pursuing civil, active goodness will not drown your faith. But insisting this lesser goodness is what real, ultimate goodness is all about certainly will.

The Christian life is the fact that you can't find God, but in words from and about Jesus, God has come close to you. True goodness from God is given apart from what you must **do**. It is given by God renaming you away from who you are as a child of Adam, bespeaking you into something new as a member of Christ. This better, passive goodness is received through faith alone, a free gift to be believed.

"You have sinned," God says. "You fall short of My glory. But I justify you by My grace as a gift, through the redemption in My Son, Jesus. Him I put forward as a satisfaction for your sin. This is to show you that My goodness is what the entire world needs first. With My goodness, I can pass over former sins and make you good, even now in this present time. This is not a matter of what you have done or will do. This is a matter of who I say you are. This is a matter of Me being the only just one, and the justifier of the one who has faith in Jesus Christ, which means **you**" (Romans 3:21–26, paraphrase).

RISE OR FALL

This is the theology on which Christianity lives or dies. It is the total reversal of all things. To natural man and natural religion, to the mind of original sin, it makes no sense. It is an affront to pride and glory and everything important about **Me**. It is the proclamation that **about Me** needs to die. **About Me** must be killed, murdered, crucified, **and** that this has already happened in the body of Jesus Christ. There, in Him, the curved-inwardness of us all was absorbed like a cosmic, evil-sucking sponge, pulling all the fruits (and the cause!) of original sin into His own flesh, which then was nailed by God to the cross and made dead, dead, dead.

Bursting forth from the tomb on the third day, it is the Christ in **Christ**ianity that changes everything. Now, religion is not about **doing** but about being ***done to***. Now you are freed to never need to find God, to never need to please God, to never need to explain yourself to God. In Jesus, God found you. In Jesus, God is already pleased with you. In Jesus' words, God explains yourself to you—both your old self and your new, both killed and raised. In Jesus, God finds you, washes you, and feeds you with Himself, purging your sin but redeeming **you**.

More so! This is the one theology that actually frees the **you** in yourself to not always constantly have to be about **Me**. Though you are never free from the imperfections and weaknesses of this life, Christianity creates in **you** a **you** that is no longer **only** curved inward. When your eyes are opened by the fact that because of what Jesus has done for you, you do not need to spend your days and your nights justifying yourself to God, for the first time you can actually stop looking at **Me**, take a gander around, and pay attention to where you really are. With eyes fixed on what Jesus has done rather than on what you need to do to find God, your eyes are opened to see you are not the only one kneeling at the foot of His cross. There are other sinners here too, men and women just like you, trapped in the inbred need to justify ourselves but freed by Christ to believe we are already justified in Him.

This is the first step in true love. But don't look at it too closely! The moment you do, the moment you say, "Hey, look, I am free to love," you've gone back to **Me**.

ME

Faith Looks Outside of You

That which . . . we have heard, which we have seen with our eyes, which we looked upon and have touched with our hands . . . we proclaim also to you, so that you too may have fellowship with us; and indeed our fellowship is with the Father and with His Son Jesus Christ. (1 John 1:1, 3)

The object of Christian faith is not faith. That is to say, salvation by grace through faith is not salvation through faith **in faith**. The object of Christian faith is Jesus—the person, work, and words of Jesus. Jesus, the man born in Bethlehem, raised in Egypt and Nazareth, testified to as a miracle worker by secular historians. Jesus, who was crucified by a real-as-you-or-me Roman governor, buried in a sealed tomb, and then, three days later, seen alive and in perfect health. Jesus, who, still bearing the scars and still claiming to be the heir to the Hebrew King David's throne forever, was seen after His resurrection, not just privately, but en masse by over five hundred who heard Him, who touched Him. This is how the Christian faith was born: Jesus Christ is risen from the dead. **It's a fact.**

Stop worrying about it so much and just enjoy it. When Christ sets you free, you are free indeed. No need to go trying to measure it in yourself. It is preached to you. "It is finished!" Believe it! What you will start to see around you are others who are also fixing their eyes on Jesus as the author and perfector of faith. Beyond them, there is also a milling, vagrant host of blind people, those who have neither heard nor believed this amazing news about who Jesus is and what He has done. All of us together, every last one, is suffering under the weight of our self-imposed decay and destruction. All of us, every last one, is desperately in need of **mercy**.

In this freedom, in this faith, Jesus' grace opens our eyes to see all those around us and their pain. Freed from peering inward and questing for yourself, Christianity unleashes your thoughts, emotions, and works to be something more than the idols by which you seek to justify yourself. Loosed from the tyranny of your own searching, these gifts are restored to their potential use in the ways they were meant to be used: to serve your neighbor. Seeing this is no good work in itself, nor any positive emotion, nor any deep thought. It is **faith**. It is trust in what God's Word has said about His created gifts. Christianity, by both Law and Gospel preached and without your having to make any of it happen, causes you to look around and find it is happening already.

With the heart unchained from looking for God within, in total freedom you will look with mercy on the sinner beside you. With your mind unshackled from searching for God, in total freedom you will find yourself learning the wisdom of creation, of stewardship, of natural law, and of history, all of which will teach you how to aid your ailing neighbors and communities. With your hands made aware of the coming resurrection, in total freedom you will find yourself putting aside the pain and the weight that so quickly entangles, moving instead at the impulse of love for your neighbor, no longer only capable of repaying evil for evil but filled with a desire to overcome evil with good. Best of all, none if it will mean anything to **Me**. You will know that none of it gains you one thing, because it is all already, entirely, and totally given: promised in Jesus. Sin will not go away. The Christian life is not the experience of victory. The broken rules we've studied in this book will not cease to tempt you, to deceive you, to hack and slash at your faith in this good news. But none of that can stop Jesus. He is the Christ, and you are His Christian, which means it is His work to regenerate you, to feed your faith, and to restore your sight so you see things for what they really are. This is faith, not to change the world, but to call a thing what it is and to believe that what it is has been made perfect in Jesus.

Indisputable as any history that the modern world accepts, more scientifically certain than Caesar crossing the Rubicon or Homer penning *The Odyssey*, the justification of Christianity is not faith in blind faith, but faith in the facts of who Jesus is and what Jesus did. Christianity is not just one more personal value or **faith-based** opinion. It is a thing **outside** the Christian and unbeliever alike. More than a bare knowledge of history, it is the redeeming **theology** of history. The empty tomb is the sign that the universe has changed. All we can observe or feel or do has now been spun on its head by the proof that one hero was born among us who has done more than take it to the next level for Himself. Risen from the dead, He is taking the universe to the next level with Him.

Hearing Is Believing

Even though many people spend a lifetime trying not to admit it, life on earth for the average Joe is about death. Everything we do and say and think and feel and pursue and chase and run from and fight for is because we are trying to find a way to get as much as we can while we still can and trying to put off losing "still can" as long as humanly possible. Death haunts us. Our fears, our doubts, our worries can all be traced back to the grave as their ultimate source. The shadow of death hangs over the entire valley, an ominous reminder that we are dust and to dust we will return. So we work and think and feel our tails off, trying to pretend it isn't so. We create dependencies and habits of denial in order to hide the thought of death from our conscious minds, because to be honest about it would drive us truly mad with fear and trembling. But our deep psyche always knows; death is there, lurking like a ravenous beast, waiting to swallow us up the moment we let our guard down.

This is what Jesus has changed. For you, in the body of Jesus death is gone. He already beat it. It could not contain Him. **And it is His promise that He will not let it contain you either**. Having risen, having appeared, having established the apostolic ministry with the power to forgive sin and all its wages by the human words

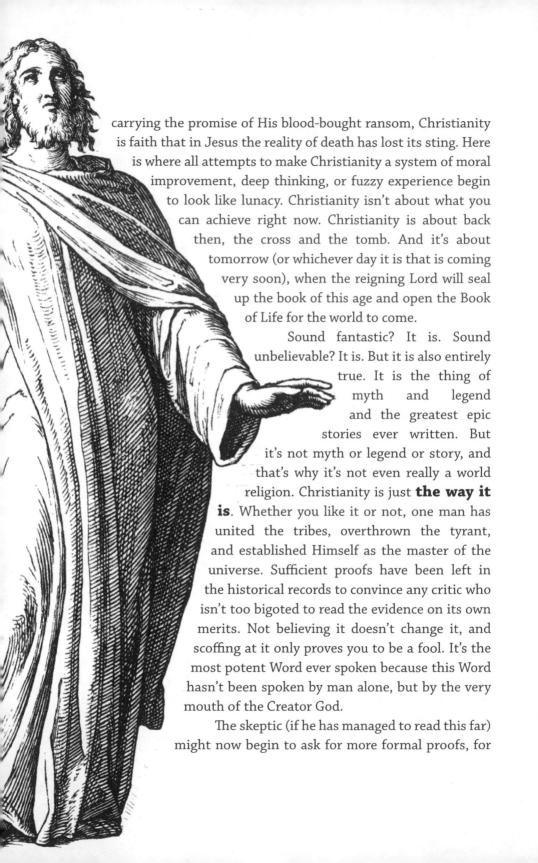

carrying the promise of His blood-bought ransom, Christianity is faith that in Jesus the reality of death has lost its sting. Here is where all attempts to make Christianity a system of moral improvement, deep thinking, or fuzzy experience begin to look like lunacy. Christianity isn't about what you can achieve right now. Christianity is about back then, the cross and the tomb. And it's about tomorrow (or whichever day it is that is coming very soon), when the reigning Lord will seal up the book of this age and open the Book of Life for the world to come.

Sound fantastic? It is. Sound unbelievable? It is. But it is also entirely true. It is the thing of myth and legend and the greatest epic stories ever written. But it's not myth or legend or story, and that's why it's not even really a world religion. Christianity is just **the way it is**. Whether you like it or not, one man has united the tribes, overthrown the tyrant, and established Himself as the master of the universe. Sufficient proofs have been left in the historical records to convince any critic who isn't too bigoted to read the evidence on its own merits. Not believing it doesn't change it, and scoffing at it only proves you to be a fool. It's the most potent Word ever spoken because this Word hasn't been spoken by man alone, but by the very mouth of the Creator God.

The skeptic (if he has managed to read this far) might now begin to ask for more formal proofs, for me to back up this claim with a laundry list of ancient textual evidence. There is a time and place for that (and those books are out there).[16] But the question I want to ask you—you who have read all the way through this book and sojourned amidst the twists and turns of the many lies painted as styles of Christianity—I want to ask you, "Why?"

Why, when you lift up your ear to the voice of Christianity wafting on the waves of media and pulpits today, **why don't you hear this preached**? Americanized Christianity has more wealth and resources at its disposal than at any other time in history. Even the empirical Rome of the Middle Ages could not wield the worldwide influence American churches hold today. Meanwhile, we hear preachers saying, "We are rich. Our mission is succeeding. We are growing. Look at us—look how our churches do it right and have prospered." But where is the evidence? The fact that the resurrection of Jesus Christ is all but absent from our popular music and writing and preaching beg to differ with this popular notion. To the soul hungry for the pure Gospel, it is clear enough we are not nearly so rich as our fine parking lots and multilevel sanctuaries would tell us to believe. Toss in the dropout rate of our children, and it becomes clear that what passes for our "faith" is "wretched, pitiable, poor, blind, and naked" (Revelation 3:17).

This is no swipe taken by some disgruntled pastor nor any boast from a backwoods cultural revolutionary. This is the voice of a thirty-four-year-old man, born and raised in the Church, who left the churches because churches had not given him a Gospel worth believing in. By the amazing grace of God, Jesus Christ looked down from heaven at my running headlong into self-destruction (and boy was I running fast and hard), and He said, "Not on My watch." He spoke a Word—that same Word—and by a faithful preacher "Jesus Christ crucified and raised!" came to my unwitting ears. Thanks be to God! So this is a voice crying in the wilderness of American Christianity and saying, "Why?"

---

16.   A good place to start is the great work done by Gary Habermas in *Did the Resurrection Happen?* (Downers Grove, IL: InterVarsity, 2009). For the more committed student, N. T. Wright's *The Resurrection of the Son of God* (Minneapolis: Fortress, 2003) is the magnum opus.

253

The Parable of the Beggar's Old Clothes

But when the king came in to look at the guests, he saw there a man who had no wedding garment. And he said to him, "Friend, how did you get in here without a wedding garment?" And he was speechless. (Matthew 22:11–12)

Why have we forgotten the apostles were committed to knowing nothing but Christ and Him crucified? Why have we sold our heritage for the porridge of worldly success? Why have we started teaching our children to rise up and dance and play rather than rend their garments and beat their breasts? Why have we looked on the white garment with golden threads brought to us by the King and decided we would rather come into His wedding feast wearing our own thoughts, words, and deeds (Matthew 22:2–14)?

It is not too late. That is the beauty of Jesus' Gospel. It is never too late until the Last Day. Our nakedness does not have to be seen, and our blind eyes can yet be anointed with the salve of His Word. Through faith this Word regenerates hearts from self-love, frees hands from the tyranny of death, and renews the mind with a view of the world that is everlasting. Given the state of twenty-first-century American Christianity, this will without question mean reproof, discipline, and repentance. But these things are the signs of a Father who loves His children, the God who refuses to let His creatures destroy themselves, the Judge who sees the ledger of our lives out of balance and has chosen to have no greater desire than to justify the debt.

Declared Righteous

Justification. It is the truth on which Christianity must either stand or fall. If we think we can fix the world, if we think we can save the churches, if we believe we hold the power to heal ourselves, then we have chosen our path, and it is the wide way leading to destruction. So long as American Christians continue listening to preachers who tell them to justify their existence by all the paths and rules discussed in this book, then we will only continue the man-made quest of setting ourselves up in the place of God. He has always opposed the proud and cast down the mighty from their thrones, and we should not then be surprised when our churches continue to fall apart, when our children melt away, and when the very hope we thought to be so sure crumples beneath us. Only a fool is astonished when a house built on sand falls down.

But if our consciences have been pricked, then we must remember this: No warning will be the thing that shall save us. The Law of God cannot show us the way. No condemnation or rebuke is by itself the answer. Those things always come back to **Me**, and nothing about **Me** really matters. What matters is the real answer Jesus sends to the question of our future. In Him, there is no **what if**. There is only *because*.

Is There Anybody in There?

Behold, I stand at the door and knock.

If anyone hears My voice and opens the door,

I will come in to him and eat with him,

and he with Me. (Revelation 3:20)

He knocks at the door not with a list of demands, not with a better business model or a new kind of worship music, but with **Himself**. "Hey, you, look here. I'm alive, and I'm alive for you. Be still, and know that I am God. **I got you.**"

This is the one hope for Christianity in America: **Jesus**. He must preach to us again. He must tell us His Gospel. He must spiritualize us with His sanctifying forgiveness. So long as there is yet one Christian who believes this, who knows Jesus was crucified but also is risen and coming again to make good on His promises, then the game is anything but up. "For the sake of ten faithful men, will You not spare the city?" Abraham once asked Yahweh (the LORD) as he pleaded for the salvation of horrific Sodom and Gomorrah. God's answer then is His answer still: **Jesus**. "Yes, for the sake of one righteous man, I will spare the world."

Believe it. ***Jesus is the rule every Christian must believe***, not a law but a promise. Jesus is the rule that inverts the paradigm, turns the galaxy on its head, reverses the shadows with cries of "Let there be light!" All of the reasons you cannot find God in heart or hands or world or religion are because Jesus is the promise that ***God finds you***. He's done it before, He's doing it right now, and He's going to keep it up forever. With glorious weakness He smashes the backward self-heroism of satanic religion by whispering, "I've nailed it all to the cross. So let go of your bootstraps! You cannot fly like that. It is better to be a doorkeeper in the house of God than to throw in your lot with the wicked."

Jesus abandoned heaven itself in order to preach and do this freedom for the life of the world. The only possible way to not receive this promise is to straight up refuse to believe it. Thank God you're too weak to do that any longer. Thank God you're BROKEN in the best possible manner. Thank God Jesus Christ justifies the ungodly. Even, and especially, **you**.

Thank God.

7

"CHRISTIAN" RULES THAT EVERY CHRISTIAN OUGHT TO BREAK AS OFTEN AS POSSIBLE

Never #7

Never follow a rule
in order to justify yourself.
Seriously.

The Seventh Rule to be **BROKEN**

The ever-Lie of all counterfeit Christianity.

You can find God: the worship
of **yourself**.

AND SO

Never Never Ever Landing
on the Wrong Side of God's Justice

WHAT WILL BECOME OF PUNK ROCK JOHN?

> Do you not know that friendship with the world is enmity
> with God? Therefore whoever wishes to be a friend of the
> world makes himself an enemy of God. (James 4:4)

The American churches of this twenty-first century stand at a crossroads. Christianity and its influence are fading from the landscape. Congregations are closing. The next generation is meandering toward perdition. All of us together are milling and wondering and waiting for someone or something to show us the way. It is clear to the waking eye that the last half-century's best efforts at mission and discipleship, while boasting of improvements, have done nothing to slow the falling apart (and perhaps have even catalyzed it).

In the name of "style," counterfeit Christianity is being preached, packaged, and sold at an alarming rate, flooding the market with dime a dozen cheap knockoffs that increasingly cynical spiritual consumers are wising up to. You can't sell Christianity as Rationalism to a rationalist. Eventually, he will figure out that he can worship his reason better somewhere else. You can't sell Christianity as Mysticism to a mystic. Eventually, she will figure out that she can worship her experiences better somewhere else. Moralism, Prosperity, and Pragmatism don't drive people deeper into the Church. They drive people out of the Church. IfWeCanJust is not the seed of hope. It is the seed of despair. Lawlessness does not bring more of us together. It drives all of us further and further apart.

Those who put their hope in the countless variations on the single lie that is summed up in the seven rules every Christian ought to break are going to find an increasingly unforgiving spiritual marketplace with little room for counterfeit Christianity, especially sold on the shelf next to more exotic world religions, each chock full of their own historical authenticity. Pious platitudes about "love" and "God" will not help us here. If we are to have any hope of passing Christianity forward

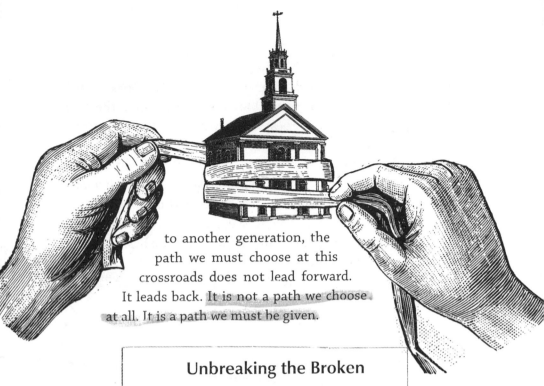

to another generation, the path we must choose at this crossroads does not lead forward. It leads back. It is not a path we choose at all. It is a path we must be given.

Unbreaking the Broken

"If the foundations are destroyed, what can the righteous do?" The LORD is in His holy temple; the LORD's throne is in heaven. (Psalm 11:3–4)

Faith that justifies not in itself but on Christ is free to call a thing what it is. It can look with integrity on the mess that we are and say, "Yes, we are falling apart. We always have been. That's what the churches always do." Justifying faith is free to know that whatever we build with our hands, feel with our hearts, and think with our minds will always fall apart because it is not **Jesus**. Jesus remains. His Word remains. Today. Tomorrow. Forever. But all the things we tack on to it, build up around it, and add to make it pretty—these things must fade and die. The alternative to such faith is blustering boastfulness that insists, "Everything is fine! Everything is fine!" when everything is clearly not fine (Jeremiah 8:11). If the blind lead the blind, they both will fall into a pit. Trying to trick the world into thinking Christianity is something it is not only succeeds in tricking ourselves into not being Christian.

In a nationally televised interview, megachurch pastor Rick Warren, perhaps the most influential individual Christian in the world short of the pope, once put his best leg forward in a bold attempt to convert talk show host and Reformed Jew Alan Colmes by asking him to "give [Jesus] a sixty-day trial [and] see if He'll change your life." He said, "I dare you to try trusting Jesus for sixty days, your money guaranteed back."[17] We can, I suppose, be thankful Pastor Warren didn't completely buckle under the pressure to back off on the whole "Jesus is the only way to heaven" thing. **But.** But if the best pitch that the best-known public Christian preacher in the entire world can come up with while being pressured about the afterlife on national TV is to offer a sixty-day warranty on the temporal experience of believing in Jesus for a better life now, then the fact that his books have gone platinum in a pan-denominational market ceases to be a victory and instead becomes an all-out indictment of our cumulative spiritual bankruptcy. If this is all we have to say to the world, then it is **no wonder** fewer and fewer people are listening. No wonder that for all the glamor of the megachurch, the average participation in one lasts no longer than five years.[18] No wonder that when those of us born and raised in this limp-wristed Christianity hit eighteen and are thrust face-to-face into a real world filled with real, aggressive, hardline worldviews armed with hard-hitting claims, organized attacks, and the appearance of substantial evidence, we walk away calling Christianity hypocritical, mythological, and superficial. No wonder. No wonder at all.

---

17.   The streaming video of the segment from Fox News "Hannity and Colmes" can be viewed at http://www.alittleleaven.com/2008/12/rick-warren-give-jesus-a-60-day-trial.html (last accessed October 12, 2012).

18.   Scott Thumma et al., *Beyond Megachurch Myths: What We Can Learn from America's Largest Churches* (San Francisco: Josey-Bass, 2007), 124–27. Also see The Hartford Institute's research at http://hirr.hartsem.edu/megachurch/megachurch_attender_report.htm (last accessed May 6, 2012), as well as the publication *Leadership Reports* at http://faithcommunitiestoday.org/megachurches (last accessed May 6, 2012), which tracks these statistics.

The more American Christianity and our churches act like the Church's one foundation is a toaster oven to be panhandled rather than a King who is coming to judge the planet, the more we cast our lot in with the wisdom of the world rather than the foolishness of God. The more we think the answer to our spirituality lies in anchoring ourselves to the winds of change rather than clinging to the Rock of Ages, the sooner Protestantism will fade into the background of modernized history.

Too many have seen the pews and seats in our churches becoming emptier and emptier and, like a man clinging to the ledge of a cliff by his fingertips, have begun to grasp for anything that looks like it might offer a momentarily better hold. Your local Christian bookstore is filled with treatises on Moralism, Mysticism, Rationalism, Pragmatism, Prosperity, and IfWeCanJust—weeds growing out of a rock face with little painted signs dangling from them that say, "Grab here, for sure." Too many consciences, too many congregations, too many souls have let go of their last grip on the rock in order to snatch at those tempting vines, only to look on in baffled wonder as the weeds pull free from the layer of dust they are rooted in.

Even as thorns prick at the palms, the hoped-for salvation comes entirely loose. You slip back. You start to drop. Worst of all, by this time your grip has become vicelike, clinging to the weed with all your focus so that in the rush of the moment you cannot even see that your trust is entirely misplaced. When the roots tear free, you fall. Your faith in Christianity is **BROKEN**.

But this is not because Christianity is broken. It is because faith built on counterfeit Christianity is faith placed in a lie. The one Lie. The same Lie. The Lie that all seven rules that every Christian ought to break ultimately boil down to. "It's up to you to find God." It's the old crow's same dirty trick. Steal the seed, and the plant can never grow.

Hanging by his fingertips as he surfs the Internet for answers and wanders into his youth pastor's office, there is only one hope, one chance for Punk Rock John, or any other of the million variations on his story. It is not that he be sent back to cast his eyes about the cliff for some dandelion to reach for. It is not that he be sent back reaching for the cliff at all. It is for a strong man with his weight grounded firmly on the top of the rocky crag to reach down and grab him by the wrist. The only hope for the one who cannot save himself is that he be saved. For that, he needs a Savior.

How Firm a Foundation

If we look around and notice that our churches are dying, closing, fading, and losing even recent converts like mist that is here one moment but gone the next, then one very possible reason for it is that we aren't preaching to the world a Gospel worth believing. Instead, we're preaching something else.

But is it too late? Is our reliance on ourselves already too strong? Are we even capable of stepping back from our personal investments and intentions in order to ask the hard questions about the last generation of money, mission, and ministry? Perhaps all the **next big things** and **spirit-led visions** and **crusades**, far from being the answer to more Church growth, have instead been the heart of the Church's decline. Maybe our attempts to enliven mission have amounted to nothing more than killing Church. What if all we have authentically accomplished is the development of a highly efficient assembly line for the mass production of counterfeit Christianity? Do we have enough integrity left to discern it, if it is found to be true? Do we have enough justifying faith left to repent, if we find ourselves in error? Or are we already so blind that the only way to salve our consciences is to insist we have done no wrong, in spite of all apparent results?

As we look down over the edge at Punk Rock John, hanging on by his fingertips, will we keep insisting that the answer is to climb down beside him and hang there as well, talking about how great a chance we have of surviving if we will only let go of the rock and grab for the weeds within reach? Would it not be better to be a man with feet planted firmly on the rock, reaching down to pull the dangling brother up? But this will only happen through our rediscovery of the **promise** that we do not build the Church. We never have. We never will. Our strength, might, good works, strong feelings, deep thoughts, and testable results can neither create nor sustain faith in Jesus. Only Jesus does that, and Jesus only does that when the heavenly Father sends His Holy Spirit so that His Word is taught in its truth and purity, and so by grace people believe this Word and are made holy by faith in it.

More Than a Feeling

Not by might, nor by power, but by My Spirit, says the LORD of hosts. (Zechariah 4:6)

Jesus Christ, holding all authority in heaven and earth, seated at the right hand of God the Father until His enemies are made a footstool for His feet, has His own plan of salvation. He has revealed it. He is reaching down by means of the Body of His Church with what appears on the surface to be the weakest and most unhelpful of things in the world: words. But these are not just any words; they are promises. These are not just any promises; they are oaths sworn by the mouth of the living God Himself, written in blood and sealed with an empty tomb.

Talk about taking Jesus for a test-drive are not these **words of God**. Talk about inviting Jesus into your heart in order to have Him change your present life are not these words. Talk about how you need to meet God halfway are not these words. Talk about what we have found in polls and statistics or talk learned by mimicking unbelievers or talk we dream up on vision quests or talk we define for ourselves in any way are not these words. The only words Jesus is sending to save the world are the words He has surely spoken. Those are the words He meant, the words He empowers, the sword of His Spirit, the place where you can know for certain He is **right now** as the power of salvation for all who believe it.

The answer isn't found by simply holding up a Bible. Verses quoted out of their context as chicken soup for the soul is not what Jesus sent to save the world. Nor is the message of salvation found in secret superspiritual knowledge buried in omega codes and cryptic matrixes somewhere behind the text. Jesus' words are the **full** texts of the Bible—the entire narrative, the simple story, the foundational truth.

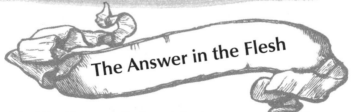

The Answer in the Flesh

And the Word became flesh and dwelt among us. (John 1:14)

This is the weapon with which Jesus assaults every evil plan and purpose of the devil. These inspired words, as history, story, and promise, are Jesus Himself. Therefore, the words of Matthew, Mark, Luke, and John are not a blueprint for life but a history—a history of God's actions in time and space, two thousand years ago, in order to save the universe. They are not words about **you** finding God, **you** letting God, or **you** serving God. They are words about a man born on our planet who is God, who came **to find you**. In every way like us, with flesh from our mother but without the sin of our father, Jesus stepped forth, the Lord of all, hidden in the poverty of a servant's form, and proceeded to be the completion of every last prophecy clung to by the most bizarre ancient people ever to arise as a nation on earth. Like a keystone finally

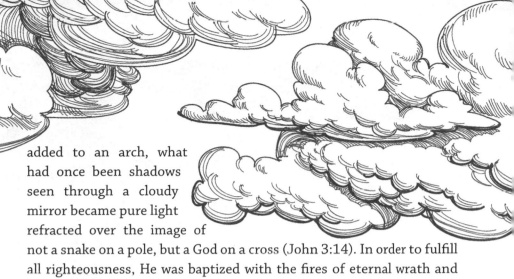

added to an arch, what had once been shadows seen through a cloudy mirror became pure light refracted over the image of not a snake on a pole, but a God on a cross (John 3:14). In order to fulfill all righteousness, He was baptized with the fires of eternal wrath and drank the bitter cup of unending punishment, not as a morality play or the catalyst for a deeper God experience, but to be the blood price and vicarious payment for our decayed morality, to mediate between the hands of an angry God and the hearts of a wayward and faithless people, and to regenerate all flesh into trust that the foolishness of God is always wiser than all of man's wisdom combined.

Will, Word

Every good gift and every perfect gift is from above, coming down from the Father of lights with whom there is no variation or shadow due to change. Of His own will He brought us forth by the word of truth, that we should be a kind of firstfruits of His creatures. (James 1:17–18)

St. Paul, St. Peter, and St. James never wrote any less of Jesus in their letters. They, like the Gospel writers, are foremost concerned with proclaiming the life, death, and resurrection of Jesus for the sake of the living, active faith that is the free gift of the Holy Spirit through those words. With a deft wielding of Law and Gospel, they write no manuals for human religion, nor do they bother with introductory jokes or quaint stories of inspiration drawn from their lives. They

preach the history of Jesus Christ, and they teach what that history means because it is the sharp, double-edged sword by which God's almighty power is saving the world, and that means saving **you**.

 This is what happened at the cross; **this** is why the cross happened; **this** is what the mercy of that cross does to you; **this** is where mercy is done to you now; **this** is what you must expect is coming next; **this** is what waiting in our life together looks like.

 Words.

Justification.

Propitiation.

Reconciliation.

Sanctification.

Doctrine.

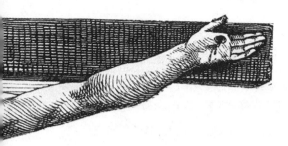

Words that will never pass away. Doctrine was what the apostles preached and taught. It was the mission they messaged with eyewitness testimony. Doctrine led to Baptisms by the thousands, and doctrine led those baptized people to confess with one voice even on pain of death by lion, fire, and sword. Doctrine—not some textbook full of diagrams and footnotes, but the essence of God incarnated into our world as words, as our history, as a man. Doctrine—God's way of miraculously taking wicked and rebellious, twisted and bent creatures, and unbending, straightening, and purifying our hearts and minds and all our senses. Doctrine—God's salving of our consciences by absolving us with promises to re-create the thing we first lost in our horrific and unprecedented fall: trust in His words.

> **Doctrine:** The old-school way of translating a Greek word that means "teaching." It's a shorthand way of summing up everything God has ever said, which we can know for certain, sink our teeth into, and build our hope firmly on.

Doctrine. Dogma. This Word is Christ, and Him crucified, for you, and not for you only, but for the life of the entire world.

JUSTIFICATION QUEST

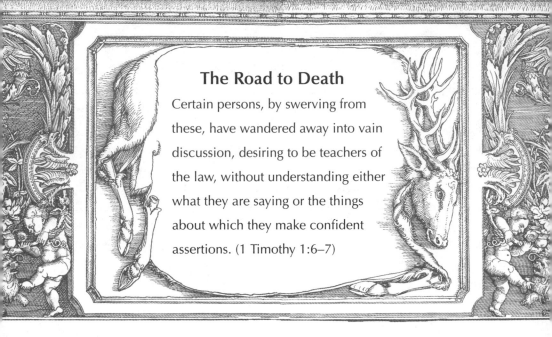

The Road to Death

Certain persons, by swerving from these, have wandered away into vain discussion, desiring to be teachers of the law, without understanding either what they are saying or the things about which they make confident assertions. (1 Timothy 1:6–7)

The great jeopardy all American churches, denominations, and Christians face in our present evil age is that by taking our eyes off of these words, we cannot help but put our hope in other words—other rules for other faiths. We invent new beliefs in words spoken not by God but by us, trusting in the words of mortal men. We call that false trust "Christianity" and then teach others to do likewise. We may take our eyes off of doctrine because we think we are looking away from some cold and lifeless history written down by hypocrites, but what we are looking away from is Jesus.

No longer seeing the author of our faith, we author for ourselves not faith but unbelief of every possible stripe. With hearts deceptive above all things, we know no end to the rules we make up in order to justify ourselves, and in justifying ourselves, trying also to justify our congregations and our denominations, our families and our vocations. This self-justification quest, though entirely normal for life lived in the fallen world, is unacceptable as a substitute for Christianity. To allow it to take up residence in the pulpit or on the stage is to welcome the essence of all decay, turmoil, and death into our churches. To spend endless amounts of time, money, and effort propping it up with yet more worthless tribute and idols while we pray for "God" to bless it is beyond disturbing.

After decades of seeing the wreckage caused by the combination of all our most radical efforts, one might think we would at least begin to question it. "Maybe these new measures aren't working?" Our intentions don't matter nearly so much as what we've actually done. We must seek a real answer. We must truly think outside the box. We must be willing to believe that even our basic assumptions (unless they are founded on clear passages of Scripture) may have been wrong for a very long time.

It is my firm belief that we, as the Church, must have enough trust left in Jesus' ability to justify us that we are open to the possibility that we need to repent of the many innovations in counterfeit Christian practice that have come to dominate the way we teach what we believe. We need to stop worrying so much about how to change or reach or fix all these other people. Instead, we should worry a little more about the authentic content of what Jesus told us to teach them. Apart from that, we can follow only one of two paths. Either we will continue to stare in wonder year after year as both attendance and commitment decline, or we will get yet more radical still, insisting that somehow an even extremer extreme solution will not have the same even extremer extreme negative net results. Both are fool's errands.

This is why St. Paul was determined to know no spirituality but Christ and Him crucified (1 Corinthians 1:23). This is why St. Peter was always ready to give an answer about the Lamb, spotless and without blemish, whose wounds are the source of every healing (1 Peter 3:15; 1:19). This is why St. John confessed, and did not deny, but confessed that if we say we have no sin we deceive ourselves, but when we confess our sins God is faithful and just in order to forgive us, to cleanse us from every unrighteousness by the powerful blood of Jesus (John 1:20;

1 John 1:8–9). This is why St. James insists that to remain steadfast under the trials of this life, we must remember the true and perfect gift comes not from ourselves, but down from heaven from the very presence of the inapproachable Father of light, by the very Word of liberating truth (James 1:17, 25).

Because the apostles all in unity believed this single, pure, and perfect faith, founded on the single, pure, and perfect person and work of Jesus Christ, they also knew these words are **the** weapon—the **only** weapon and the **ultimate** weapon—with which the Spirit assembles a people in His name, against which the gates of death and hell can never prevail. Even the perfectly just wrath of God against you, against your every real sin of thought, word, and deed, against your own faults and your every most grievous fault, against your original sin and your manifest sins—even this righteous attack against your very real evil can only pass over you when you are defended by the sword of the Spirit bloodied with the words of Jesus and the shield of faith, not in what you think, but in what He has clearly said.

These words are the future of the universe. These words are the new creation of a new heavens and a new earth, where Christ will reign on David's throne. These words are the mission—God's mission to save **you**.

THE WRONG SIDE OF GOD'S JUSTICE

The true danger for all the words floating about today as counterfeit "Christian" rules is that the great majority of them are not Christian at all. They are lies, tares sown in the field of faith by the devil (Matthew 13:27–28), who with his deceiving and murdering day and night desires that you never find rest or peace for your soul. With these inveigling words he tempts you into placing yourself back under the justice of God by putting your faith in your ability to keep the Law—whether God's true Law or some laws you made up on your own. It doesn't matter whether you seek this self-made living up to God's justice through your heart or your mind or your hands. These rules are all one and the same bent word, the same Lie: "**If** you . . . then God will . . ."

Such words force you to believe your only hope lies in proving yourself, earning your worth, justifying your future. Such words place you into a courtroom, where God is the Judge and you are both the defendant and your own advocate. In this courtroom, even the good things God has given you—such as morality (which is love) and emotion (which is community) and vocation (which is purpose)—even these good things become your idols, little statuettes you hold up to God as if to say, "See, God. I have this. This is good enough to trade in a plea bargain, right?" But these are not only **not** good enough, they were gifts from Him to you in the first place! They were never meant to be the source of your relationship with Him, nor your eternal value in His sight.

Your hands were never meant to build a path to God: **Moralism** is a rule for counterfeit Christianity.

Your heart was never meant to divine an immediate connection with God: **Mysticism** is a rule for counterfeit Christianity.

Your mind was never meant to think your way around God: **Rationalism** is a rule for counterfeit Christianity.

The material world was never meant to define your relationship with God: **Prosperity** is a rule for counterfeit Christianity.

Spirituality was never meant to be an "If . . . then . . ." pact with God: **IfWeCanJust** is a rule for counterfeit Christianity.

Freedom was never meant to be a cover-up for evil: **Lawlessness** is a rule for counterfeit Christianity.

"You can find God" is a lie: it is the ever-Lie, which the original liar has been lying with since the beginning. It is the root of all counterfeit "Christian" rules. It is the source of doubt. It is a no-good, dirty trick meant for nothing other than to leave your faith in Jesus **BROKEN**.

There is only one Christian rule, and it is not for you to **do** but for you to **believe**. It is not a command. It is a **promise**. The Day of Judgment is coming, and God has already judged you according to yourself and found you wanting, guilty unto damnation. **But!** Even better, He has found and done this judgment not to and in you, but to and in **Jesus**. Jesus' wounds are your wounds. Jesus' torment is your torment. Jesus' death is your death. **And Jesus' resurrection is your resurrection.** Jesus' reign (Jesus' rule over sin, death, and the devil—Jesus' rule of everlasting innocence, righteousness, and blessedness) is your reign.

Jesus' rule, that is, Jesus' reign, is the only Christian rule that puts you on the right side of God's justice. Under Jesus' rule justice and judgment are entirely overcome, flipped on their head and set in another direction altogether, polarized and reversed so that your curse becomes the ultimate blessing. Under Jesus' rule God's wrath against all sin is turned away from you; your death, died by Jesus, becomes your eternal life. This is authentic Christianity, the ancient, future religion **given** by God. It is the holy spiritual faith that with joy can sing, "You will come to be our judge" because we already know what this judgment will be! Mercifully placed under the rule of Jesus, we hear our Lord say, "I have you. I bind you. I cover you. I heal you. I will never leave you nor forsake you. I wash you. I feed you. I forgive you. I adopt you. **You are Mine.**"

Tree of Life

Christ redeemed us from the curse of the law by
becoming a curse for us—for it is written, "Cursed
is everyone who is hanged on a tree." (Galatians 3:13)

Jesus' rule is the only Christian rule your life and death hang upon keeping—not doing but **believing**, not by works but by **faith**. Faith in what God has said and done. Faith in the reign and kingship of Jesus. Faith that the Scriptures can never be broken. Faith that the Spirit creates faith by His human words, which, coming from the mouth of Jesus, now are the lamp for your feet, the light for your path, the rock upon which your house will always stand, and the reason you are free to break all those other man-made rules as often as humanly possible.

The grace alone of Christ's words casts aside every lie that hinders and the striving after the wind that so easily entangles. This grace is the promise that Jesus was broken for you, that He did it all in order to save you. This grace is the promise that the weight of the **Me** ever seeking to drag your chin back down to look inside yourself for answers cannot overcome the antidote of His words, which are constantly and totally true, doubly so because they are outside of you. This grace calls the devil's bluff for you, in your place, replacing it with a voice of guidance shouting out to you over and over again so that you don't have a chance to look down for long, but are compelled to look back up and there to see the new man, the man who is outside of you, crucified for you, constantly giving you yet more grace alone.

Little children, you are from God and have overcome them, for He who is in you is greater than he who is in the world.

(1 John 4:4)

Your original brokenness is answered by this grace spilled out of Jesus in promises authored, perfected, and completed even and especially at the moment when all the gates of hell and hades were most arrayed against Him. He died for you. He rose for you. The battle is over; the victory is won. This is the true Good News. This is the Gospel the Bible speaks of. There is nothing you must do but hear of it, and that is not up to you either. That is what the Church is for. That is what it means to be Church: together, where the Son of God who was **BROKEN** in our place speaks His oath to us, promising He has put us on the right side of God's justice forever. This is a free gift, regardless of the state of your heart, mind, or spirit. It is a promise from almighty God, which means it is doubly solid and entirely true.

That's it. That's the only rule of Christianity. Jesus reigns over sin, death, and that that dirty old crow, the devil. Jesus says, "I forgive you," and this means light and life and salvation. Period. You can put the book down. It's more than okay. It's absolute absolution. Go. You are free.

Jesus said, "I will build My church."
—Matthew 16:18

THE ONLY TRUE CHRISTIAN RULE

The Truth

Because your salvation is not dependent on you, but has all been done by Jesus and credited to you as righteousness, you will never never ever land on the wrong side of God's justice.

The Only True Rule

Go. You are free.
God finds you by sending the words of Jesus.

Art on pages 95, 154, 155, 229, 243, 248, 252, 259, 261, 268, and 269; ©iStockphoto.com.

Art on pages 1, 12, 27, 30, 38, 52, 58, 112, 113, 115, 118, 119, 125, 131, 135, 136, 140, 142, 150, 161, 162, 169, 175, 180, 187, 200, 216, 222, 227, 234, 235, 237, 239, 253, 254, 262, 266, and 276; © Shutterstock.com.

Art on pages 3, 8, 9, 10, 11, 18, 20, 23, 51, 61, 63, 64, 77, 82, 83, 86, 88, 105, 138, 156, 178, 250, and 278; © Harters Picture Resource for Collage and Decoupage, Dover.

Art on pages 6, 7, 8, 12, 13, 23, 34, 38, 46, 56, 71, 77, 85, 122, 147, 150, 164, 198, 207, and 220; ™Picture Sourcebook for Collage and Decoupage, Dover.

Art on pages 41, 48, 88, 100, 101, 109, 120, 135, 157, 189, 190, 205, 232, 239, 270, 274, and 275; created by Albrecht Dürer. Public domain.

Art on page 51; Courtesy of the Digital Image Archieve, Pitts Theology Library, Candler School of Theology, Emory University.